THE FORCE

'Robert Chesshyre's first-rate book, *The Force* which, unlike too many books about the police, is not marred by either political bias or lack of objectivity . . . his criticisms should be required reading for every police officer from Sir Peter Imbert downwards.

'His book deserves to be taken seriously. It also happens to be a good read. Written with pace and style, it contains a number of chapters of genuine excitement and human interest.'
Times Educational Supplement

Robert Chesshyre

THE FORCE
Inside the Police

PAN BOOKS
in association with Sidgwick & Jackson Ltd

First published in Great Britain 1989 by
Sidgwick & Jackson Ltd

This edition published 1990
by Pan Books Ltd,
Cavaye Place, London SW10 9PG
in association with Sidgwick & Jackson Ltd

9 8 7 6 5 4 3 2 1

© Robert Chesshyre 1989, 1990
ISBN 0 330 31458 0

Phototypeset by Input Typesetting Ltd, London

Printed and bound in Great Britain by
Clays Ltd, St Ives plc, Bungay, Suffolk

Contents

Author's Note

I am, naturally, well aware that more than one in ten London police officers are women, and that the proportion is rising month by month. Except, however, where I refer to specific policewomen or write about them as a separate group, I have stuck to male pronouns. I have not been motivated by male chauvinism – I believe the rising number of women will progressively ameliorate police/public relations, increase the brain-power within the force, and lead the police towards less confrontational solutions – but by a hatred of the inelegant alternative of endlessly repeating 'he or she' and 'him and her'.

Acknowledgements

A great number of police officers and civilian employees of the Metropolitan Police have helped me with this book. Very few had any reason other than decency to give me their time. No one in the Streatham division was antagonistic to me or even visibly suspicious of an outsider with a notebook prowling around a police demesne. It remains the great pleasure of my trade that most people are happy to talk at length about themselves, their attitudes and their jobs, and I became known on the division by the friendly appellation of 'Bob the Book'. The interpretation of what I was told is entirely my own (as are the mistakes). I owe many people thanks, and those I do not name here will know who they are; some will probably be relieved not to be named.

Those who cannot escape being singled out (and are in any case already too well associated with my project to deny having helped me) are: Chief Superintendent Roger Street; Superintendent Ian Buchan; Chief Inspector Pat Hook; Chief Inspector David Rees; Detective Chief Inspector John Walsh; Inspector Ian Hogg; Inspector Don Broadbery; Detective Sergeant Colin Bush; PC Chris Birkitt; PC John Fogg-Elliott; Detective Inspector Brian George; Detective Superintendent Brendan Gibb-Gray; ex-Chief Superintendent Sheila Ward; Mr Peter Roe; Mr David Rangecroft; Chief Superintendent Mike Farbrother; Divisional Officer Leonard Blomstrand; Deputy Assistant Commissioner Bob Innes; William Storey and Richard Paris.

I would also like to thank my professional colleagues, my agent Gill Coleridge, of Rogers, Coleridge and White, who inspired me to tackle this subject; William Armstrong and Carey Smith of Sidgwick and Jackson for their enthusiasm and support throughout the writing; and Judith Hannam of Pan for nursing the paperback into publication.

Preface

'The force doesn't know where it is going. If there is a blueprint, it doesn't percolate to the troops. The men on the ground are becoming increasingly cynical about their leaders' abilities. Most feel that the "guv'nors" couldn't organise a piss-up in a brewery. New systems are constantly introduced; they don't work, and they melt away again.' – An officer with over twenty years' service

'You can't afford to be a liberal when your teeth are being kicked in. There are educated people who make you proud to be in the same service, but it's an old bullhorn type you want to see coming round the corner when you've got a couple of yobs on your back.' – Police Federation official

Superintendent Ian Buchan, second-in-command of the Streatham division of the Metropolitan Police during the winter of 1988/89, welcomed each batch of new recruits on arrival to what he termed their second 'family'. I also – as a totally unknown quantity licensed to eavesdrop on every word – was welcomed into the family. Very few questions were asked; very little was denied me. Whenever I was quizzed on my attitude towards the police, I made it clear that I travelled with an open mind. Although I came with the blessing of the 'Yard', I was given a totally free hand. No one, I hope, was under the illusion that I was writing police propaganda. Mr Buchan's boss, Chief Superintendent Roger Street, recognised that I would not approve of everything I saw; he merely asked that, before I criticised, I asked the question 'why?' things or people went wrong. This I have tried to do.

I decided to concentrate on London, not from any metropolitan bias, but both because I live there and because I suspected the troubles that worry the public and confuse the police are at their most acute in the capital. The Met is huge, comprising 74 divisions, 28,000 police officers and 14,000 civilians – a vast, unwieldy organisation scarcely susceptible to control or direction. I made my first approach to the Kennington division, but, when the then Chief Superintendent moved on, I was skilfully 'steered' towards Streatham and its Chief Superintendent, Roger Street. It was a good choice on both counts. Streatham, six miles due south of Westminster, is, in police terms, a busy area with a fair mix of work: it has neither the exceptional problems of, say, Brixton, nor is so sleepy that I would spend six months observing police officers sticking parking tickets on Volvos. Mr Street – every inch a cop even out of uniform – is a 'liberal' by police standards, but metaphorically he wears big boots. His career had embraced both service in the Flying Squad and time out to take a degree at the London School of Economics: a man with his track record at the sharp end of policing is able to ride roughshod over the canteen prejudice against intellectual cops.

By chance I had hit on a good moment to make my approach. The anxiety from which the police were suffering had created an unprecedented spirit of *glasnost*. Sir Peter Imbert, the Metropolitan Police Commissioner, was restless and keen to refurbish the image of his force. His own men were voting with their feet; applications to transfer out of London were running at record levels. And the public was less happy with the police than at any time this century. I was several times rocked back on my heels by the vehement hostility to the police expressed by acquaintances I told of my project.

I faced two professional dangers. The first, that I would get sucked in and become a quasi-cop; this temptation was, I confess, quite appealing, fulfilling a Walter Mitty urge which I found especially strong when I had the chance to follow a murder inquiry. To some extent I began to think like a policeman; I now watch unknown people in my street with a different eye. The man with a ladder might be a decorator, but he might also be a burglar; the loitering youth could be waiting for a friend, but he could be sizing up houses. An American professor who spent some time with the police told me that the first time he went out on patrol and saw a lone man late at night, he said to himself: 'I wonder what that guy's doing?' A few months later it was: 'What the hell's that sonofabitch up to?' I never became that involved, but I understand what he meant.

The second danger was that, however familiar a figure I became, I could never be sure that my presence was not affecting the way police officers behaved. 'How will you know when we are telling the truth?' one policewoman asked. If anyone was inclined to thump prisoners, he was not going to do it while I was in the van; if anyone was racist, he was not going to abuse blacks under my nose; if a beat officer habitually took an afternoon nap somewhere on his rounds, he was going to forgo the pleasure when I was with him. On my first visit to the cells, a sergeant showed all the solicitous care for his charges you might expect of a ward sister in a private hospital. Did this one want an extra blanket? That one a cup of tea? Maybe the milk of human kindness did flow through the sergeant in exceptional quantities, but it seemed unlikely that he would be quite so caring when there was not a man with a notebook at his elbow.

I also faced a problem interpreting what people with powerful reasons for disliking the police had to say. When I visited a young burglar whom I had watched being interviewed at the police station, he told me horrifying stories of what would have happened had I not been present. I actually didn't believe a word he said on that score. But before I left, several officers said to me: 'You've been here a long time; you've been allowed to go where you want; you haven't seen anyone beating a prisoner.' Ergo, the argument ran, beating prisoners (or whatever malpractice was under discussion) didn't happen. However, because I did not see something does not mean that it never occurs. There is enough evidence of police abuses for my certification of good behaviour to be weak evidence for the defence. Occasionally I suspected that an officer protested too much; with a very small minority I was glad that I was discussing theory over a cup of canteen tea rather than sitting eyeball to eyeball 'assisting with inquiries'.

My aim, in any case, was not to expose, but to examine and report on a group of people whom we civilians inevitably treat as a distinct social tribe. The brief I set myself was to be a fly on the wall: I wanted to spend enough time with police officers to hear them properly. I also wanted to go into the community to see the police as others saw them. Police officers are frequently close enough to touch – walking the high street, policing football matches, directing the traffic – and they are never more than a phone call away, but, for most of us, they might as well belong to another world.

Although I give Streatham a local habitation and a name, the picture I draw of police and policing is intended to be relevant across Britain. I had considered disguising the place and making all the people anonymous, which would have made my life easier and lessened the chances of injured feelings, but it would have stripped the book of an essential element of reality. To a great extent, the environment makes the cop, and is crucial to determining how individual officers exercise their vaunted discretion. The policeman walking along your road will disregard a large number of transgressions, from untaxed cars to kids dropping litter; what he acts upon will depend on his workload, local expectations, and such mundane considerations as whether he is nearing the end of his shift.

What I learned very quickly was how uniforms, shift work, policemen's shibboleths, and physical isolation combine to set the police tribe apart from the rest of us. An American police chief said: 'The police world is hermetically sealed. We repeat each other's myths. We only talk to each other. The cops are not communicating with the outside world and never have. We learn our own things. You discover you can't talk to civilians.' The same stories, prejudices, fears work their way through the canteens, into police vans; then, via the columns of police publications, into other canteens and other vans. If I had a pound for every time I was told the same (often apocryphal) anecdotes, I would significantly augment my earnings from this book. The profession lacks a philosophical underpinning: few officers think hard and thoroughly about the wider aims of the job. Opera-loving cops who spend their holidays on archaeological digs are an entertaining figment of the imaginations of well-educated thriller writers. A chief inspector said: 'Our whole being is channelled towards one end – producing people before magistrates. If we lose that *raison d'être*, we might as well pack up and go home.' But, behind these surface certainties – the 'take charge' demeanour of everyday policing – I detected a gaping void. 'It's hard to know where we're going on this job, where we'll be in ten years' time. We're bumbling along in our usual way,' said a long-service Streatham PC.

Together, the isolation and the uncertainty create a generalised paranoia. I pointed out until I ran short of breath that the police emerge with far more support from public opinion polls than, for example, politicians and journalists, and that, when the chips are down, they usually receive unqualified support from the popular media. But Item One of the police creed is that they are a misrepresented body of people, continuously under a hail of ill-informed criticism. There is criticism in this book, and that will not escape the eagle eyes of my police readers, but I would ask them to step outside the tribal reserve long enough to weigh the merits of what I report. 'Is this going to be a "bad" book?' asked a sergeant, who just reeled off a string of familiar police bellyaches. What he had in mind was not its literary or even journalistic merits, but whether it was going to be pro- or anti-police. 'If it is, you'll have to go into hiding. There'll be twenty-eight thousand police officers after you.' He was, of course, joking.

1

'The Police Force We Deserve'

The charge room and cells are the dark heart of a police station, where the accused come face to face with the consequences of their transgressions. For some, arrest is a matter of inconvenient routine, an unwelcome but not unexpected interruption to a shiftless life of petty crime; for others, like many drinking drivers and shoplifters, it is a once-in-a-lifetime humiliation; for a small minority, a police station cell is the gateway to many years of incarceration. The police, ever on the hunt for sanitised nomenclature, officially call this epicentre of their operations 'the custody suite'. But no playing with words can soften its hard purpose or its hangdog air. It is a casualty department, a claimants' office, a dingy waiting room at some far-flung outpost of a railway system; it is a place, not just of temporary persons passing through, but of defeated people at their lowest ebb. It is claustrophobic, bureaucratic, harsh; people arrive and depart in handcuffs; while they are there they are 'prisoners'. For the police, and for their more habitual customers like prostitutes, the bleakness is relieved by a determined jokiness.

'You need a sense of humour in this job. You've got to be happy or the days drag on.' A custody sergeant was addressing a large, bearded, black man who had been brought from court in handcuffs, and was about to be bailed on a number of robbery charges. 'Where have you been? The Scrubs? I suppose that was for something you didn't do either.' The sergeant typed with one finger as he talked. Peck . . . joke . . . peck . . . joke . . . 'He's got how many girl friends and four kids, he wouldn't commit a crime like that, would he?' The phone rang. 'Come on,

1

work your ticket, answer the phone. Prisoners in the old days used to be good; now they don't want to do anything.' The typing resumed with the rhythm of a slow-motion woodpecker. 'Which court were you at? The Bailey? That's one court I don't mind waiting at. Pretty pictures and nice mosaics on the walls.'

A few yards away an Asian woman, wearing the uniform of a check-out girl, was having her property listed and transferred to plastic bags. Handling prisoners' property is a time-consuming process, hated by the police and often about as useful as counting grains of sand. The woman was being quietly degraded, as each personal possession was laid out before her and examined; family photos, religious pictures, letters. She never spoke or lifted her eyes. Her supermarket manager emerged from an inner room, and left without a glance at the prisoner. An umbrella went into the plastic bag; by now there were three rows of property for the cashier to sign for. It would probably all be returned to her within a couple of hours. The jokey sergeant complained that his typing finger hurt. 'Why don't they issue us with word processors?'

The door opened and a wild and drunken man was dragged in by two PCs. He was shouting that he had a complaint to make. He wouldn't sit down. Eventually his captors kicked him behind his knees – without, it must be said, undue force and with the sole purpose of getting him to sit. 'Violence. That's all you know,' shouted the drunk. 'What's your number?' He began blowing raspberries. The sergeant broke off his battle with the typewriter and intervened: 'Listen. This is my charge room. If you want to be treated civilly, you behave civilly. If you don't, you'll go to the cells until you're sober enough.' The plea fell on deaf ears. 'I've got a complaint to make. I'm sober. Give me a breath test.' Off to the cells he went, his shouting gradually receding, leaving the police to go through his property, which included a Millwall supporters' club key ring and a Conservative Party membership card. He had been arrested, apparently, for refusing to pay for an Indian meal and for throwing things around the restaurant.

In the background, detectives were trying to sort out an unholy mess involving three brothers caught up in a fracas. Two were being sent home with apologies. 'Sorry to drag you all in, but it was best to get it sorted out.' The police had eventually established that the third brother had been in a fight with a friend. One of the departing brothers was advised to keep his aggressive sibling away from the assaulted friend, 'or he'll be done for contempt of court'. The sergeant wanted to know whether he should retain the third brother's boots as evidence. In a side room, a procession of scrubby whores – short skirts, fishnet tights, fake fur jackets – were being booked in, gossiping about past arrests and sergeants they had known. Amidst the mayhem a boy was being finger-printed.

The scene was Gipsy Hill police station, the second of Streatham's two 'nicks', and the highest police station in London; from the roof on a clear day there is a fine panoramic view from the Surrey hills in the south to Hampstead in the north. In the middle distance are St Paul's Cathedral, the City office towers and Westminster, where the laws that are enforced in the custody suite below are promulgated. It is not a view that prisoners get to enjoy; there are no windows in the charge room, which is lit by a raised skylight past which the wind slices with an eerie whistle. In the early hours, when the police station for once is quiet and its prisoners are stretched on blue plastic mattresses, it is possible to imagine oneself deep inside a remote fortress on a gale-lashed shore.

It is a functional place, this heart of darkness. A long series of joined desks, screwed to the floor, face the prisoners' bench. Prisoners' names, their alleged offences, the times at which their detentions must be reviewed by a senior officer, forthcoming court appearances, remarks – 'possible HIV positive' read one – are entered with black markers on a white board. Like a recording angel, a sergeant painstakingly enters every action and decision concerning each prisoner in a custody record. A host of notices, pinned and Sellotaped to the walls, advise and warn. Prisoners are told their rights – to summon a lawyer, to phone

3

a friend. Police are advised to wear gloves when dealing with blood and vomit because of Aids and Hepatitis B; a chart shows how to communicate with the deaf using the finger alphabet. Against one wall there is a brass rod, marked in feet and inches and screwed to a polished wood board, for measuring prisoners who do not know how tall they are. Fingerprints are taken in a room the other side of an open door – 'think before you ink', enjoins a poster; a camera is permanently mounted for mugshots; across the room stands the Breathalyser, a surprisingly large, grey machine, the height of a man's chest.

Behind the sergeant, a door leads to a small surgery, where women prisoners are searched and police doctors pay regular calls. 'The man will live,' said a youngish doctor with flowing fair hair, a bright check sports jacket and a luxuriant moustache. He had been called to a prison escapee, who had complained of spitting blood but who, I suspected, wanted a break in what would otherwise have been a long, dull day. Neither the custody sergeant nor I could read the full medical diagnosis, but we could read the fee: a policeman made a rapid calculation, comparing a doctor's earnings to his own. 'Ten minutes of a doctor's time is worth eight hours of a PC's,' said one. The contrast was a perennial source of charge room discontent, but, when the calculations were complete, the police usually added the grudging admission: 'Still, they had to work hard to get there.'

The custody sergeant's right-hand man, a PC known as the 'jailer' – an unpopular job since its main responsibilities are coping with dreaded property – counted the prisoners out and counted them in, marking their exits and entrances on the scoreboard. 'It's rotten when it's busy, and it's rotten when it's not,' said the sergeant. Usually it *was* busy. All manner of people occupied the charge room bench, from children arrested for vandalism to men seized at gunpoint in the commission of armed robbery. The charge room daily became a stage on which were played endless tragedies, the shifting casts a never-ending tide of the greedy, the desperate, the wicked, the cruel and – like a vast army of

4

spear-carriers – the inadequate. Briefly they occupied the spotlight. Some swaggered – the escaped prisoner gave his occupation as 'burglar'. Some blustered – a large black girl in a tracksuit, who looked as if she should have been winning gold medals for Britain rather than thieving from shops, lied and lied. 'She's a full-time occupation, this one,' said the sergeant. 'I only lied about my name and age,' said the girl, lying again. Some were so stunned, they could only blink, like the teenaged armed robber sitting miserably in a white disposable boiler suit – his own clothes had been taken for forensic examination – knowing that his life was over before it had properly started. Most were just dejected. Onto endless forms went their names, their heights, the colour of their eyes, full descriptions of their tattoos, when they had last worked, how much they earned, whether their girl friends were pregnant, how much rent they paid, their dates of birth. Sometimes they would be asked the same questions three times in twenty minutes. They will know the ropes on Judgement Day.

'Johnny's' little drama was typical. He was a deeply unhappy young man who had smashed a window at the bail hostel where he lived. The police wanted to caution him and send him on his way, but the hostel would not have him back unless he was charged with criminal damage. The youth certainly did not want to return, claiming that he was bullied there by other boys. For over an hour an inspector, the custody sergeant, the gaoler, the arresting officer wrestled with this mess: they telephoned the boy's solicitor and his probation officer, they spoke to the hostel, they questioned the young man. 'My life is just a total misery at the moment. Nothing is going right. People kick at my door, they beat me. No one's going to witness it, are they? I can't handle it,' said the prisoner. 'I'm going to continue doing more and more damage because it is wrong if I stay in these places. All I have got to do basically is get some work and then find a bedsit.' Sitting on the bench in his anorak with its broken zip and his torn jeans – exposing, when asked by a PC, the eagle tattooed on his back and the football club name on his arm – it would have been as realistic for him to dream of becoming a brain surgeon. He was hopelessly vague and pathetically slow-witted. 'Is "p.m." morning or night?' he asked. Nobody wanted the boy, probably nobody ever had; certainly there was no mention of his parents. A police officer said, not without pity: 'This one's going to go down and down. Where we fall down is that we cannot cure, we can only suggest.' That boy's sad face, his lips and eyes trembling on the brink of tears, was its own crystal ball: what the boy needed was love, what he would eventually and inevitably get would be endless small gaol terms. A Solomonic judgement was arrived at: for the moment the young man would not be charged, but would be bailed to return two weeks later. Something might turn up.

Each period of the day had its moods: the evening confusion when the drunks and prostitutes cluttered the system, the morning calm after the vans had removed prisoners to court, the afternoon when the shoplifters were shuffled in. But the moment I found most bizarre was the dawn, when cleaning ladies, in aprons and red rubber gloves, arrived and busily mopped their way round recumbent figures stretched on the cell floors; it was not unusual for there to be three prisoners to a cell. One typical morning the cells stank of stale clothes, drunks' breath and urine; a large number of badly hungover Irishmen were among those present. 'It was me who was assaulted, sure it was,' said one with several days' growth of beard. Mop, mop, went the ladies. 'I'm not here to enter into the rights and wrongs of it,' said an inspector. Mop, mop. 'I'll smash the head in of the bastard who urinated in the corner of the cell.' Mop, mop. 'Cool it, or you'll be in more trouble.' Mop, mop. 'We're cream-crackered,' said a sergeant, surveying the scene.

Most police officers have one very specific goal in mind, to produce guilty people before the courts and see them justly convicted. Everything else – specialisation, community policing, public order – pales beside that aspiration. Some may rise to be senior detectives and charge professional criminals with serious crimes, but hour-in, hour-out across the country, minor malefactors are being brought under arrest to places like the Gipsy Hill charge room.

'Why are you lying to me, Tommy? All this is a lot of crap, isn't it? I think you've been caught bang to rights.' The speaker was a police constable, who a few years before had been, by his own admission, a 'bit of a lad' himself. Before him, seated at the other side of a table, was a thirteen-year-old boy, accused of burglary. 'I haven't done no burglaries and I never would. I haven't done anything, see.' The PC tried another tack: 'Listen to what I say. This is serious, more serious than taking mopeds. Decent people have to put grilles over their windows to stop people like you stealing what they've worked hard to earn.' Sitting beside Tommy was his stepfather who chipped in from time to time: 'I'll give you a leathering if you're lying. Better than Ronald Biggs, you are. If you're telling porkies, I'll kill you because I haven't had my tea yet.' He turned to me and winked, as if to say, 'What a lad.' Under the twin barrage, Tommy stuck to his story: he knew nothing about the burglary, and had been with a friend at the time. In longhand the PC first wrote down the questions, then read them out and finally transcribed Tommy's replies.

What was under investigation was a burglary on a council estate. It had been spotted by a vigilant neighbour, who had called the police. Tommy fitted a description given by the neighbour, and had later been named by another youth who had admitted taking part. Tommy was well known to the police, mainly because he was often still running about the estate after the pubs closed. He was bright, cheeky and dishonest. I had been in a café one night with a policeman when Tommy came in. 'If you hadn't been here, I was going to steal a Coke,' he said with a wide grin. 'As you are here, can you lend me 30p?' The evening Tommy – whose real father was serving a long prison sentence – was arrested, the family had been gathering for tea, and were not, therefore, pleased to be interrupted. 'I'm not going to no poxy station. I've already got to go back on Sunday [in connection with another crime committed by Tommy]. I've got a stinking cold,' said his mother. Reluctantly, the stepfather agreed to come: 'If you're not telling the truth, I'll give you a thick ear,' and then added, 'He's always admitted the other things he's done; I'll give him that.' Tommy himself didn't want to miss *The Bill* on television. Where he was going he would be starring in his own episode.

At the station he was read his 'rights', including his right to a solicitor. 'Yes,' he said, 'I'd like to have one.' His stepfather jumped in: 'Why? Have you got anything to admit?' The PC added: 'You're wasting your time; he's not going to do anything.' He had in mind that the hour was already late, and that the boy had his stepfather to guard his interests. Had Tommy insisted, a lawyer would have been summoned. But he didn't, so no solicitor. The PC disappeared to find an interview room and prepare his questions, leaving Tommy to the attention of a custody sergeant, who was chomping his way through a corned beef and pickle sandwich. 'How many times have you been in trouble?' 'Hundreds,' replied Tommy who had been delighted to see a motor scooter he had stolen in the police yard, tangible evidence of his delinquency. 'By the time you're seventeen,' replied the sergeant, 'you'll be put in prison every time you're arrested. It's not very clever.' Then, behind Tommy's back: 'He's a right little toe rag.' The stepfather hastened to agree: throughout the evening his emotions hovered between parental pride in the criminal potential of his stepchild and exasperation that he was still being kept from his tea.

The interview was conducted in a miserable little room, lit by a suspended neon light. The only decoration was a map of the Metropolitan Police area. There were cigarette ends and a dead wasp on the floor alongside a small rectangle of grey carpet; the yellow paint stopped at the picture rail. The interrogation, which lasted an hour, was persistent, but Tommy wavered only slightly, finally admitting he did know the block of flats where the burglary had taken place. 'I'll give you this, you're a fucking good liar. You'll make a good little villain when the times comes,' said the PC, adding that fingerprints had been found on a broken window, and had been sent for identification. 'They won't be mine,' said Tommy. When the questioning finished, Tommy signed each page of the statement, gripping a red ballpoint pen tightly in a grubby left hand. 'May I have a sweet now?' he asked as he concluded. The PC had a final word with the stepfather: 'You make up your own mind.' 'I already have.' 'It's up to you what you do' – pause – 'within reason, of course.' An inspector drove Tommy and his stepfather home and delivered the final homily of the night: 'Rides in police cars can be less pleasant than this one. You've brought a lot of grief to your family. Try to keep out of trouble.'

A month later the prints came back from Scotland Yard: they *were* Tommy's. I was both dismayed that Tommy had, despite his protestations, committed the burglary, and yet pleased that the PC had been vindicated. He was a decent man, who sought to tread a careful line between discretion and the full vigour of the law. In retrospect his handling of Tommy was certainly understandable: he *did* know that Tommy was lying, and the victim had been sufficiently upset both to put bars across her windows and to move out for a few days, unable to face the prospect of sleeping alone in her own home. Tommy finally 'put his hands up' to the burglary and was given an official 'caution'. It was by no means his first offence, and shortly afterwards a place was found for him in the boarding school for unruly boys to which the boxer Frank Bruno once went.

'We got a result,' said the PC. It was a rare achievement. A vast percentage of burglaries are no longer fully investigated, allowing the police to concentrate on crimes they have the best chance of solving. There is no such thing as a 'typical' crime, but hours and hours of police effort are occupied on such offences as Tommy's.

When Tommy was arrested, I was a few weeks into the six months I was to spend with the Streatham division of the Metropolitan Police and, briefly, with other departments of Scotland Yard. My point of departure for this book was the perception, arrived at both through following the public

9

debate and, increasingly, listening to private concerns, that our police forces were in crisis. Despite their comparatively high standing in public opinion polls, their support was being rapidly eroded, and they as a consequence were demoralised and unsure of their role. For twenty years there had been a gathering social disaster as reported crimes quadrupled from 900,000 in 1968 to nearly four million in 1988; within that statistic, acts of violence, including murder, rose from 25,000 cases to 125,000, and 'muggings' from 4,400 to 33,000. A recent slight dip in the total figure (achieved largely because people have started to take better crime prevention measures against burglary) was undermined by the inexorable rise in crimes of violence – up 16.9 per cent in 1988 over 1987, and sex offences – up 16.4 per cent.

In the face of these statistics, the credibility of the police was in severe jeopardy. Crime – or, more accurately, the fear of crime – had become one of the major public preoccupations. Half the women questioned in a poll said they were too frightened to go out alone at night. The rich were increasingly employing private security firms to protect their homes; the middle classes were hastening to neighbourhood watches; the poor in some areas were forming bands of vigilantes; Guardian Angels arrived from the United States to patrol the London Underground, and proved unexpectedly popular, forcing the police hastily to moderate their instinctive hostility towards citizen armies. Indeed, the 'professionalisation' of the police was a large part of the problem. 'Leave it to us,' they had said. We did, and we were taken to the cleaners; naturally there was a loss of confidence.

Sir Peter Imbert, the Metropolitan Police Commissioner, acknowledged that esteem for his officers had dropped so low that some juries had become reluctant to convict on police evidence. Loss of faith in the police was no longer concentrated among their traditional (left wing) political opponents, nor among inner city ethnic minorities. The new doubters were solid citizens who had seen their burglaries unsolved; who had been treated with arrogance when stopped for minor traffic infringements; who had heard stories from their children of police abuse of power. One of Imbert's first actions was to devote £150,000 to an outside examination of the image of his force, a use of scarce resources that attracted considerable derision in police canteens. A Scotland Yard civilian employee complained: 'We suffer from this dreadful desire to point a torch up our backsides all the time.' But the public was demanding more light. There were calls from several quarters for a Royal Commission, a sure sign that the institution was in disarray and that no one had the faintest idea what to do.

At the heart of the general dissatisfaction lay specific public concerns: do the police fix evidence to secure convictions of people they 'know' to be guilty? Do they use excessive violence against prisoners or demonstrators? Do they harbour prejudices, such as racism? There is no empirical way of answering the above questions: what happens in interview rooms, in the back of police vans, or down dark alleys is known only to those who were there. Occasionally a random swivel of the public searchlight catches the police going about vile business: the author Roald Dahl saw officers beating a black man in Hyde Park; a TV crew trying out a new night-time camera filmed police assaulting a motorist; a man was paid £30,000 damages after a jury decided that he had been framed; a suspected robber awaiting trial in prison used a smuggled tape-recorder to expose a corrupt detective; the inquiry into the Hillsborough disaster exposed arrogance, incompetence and appalling insensitivity in the face of grief and bewilderment.

Policing is perhaps *the* vital function in a tolerant, democratic nation. Those who fulfil that function cannot expect unqualified support regardless of their performance; what is at stake is too important. Abuses of police power threaten the wellbeing of a society that operates on the core assumption that right will be enforced over wrong. When corrupt police put that assumption in jeopardy, we need to shout our warnings as loudly and continuously as we can. We accept that abroad the police often symbolise the nature of the regimes they serve, from corrupt and inefficient forces in some countries to ruthless and authoritarian forces in

11

others. We categorise some nations as 'police' states, and think of others like South Africa or the Soviet Union largely in terms of their secret and not-so-secret police forces. The deadly violence of the United States is reflected in its gun-toting police. Britain's own self-image as a tolerant, decent society was sustained for perhaps twenty years after the Second World War by the *Dixon of Dock Green* notion of unarmed police maintaining law and order with the full consent and support of the people. A very senior policeman said: 'A police force cannot operate in the face of sustained hostility; we haven't the luxury of the barrack gates to retreat behind; we cannot live without the consent of the public; we are part of the community.' The fact that the British police are in self-confessed crisis says as much about society as about the force itself.

Few rank and file police officers grasp the centrality of their relationship with society. They are preoccupied with their own gripes, the first of which is that they are not merely unloved but actively hated by malignly motivated sub-groups like politicians and journalists, who poison the well of public opinion. The second, often seen as a conse-quence of the first, is that they are severely under-resourced. This charge, without access to the books, is impossible to answer. I did see and learn of many occasions when there was an obvious shortage of officers; I also saw wastage. Many of the civilian support staff, employed to free police officers to 'return to the beat', are badly paid and worse trained. The crime support group (CSG), charged with preparing papers for the Crown Prosecution Service (CPS) and so for court, was under impossible press-ure; case papers were often late and occasionally lost. The CPS itself is a police *bête noire*, blamed for all manner of inefficiencies; officers pine for the days when they presented their own cases in court. With the then Home Secretary Douglas Hurd sitting next to him staring into the middle distance, the leader of the Met branch of the Police Feder-ation told its 1988 annual meeting: 'One wonders if some Crown prosecutors are really lawyers or the archetypal social worker. Many of our customers, when asked "Do you want a solicitor?" reply "You don't need one with the CPS." '

For many years, the police kidded themselves that they could cope with society's problems on their own. There is still a delusion, shared by cops and their 'unions', that the police stand alone in defence of values long since abandoned by the likes of teachers and social workers. 'The police service is by far the most stable social factor in our society,' said one senior officer, adding, somewhat contemptuously, that in his opinion society now had a better police force than it deserved. Amongst themselves, officers promote the notion that they are the sole bulwark against Britain's descending into the kind of society once presided over by Idi Amin. In London they are the Thames barrier without which the capital would be inundated. Even senior officers seldom pause to consider whether additional money might not be better spent outside the police force, for example, on improving the quality of life on rundown estates, or even on building more prisons! A former Home Office economic adviser produced a theoretical model that showed that longer sentences and more prisons would be a dramatically more effective use of money to combat crime than more policemen. But, of course, police work *is* profoundly affected both by the nature of the local community and by influential organisations such as local authorities. The police do not operate in a vacuum. As Britain has become less cohesive, and as the problems of race, class and education have proliferated, so the police job has become harder. An experienced PC said: 'Ten years ago if a child was going wrong, a head teacher would call in the police, parents. All hell would break loose. Estates hung together.' Today, we have Mrs Thatcher's words for it: 'There is no such thing as society.'

The 'leave it to us, we can be trusted' mentality often breeds contempt for mere civilians. Police officers become exasperated by our fecklessness. A PC who had just been to a house that had been burgled four times was beside himself at the stupidity and laziness of the householder. 'Most people simply do not want to know when it comes to taking preventative steps. They demand "What are the police doing?" and don't even mark their property,' he said. 'Kids rob cars at eight and nine in the evening, bold as you please. People pass by, but they don't want to know. Then they have the cheek to tell us about it afterwards. It's not as if the criminals were great big thugs; they're small children.'

The ultimate grievance, into which are rolled most of the others, is the belief that the criminal justice system is weighted against the police and in favour of the criminal. A civilian working with the Met said: 'Society wants police officers to catch and convict offenders, while making it as awkward and difficult for them as it can. There has to be a balance between a fair trial and the maintenance of law and order. Most police officers would say that we have got that balance wrong. It is not longer a question of whether the accused did it, but of how sophisticated he is in manipulating a system that benefits no one except a few criminals and a lot of lawyers. Most trials are not justice at all; they are intellectual exercises between intelligent people who don't always know best. The man in the street doesn't get justice, and that riles coppers.' One such riled copper said: 'We are losing the battle on the streets because the yob is protected by the technicalities of the law, while the policeman has no such protection.'

We think about the police on several levels. As a society, we are concerned that they should be efficient yet not overweening; as individuals, many of us suffer from police phobias. A senior officer said that even he feels alarm when he spots a police car in his driving mirror, and worries about his speed and whether his brake lights are working. When a beat PC rang a suburban doorbell merely to tell the occupier she had left the door open, the woman was almost breathless with panic: 'Oh my God, I was trying to remember everything I might have done wrong in the past five days.' We all break minor laws – mainly motoring ones – and occasionally we feel tempted to break bigger ones. What might our baser urges lead us to if there were no police? They serve as society's boundary posts. They are also the carriers of desperate news, which, down the centuries, has never been an easy or popular role. A man whose teenaged son had been murdered answered the door at three in the morning to find a policeman. 'He didn't have to say a word,' he said later. A slightly shocking recruitment advertisement for the Metropolitan Police, showing a crushed bicycle and a blanket thrown over a dead child's body (one upturned hand is poignantly exposed), advises the would-be recruit: 'People expect the worst when they see a copper, so don't beat about the bush.'

What the rest of us don't always appreciate is quite how uneven policing can be. You are, I was told, more likely to be stopped for a minor traffic offence, such as jumping red lights, in Westminster than in south London, because the small resident population and comparatively low crime rate place relatively few demands on Westminster-based officers. Late night rowdyism which might pass without action in a high street could lead to arrest in an adjacent residential street. Such examples are not contentious, but it is the application of this discretion that lies at the heart of much of the unhappiness with the police. Why was this one (black) arrested, when that one (white) was not? There may be a perfectly just answer – there may not – but it is a minefield to negotiate. Every day the police make not just practical, but moral judgements. A chief inspector said: 'Parliament decrees what will be lawful and what not, and the police, given the limited nature of their resources, are entrusted with the discretion as to what has priority. Why we choose to enforce certain things comes to a moral standpoint, to what we feel is repugnant.'

Some crimes are more clear-cut and exciting than others, which – given that most police officers are attracted by fast action – also determines how they use their discretion. The same chief inspector said: 'The high speed chase and arrest of some "scrote" [police argot for a young, worthless yob – derived from the word 'scrotum' and interchangeable with 'toe rag'] who has nicked a car has more appeal than arresting a man who has hit his wife. The car thief is usually a pathetic beanpole of a fifteen-year-old, but the arrest of the husband will end in grief with a hostile witness and an abandoned case.' He added: 'Even alienated youths will say "We want a police service." But they don't want us to pick on and harass them. It isn't the idea of police they are against. It is the way that individual officers perform their tasks which, in their view, results in them being harassed. It is the PC on the street who has the business of interpreting whether they are going to be stopped and arrested, not the senior officer.'

It is also the PC on the street who bears the brunt of the accelerating level of violence. Policing is not only a very dangerous job, like coal-mining or deep-sea fishing, but one in which the danger takes the form of unpredictable violence. Every day a police officer reports for duty he faces potential attack. In my limited time at Streatham, four officers I knew personally were assaulted and off work as a consequence. In 1987 there were 17,000 assaults on police (4,534 of them in London); 111 officers have been killed on duty in the past seven years. There are other dangers: talking a potential suicide off a roof, rescuing people from fires. I suspect that the rest of us underestimate this bravery. It is a quality that nearly all of them share, regardless of their other characteristics. A very senior officer said: 'The vast majority of police have a great sense of duty which the public doesn't understand very well. They will act with near stupidity. When they hear a member of the public calling for help, their whole instinct is to get there. Wives and girl friends may tell them never to do anything so foolhardy again, but they will.'

Violence against the police is inextricably linked to their mandate to apply necessary force on our behalf, and the debate swirling around their proper function returns like a homing pigeon to one central (and contentious) issue: is it a police *force* or a police *service?* It is, of course, a bit of each, but, stripped to its bare bones, the question divides the police into two camps. There are powerful voices (including Imbert's) on the side of service, but many subscribe to the notion that it is primarily a matter of force. A south London probation officer said: 'It is a police force.

16

Officers who think otherwise are marginalised, considered by their colleagues to be wet, windy and boring, without ambition. Or they are at such a high level of management that their approach does not filter through. There is a serious problem getting the troops to do what they are told. The behaviour of the police routinely reported by our clients shows there is an enormous disparity between what actually happens and what should happen by the book.' John Stalker, the former Deputy Chief Constable of Manchester who tried to investigate the alleged 'shoot-to-kill' policy of the Royal Ulster Constabulary, put it thus: 'If it comes to a choice between policemen playing table tennis in youth clubs or catching burglars, I suspect I know what the ratepayers' priority will be.' Mr Street addressed the dilemma somewhat more subtly: 'You have got to be a realist. However deeply committed you are to the community aspects of policing, you have also got to uphold the rule of law, and safeguard life and property. If what you are doing is not related to that, you must question why you are doing it.' Some policemen may look like big teddy bears, but every policeman, even when occupied in teaching children to ride bikes safely or in standing on school crossing duty, carries a pair of handcuffs on his belt and a truncheon down his trouser leg.

Public faith in the police is, paradoxically, threatened as much by the unswerving support the police have received from Mrs Thatcher's three governments as by the intermittent sniping indulged in by left-wingers. The police budget for England and Wales was increased by 52 per cent in real terms during Mrs Thatcher's first ten years in office, and in 1989 it stood at four billion pounds (one billion of which goes to the Met); police manpower increased by 10 per cent in the same decade, and stands at 130,000 officers (with more on the way to deal with rural 'lager louts') and 42,000 civilians. Individual police have never been better off. A young constable, who had abandoned teaching for the police, told me that he earned over £16,000 with rent and London allowances. Millions are poured into technology to support police operations: police stations are being torn

17

apart to install computers; armour-plated Landrovers, costing £50,000 each, sit in a hangar near Heathrow, ready for the next Broadwater Farm riot or deranged 'Michael Ryan' gunman; central London is dotted with television cameras linked to a control room in Scotland Yard from which public demonstrations can be monitored and policed. While the government seems quite prepared to assail the health service, schools and even the legal profession, the police appear to be untouchable. And that breeds public resentment.

Education, for example, has been increasingly subjected to performance yardsticks, and 'consumers' have been given vastly greater say in the running of schools, but the operation of the police – in deference to their 'independence' – lies beyond scrutiny. The professional audits of the police, carried out by the Inspectorate of Constabulary, have been so shrouded in secrecy that, until recently, not even chief constables or police authorities saw them. A researcher said: 'The police find it difficult to deal with people who appear to undermine what *they* say the facts are. We get given partially adequate answers, but they do not satisfy those who have adequate knowledge.' The reason, she suggested, why schools and not police forces are returned to the 'people' is that while the government is prepared to trust 'parents', it does not trust the 'people' likely to control inner city police forces. The spectre is raised of police forces in thrall to 'loony Left' councils.

In San Diego, California, the local force emblazons the slogan 'America's Finest' on its cars, and sets itself such targets as responding to a 'crime in progress' within three minutes, and an urgent call – like a summons to the scene of a burglary – within seven. A minority of British police forces have adopted 'policing by objectives', but most Britons would still be hanging on to the phone long after the citizen of San Diego had a cop on the doorstep. A chief superintendent said to me: 'The quality of our intake is the highest it has ever been, yet our relations with the community are the worst they have ever been. The police cannot absolve themselves from blame for this breakdown.'

Individual middle-level officers are stranded between the two concepts of 'service' and 'force', like batsmen unable to regain their ground at either wicket. They are entrusted with devolved responsibility, but have little back-up or training with which to exercise it. The Police Federation, which represents all officers below the rank of superintendent, believes that the primacy of budgets has perverted police priorities. A senior official said: 'An inspector thinks that his most important task is to keep the overtime down and stay within budget. No one understands the science of management as applied to policing. Traditional management training has to do with the profit motive, but how do you manage a non-profit service? "Watch your arse" should be translated into Latin as a motto for senior officers' messes. That sounds cynical, but it's accurate.'

It is true that a substantial proportion of senior police time is spent on 'management' rather than 'policing', but the public is concerned with the service it receives, not the problems of those who deliver it. The temptation for many is to resort to calling the police names when officers transgress or things go wrong. That may relieve the feelings, but it tends to be a self-fulfilling exercise. A Yard employee said: 'If you constantly tell someone he is a bastard, arrogant, thick, stupid, he will not only come to believe it, but will act that way.' But name-calling will persist as long as the service the police deliver continues to be flawed by inefficiency and off-hand attitudes. One burglary victim told me that twelve officers rushed to his house when he dialled 999, but not one carried out any meaningful investigation although there were 'Sherlock Holmes' sized clues like footprints outside the window. Another victim complained that the officer who came to her burglary was incapable of departing from what was obviously his standard brief, and therefore could not absorb and act upon the unique features of her break-in. A third was sufficiently angry to call the station to complain that officers had been slow in responding to her burglary and rude on arrival. When I told people I was writing a book about the police,

19

I was assailed by such anecdotes, and these dissatisfactions are increasingly finding their way into print. In December 1988, the editor of the *Mail on Sunday*, Stewart Steven, launched a coruscating two-page polemic against the Met under the heading 'YOU ARE UNDER ARREST'. He had been detained after an altercation with a police officer which started when he blew his horn in congested traffic. He wrote that he had discovered – albeit late in the day – what many less advantaged people had clearly known for some time: the comfortable notion that the British police were the best in the world was being eroded by an attitude which, if allowed to fester, threatened society's most important values. He continued in an indignant vein: 'policeman whose soul has been corroded by power . . . arrogant . . . a menace . . . a bully whose uniform permits him, he believes, to ride roughshod over the community . . .' Mr Steven then told the story of his escalating encounter with a west London policeman. He was, by his own account, seized and frogmarched to the police station; bruises were visible, he said, several days later. His conclusion was:

> If this man can treat someone like me in the way he did, how does he behave when confronted with less privileged, less assured and, yes, differently pigmented people he comes across? This incident . . . has profoundly altered the way I now view what is going on in our country. Where before I tended to disbelieve stories of police violence, I now tend to believe.

For the record, Mr Steven was fined £25 for unnecessarily blowing his horn. He immediately said he would appeal.

The following Sunday, the paper's readers had their say, and nine out of ten either supported Mr Steven or added their own unhappy experiences. Middle England, which could in the past have been counted on to give unswerving support to the police, was deeply angry and disturbed. One solid citizen told how he had been arrested after *passing* a Breathalyser test. A woman described how her son had been confused for another man, taken from their home, and put in a cell; the arresting officers were 'abusive, arrogant and very forceful'. When the mistake was discovered, there was no apology, simply a letter to say that the matter was not being taken further. A former member of an RAF bomber crew wrote: 'I believe I wasted five years of my life flying over Germany dropping bombs to prevent their authoritarian methods reaching our shores.'

At the canteen level, the tendency is always to dismiss similar complaints by aggrieved members of the public on the assumption that people who have such experiences usually ask for them. One PC told me how a complaint had been made against him because a motorist objected to the way he had raised an eyebrow. But, long before the Steven fuss, senior officers (Imbert included) had been concerned about the damage that the accumulation of minor malpractices was doing to the force image.

As I started this book, Wolff Olins, an image consultancy firm hired by the Met, produced 'A Force for Change', a report into the 'corporate identity' of London's police. The Olins team, who interviewed 250 people, found much to criticise. The force, they said, was shrouded in obscurity, deeply divided and bad at communication both internally and with the public. The report decided: 'The Met is uncertain of its role. This uncertainty manifests itself in a wide divergence of views on what is proper police work.' It highlighted a shabby 'Sellotape culture': 'This atmosphere is bad for the force, it contributes to an uncared-for feeling, it is also bad for relations with the public. It represents an antithesis of the service idea.' Olins drew attention to the paradox that, while the vast majority of people neither know nor care about the entirety of police work, they are fascinated both with the more glamorous aspects of policing and, naturally, with anything that touches their own lives. 'The combination of ignorance and interest is highly volatile. It explains why, in any one week, London's police may be both praised and attacked by the same newspapers,' said the report. Even police approval ratings can mislead,

21

because they disguise the highly concentrated nature of much of the antagonism towards the force. A favourable poll does not guarantee that police will not be spat at or abused on the streets of Brixton. The report touched on the powerful police pecking order; the unsatisfactory complaints system; and poor police/public relations. 'Police, like other social groups, need to feel wanted, admired, cared for, but they are, as they see it, sometimes misunderstood, misinterpreted, vilified, even from time to time physically and verbally abused and this inevitably affects their attitude to the public.' Olins concluded with a call for a reinterpreted 'mission statement', which, he suggested, should come down somewhere between the 'service' and 'force' extremes: 'It should give equal weight to crime detection, crime prevention and providing assistance to the public when in need or the victim of a crime.'

Senior officers, who for years had been saying many of the things Olins found, were glad that an outside body had confirmed their analysis. The £150,000 price tag might persuade the powers-that-be to take it seriously, said one. On the lower deck there was, as usual, resentment of the way the press highlighted the criticisms. Olins himself felt obliged to salve the wound by giving an interview to the Met newspaper, *The Job*. 'Much of the Press has mischievously made capital out of our observations . . . they have quite unashamedly gone for what makes the best headlines. I can now understand why police feel so often that they get a raw deal from the Press.' There was also harmless canteen mirth at Olins' proposals to brighten up police station reception areas with pot plants. One Streatham PC said: 'Doesn't he know what sort of people use those waiting rooms? The woman who comes out of the bushes and sleeps on a bench, people dripping with blood.'

The vast Metropolitan Police territory is divided into eight 'Areas', each of which is larger than most provincial police forces. They provide the divisions with pooled services, including traffic police, mounted police, dog handlers, senior detectives for murder and similar inquiries, some training, and Territorial Support Group (TSG) units, deployed for manpower-intensive operations. (Armed officers come directly from a branch of the Yard.) The Streatham division, occupying the midriff of Four Area, is a squat, amorphous slice of south London, best known outside its own environs for the Streatham Ice Rink and the High Road, a permanently bottle-necked section of the London/Brighton A23.

If the Gipsy Hill charge room – where 'Tommy' was questioned – and the cells were the sharp end of the Streatham division, the second floor at Streatham police station itself – a cosy eyrie beneath the eaves of a red-brick Edwardian building – was the think-tank. Here the most senior officers had their offices, and here strategy was devised. The first event of each day was 'morning prayers' in Chief Superintendent Street's office, when the senior management team, the duty inspector, and the woman sergeant who ran the divisional computer assessed the day's problems and possibilities. The gathering was chaired not by Mr Street but by Ian Buchan, the Superintendent. Formally, Mr Street's job was to devise policy, and Mr Buchan's to implement it, but their two roles inevitably merged. The other members of the management team for most of the time I was there were: Detective Chief Inspector John Walsh, the 'crime manager'; Chief Inspector Pat Hook (Operations); Chief Inspector David Rees (Personnel and Support), who was on exchange from the Kent County Constabulary; and Mr Peter Roe, who was divisional administrative manager. As a civilian, Mr Roe carried the least clout, but in September 1988 was, with just over one year's service in Streatham, the longest-serving member of the team, a fact that betrayed the alarming lack of continuity in divisional policing. He also was moved shortly before I left.

Morning prayers was a *tour d'horizon* of overnight events: major crimes, which would include worrying ones like 'burglary/artifice', the name given to burglaries carried out by people posing as bogus officials; local embarrassments, such as a wrongful arrest due to a muddle over names; sensitive issues, such as crimes with race or community implications; housekeeping problems. There were also reports on meetings with the community or at Scotland Yard. The meetings, and the weekly policy group gatherings, were relaxed and (up to a point) democratic. An inspector said: 'Even if you lose your corner, you have an opportunity to put your side of the case.'

Roger Street was a local man. His great-grandfather had been catering manager at the Crystal Palace, and his relatives still lived on Streatham's 'ground'. Unusually for a former senior detective – his office was decorated with photos of bank robbers caught in the act by hidden cameras – he had become wholly committed to community policing. With great pride he presented me with a report he had produced in his previous job with the Yard's Community Involvement Policy Unit, entitled 'Policing the Urban Village'. His well-stocked bookcase included *The Police and the Public*, *Les Misérables*, *Capitalist Democracy in Britain*, and *Vineyards of England and Wales*. The journal of his *alma mater*, the *LSE Quarterly*, nestled on a side table together with the *Spectator*. He lectured to the Howard League on penal reform, and professed himself happy in the company of academics. He didn't suffer fools (or even foolishness) gladly, which sometimes made him seem rather brittle. He pushed his management team to the limits, he said, even if that meant the strains sometimes showed. Giving less than the best was, to him, unpardonable: 'Policing is a public service of the utmost importance: it can make the difference between life and death.' He was, he once told me, surprised by how far he had risen. While, as he put it, thoroughly in tune with objectives of policing, he did not come from a family of achievers, and had not supposed that he would reach the higher ranks. But, now that he was a senior officer, his ambition had been stirred.

He wrestled continuously with the dichotomy between 'force' and 'service'. He had, he said, recently been mildly upbraided by a fellow senior officer: 'The trouble with you, Roger, is that you're always thinking about the community.' But he would not have risen through the Flying

Squad to chief superintendent on notions other police found woolly or soft. As divisional commander, he played several parts. At times he was the headmaster, attending the divisional rugby matches, or congratulating the boys and girls on a good piece of work. In this role he would also upbraid. Having thanked a group of young police constables for catching a team of youngsters trying to rob a bus driver, he told them off roundly for parking the 'nondy' (nondescript) – an ancient, unmarked builders' van used for observation – in the station yard and so potentially betraying its identity to any shrewd student of police practice. As 'headmaster', he was, to a limited degree, a moral guardian: he decreed one day that pin-ups should be taken down. 'I see no reason why a police station should have naked women on the walls.' I was never quite sure how such edicts were put into effect; there were certainly some nudes on walls many weeks later.

Although a uniformed force, the police are not disciplined like the armed services, and it shows. Police station garden beds are untended; litter proliferates even on station steps; a broken window at Gipsy Hill remained broken for several days; the clocks on the top floor at Streatham had stopped at 2.23 – I suspect during the great October storm of 1987; an injunction to ensure the main door was closed as defence against the IRA was sometimes not acted upon. There is, as one inspector said, 'a lot of power slushing about', but it is diffuse, and difficult to mobilise on comparatively trivial issues.

Mr Street was also a crisis manager, perpetually on the alert like a coastguard responsible for defences against a stormy sea. After an eruption of trouble at a High Road night spot on Christmas Eve, he spent much of Christmas Day ensuring there were sufficient troops on the ground to cope with a possible repeat on Boxing Day. In this role, he can never wholly relax; the phone may go at any hour, advising him that 'the wheels have come off' (police parlance for a crisis).

Roger Street's number two, Ian Buchan, was a Scot from near Inverness, whose boyhood ambition to become a professional golfer was reflected in a handsome Metropolitan Police golf trophy which decorated his office windowsill. His father hadn't the money to launch him as a golfer, and on impulse the teenaged Buchan, whose horizons had been limited to one trip to Aberdeen, answered a Met Police ad. His most recent post had, like Mr Street's, been in community relations, where he had sought to find ways to draw more blacks into the police force. His ideas were variously described to me as visionary – 'the rest of this carthorse may catch up with him in twenty years' – and naïve. He excelled at public meetings, where his charm transported his audience smoothly over the roughest terrain.

Mr Roe had the least enviable job among the senior management team: his daily report was usually devoted to the juggling of his civilian staff and the placating of police colleagues whose typing and other work had not been done. 'We're always the tail end charlies, rushing to pick up the pieces,' he said. He was philosophic about the brickbats which the police threw at his team: civilians were there, he said, to support the police and soak up their stress. They had to make allowances when a policeman was rude; after all, he might just have come from a ghastly accident. (He might also, of course, simply be an unpleasant person in a foul temper.) Roe was being diplomatic: the grudging attitude of police officers to civilians is one of the reasons why civilians are hard to recruit and retain.

The large majority of police officers were then assigned to 'reliefs', which, despite their name, operate a round-the-clock shift system and carry out the basic station duties. Relief officers man the front desk and the communications room; they lock up prisoners; they operate the computer and the message switching centre; they drive the vehicles; and, if any officers remain when the essential duties have been assigned, they walk the streets. A minority will always be absent, at court, on courses, on 'aid' at football matches and demonstrations.

A relief officer knows for a year in advance exactly what his shift pattern will be; if it is broken without sufficient warning, lucrative overtime payments are triggered. While it lasts, which may be for many years, membership of a relief is the core experience of an officer's life. Loyalty to 'justice', the 'job', the wider police force or even to the division are distant and theoretical concepts; dependence on the relief is paramount. A PC, recently in the army, said: 'You identify with all the people on your relief; you can always turn and ask them. They're the people you rely on in a tricky situation; they're only a radio call away. If you can't get on with the relief then it's pointless doing the job.' The relief inspector – the 'guv'nor' – is a powerful figure, who determines how his men and women are assigned, what courses they go on, how, therefore, their careers will develop. For the majority of London police, the force of 28,000 officers is shrunk to a community of about 45 people, with whom they will share both the many hours between responses and the excitements and dangers when they occur. Out of about 260 police officers in Streatham, nearly 200 were attached to reliefs.

Reliefs work a complicated shift pattern: at Streatham it was seven straight 'nights', 11.00 p.m. to 7 a.m; back that same day after what is known as a 'quick change-over' for a 'late' turn, 3 p.m. till 11 p.m., and the same the following day; then two days off, followed by three 'earlys' – 7 a.m. to 3 p.m; two more days off, five 'late', four 'early', long weekend, and the pattern begins again. Its logic appears crazy; one retired senior officer said it defied the natural rhythms of the circadian cycle, and an inspector, in the foothills of middle age, told me he found the night shift so debilitating that it took him two weeks to recover. 'By then it's time for nights to come round again; knowing they're ahead takes the edge off the long weekend. You're always out of sync, and it's hard to get to sleep – you find you're watching all kinds of rubbish on TV,' he said. Most younger officers, however, thrive on it; one PC who had left the force rejoined largely because he had come to enjoy having time off when others were at work. He had found that being free only at weekends cramped his style.

To provide this twenty-four-hour cover, a division is split

into four reliefs – 'A' to 'D'. Each shift begins with a parade of those few officers not already earmarked for a specific task. In the fairly recent past this was a semi-military ritual, with policemen standing at attention and presenting truncheons. At Streatham, officers sat, notebooks on knees, while a sergeant read out the day's duties, calling each officer by his number rather than name. He also designated each officer's time for 'refs' (refreshments) – police officers measure out their lives with tea and chips. One December night, 'A' relief, with six PCs and one WPC on parade, was coming on duty. A PC assigned to walk the High Road rolled his eyes and moaned; the inspector said with a smile: 'The fresh air will do you good. I thought you'd enjoy a walk after being tied up in the "comms" [the communications room] all week.' Another officer told to ride in the van gave an exaggerated 'phew' at his escape from foot-patrolling on a cold night. It was time for the first canteen break of the night.

Ian Hogg, the 'A' relief inspector, is a tall, well-built Yorkshireman, the apotheosis of a 'copper'. He came to London as a police cadet in the mid–1960s and is married to a former WPC. His daily problem was to juggle his available officers to cover the obligatory jobs while still leaving a few pairs of feet to pound the beat. On each shift, officers were needed for the area car, two vans, two pandas, the communications room, the front offices at both Streatham and Gipsy Hill, the 'custody suite' and the cells. Allowing for those tied up with other commitments, Mr Hogg was lucky if there remained two or three 'walkers'. Duty inspectors have budgetry responsibility but little control. Officers would be earmarked for court, for example, only to turn up to find they had been given the wrong day, and the wasted time was paid for out of the relief budget. Two rather morose officers – a man and a woman – explained they had attended court in the morning as witnesses in a shoplifting case; the case had been held over till the afternoon, when it was thrown out because of conflict of evidence. The sum involved was under five pounds. Such waste of manpower and money happened all the time. The

theory behind passing financial responsibility down the line
is to alert inspectors to the cost of the resources they command, and therefore to encourage them to be frugal and
accountable. In practice, since they have so little control
over events or the demands on their men, they have responsibility without power. A senior PC said: 'Policing isn't an
industry, and crime can't be budgeted, yet senior officers
sit down with slide rules. If we need a couple of hours
overtime, we have to beg or burgle it. Executive officers go
through expenses to claw back pennies. We can't work
under these conditions; morale has gone down and frustration up. We're told we can't do things because the pot
is empty. If the public knew, they'd go potty. What we are
saying to them is "we can't deal with your problem, because
we have got no money".'

However far an officer rises, his first two years are spent
on relief and (inescapably) in the canteen. Here, he not
only takes his 'refs' – he must be available throughout the
eight-hour shift – but writes up his notes, completes his
interminable reports, takes part in meetings, briefs and is
briefed; recruits in their early days on the street duties
course seem scarcely out of the place. Physically it is the
centre of the operation. At Streatham along one wall were
a fridge, a cooker and a microwave, so when meals were
not being served officers could cater for themselves. In one
corner there was a dart board, which I never saw used, and
a Pepsi-Cola machine. A Space Invader video game near
the door was keenly competed for; zapping aliens filled in
the time after the *Sun*, the most popular newspaper among
the police, had been thoroughly digested. Traffic wardens
– tolerated, like blacks in the Deep South before Civil
Rights, so long as they don't become uppity – shelter from
the rain and the exigencies of their unpopular job. Retired
police officers, working at the station as civilians, hold daily
card schools. If you want to find someone, the canteen is a
sensible first place to try; if he is not there, he will probably
turn up. The close-knit world of the relief and the physical
environment of the canteen combine to create what is
known as 'canteen culture'. This is the below-the-stairs

attitude to the job and the world which is a far more powerful influence on a police officer's behaviour and beliefs than the official policies devised at the top. A man who had made a close study of the Metropolitan Police said: 'Canteen culture is the total reversal of official culture. "Governors don't know how tough it is. The world is full of villains. If we went, then London would stop." They have mad, romantic notions of quelling this heaving underworld, seething with vice and crime.'

The perception of senior officers as out-of-touch panjan-drums is an invariable canteen theme, and is linked to the complaint that the police are poorly led at the very top. 'The Met is a bloody great galleon going nowhere. There are very few senior officers with leadership qualities. We don't see our own senior officers from one year's end to the next,' said one experienced constable. PCs are constantly on the look-out for evidence of senior officers' failings. After an armed robbery, a senior officer called the charge room to find out what was going on. When he was told that there were two prisoners, but they had been arrested by officers from a neighbouring division, he commented that it was a pity they hadn't been 'nicked' by Streatham men. It was probably a joke, but it did the rounds for several days: 'That shows what sort of governors we've got.'

The canteen antithesis of the Identikit senior officer is the noble PC, his feet anchored to the ground and his head stuffed full of common sense, who gets on with his job, uncorrupted by thoughts of promotion. Such officers are renowned for their 'instincts' – a far more valuable qualifi-cation below stairs than education or training. 'I've had a few good bodies in my time, but 'X' is a real thief taker. He'll be walking along the road and a burglar will pop out of a window in front of him. Some complete idiots can't help falling over good bodies. They just stop a car on instinct, and find a wanted man in it,' said one PC, subscrib-ing to the theory that good coppers are born and not made. Instinct, however, let both these men down later that night. They were looking for a man who had carried out an attack, and, from a vague description, jumped to the conclusion that it was a well-known local 'scrote'. Said one: 'He's a right little shitbag; he wouldn't hesitate twice to give you a dig.' On this occasion he was the wrong suspect.

It would be difficult for a young officer to dissent too vocally from canteen values and remain one of the boys. A senior officer, who acknowledged that peer pressure was intense, said that some police wore 'an overcoat of values to hide other values underneath'. As a young officer, he himself had simply put his newspaper over his head when the routine prejudices were being paraded. He had, in any case, found his first ten years so demanding that it was only when he was sent on a course at Bramshill college (where senior officers from throughout Britain are trained) that he had time to think about the wider aims of policing. If an officer was good, he said, he could achieve credibility 'by prowess at such fundamental tasks as catching criminals'. He could then withstand the 'odd' label. One of Streatham's most popular PCs was a university graduate who spoke several languages, read Thomas Hardy in the canteen, talked in a clipped voice, was unashamedly enthusiastic about everything that came his way, and rode a bicycle on his beat. But in less self-confident characters, the survival of the brightest depends on chameleonic qualities. Good policemen, said a university graduate, do rise to positions where they can make a difference: 'Well-educated people are coming into the force, but they will need time to marshal their thoughts.' He added that making an impact takes patience; the out-and-out 'crusader', even at the highest levels, tends to run into a brick wall.

The area that comprises the Streatham division has been coming down in the world for a generation. There is, certainly in the evening, a faint air of menace on the High Road as revellers topple out of the restaurants and clubs; the pavements are litter-strewn and the incidence of mugging fairly high. It is the sort of environment in which you look over your shoulder when drawing money from a cash dispenser. To the west of the High Road, there is a highly unlikely, but renowned, prostitution district, which sets the police one of their chief challenges. Streatham's heyday

had been the late Victorian era when prosperous City busi-
nessmen built large villas there to take advantage of the
three railway lines that pour commuters back and forth to
central London like the tide. Today, when an elderly person
dies, his house is likely to be converted into flats since his
children seldom want a big home in a fading area. First
time buyers don't remain very long. Some parts of London
have retained the feel of an urban village – even Brixton
makes efforts – but traffic runs through Streatham in all
directions, rendering it a kind of sieve. Multiple occupancy
is a blight; front gardens are neglected, houses unpainted;
during the day many are deserted, providing the perfect
opportunity for burglars. While the national burglary rate
was at last declining, Streatham was suffering as never
before.

Until recently the district was almost totally white; now,
accelerating migration from neighbouring Brixton is stimulating some fairly raw racism. During one afternoon I spent
with a PC, virtually everyone we met made racial comments, either overtly or by unmistakable implication. A
mechanic put the ills of inner London life down to 'the
brown chappies', to whom he referred several times. A
retired businessman suggested that blacks were anti-police
because of their different experiences 'at home'. 'So many
of our coloured people seem to think that the police are the
right arm of some terrible dictator,' he said. Rape and the
use of knives, he added, were 'foreign to this country'. (He
spoke in the week that marked the centenary of Jack the
Ripper.) He was trying to sell his home to escape from
living close to a council estate which housed many blacks.
To him, the decline of Streatham appeared a microcosm of
the decline of the mother country. 'Most of our troubles
can be related to poor education, the lack of a Boys' Brigade
and Scouts, the lack of religious education. We teach history in a backhanded way, almost as if apologising for our
achievements,' he said. A neighbour had watched 'coloureds' taking evasive action at the approach of the police:
'Ninety-nine out of a hundred cross the road when they see
a policeman.' For him, society's ills could all be traced to

the alien wedge of immigration. 'If you had the camaraderie, the way of life before the war, when a policeman could
smack a little boy around the ear . . . It's a great shame
that a policeman's power has been eroded. I had enough
thumps from police when I was young: it did me no harm,
it made me respect them. It doesn't matter whether respect
is genuine or comes from fear.'

Traces of Old Streatham exist only in a handful of buildings, chiefly the parish church, which stands eighty yards
from the police station. It was at this church that Dr Johnson, during the fifteen years he visited his friends the
Thrales at Streatham Park, worshipped. When he departed
for the last time, he recorded in his diary: *'Templo valedixi
cum osculo'* – 'I say farewell to the church with a kiss.' The
tranquillity of that scene might, however, give a misleading
picture of the historic state of law and order in the area now
policed by Messrs Street and Buchan. Frederick Arnold, a
local nineteenth-century historian, wrote: 'It is a fearful
and horrible fact that few churchyards have so many people
buried within their precincts who have been "found dead",
foully murdered, in many cases, by the numerous footpads
who infested the roads in times gone by, as God's acre at
Streatham.'

Mr Street listed his priorities as the robberies, burglaries
and assaults to which a transient and demoralised inner city
population is highly vulnerable. A community on the slide
is like marginal land on the edge of a desert. As the trees
are uprooted, the desert encroaches; as stable citizens move
on, their places are taken by the defenceless and the preda-
tory. Fear creates openings for criminals: people become
wholly concerned with their own survival. As well as housing ordinary people who find it difficult to cope, a neighbourhood of bedsits and single people becomes home to
both discharged prisoners and mental patients. Inevitably,
alongside the disadvantaged, live the dangerous. The *South
London Press* feeds its readers a bi-weekly diet of horror:
'Three drink- and drug-crazed men murdered a complete
stranger for his pint of beer . . .' and 'A father of two was

brutally tortured with a stun gun while his family were imprisoned in another room by masked gunmen . . .'

The Streatham division has its share of such horrors, but the bulk of its crime was not the stuff of headlines. Mr Street said: 'Most police work is ordinary, everyday stuff – kids arrested for shoplifting, people locked out of their houses. These things are vitally important to the lives of the people concerned, and in terms of manpower are as demanding as a bank robbery. But, because they *are* so demanding, they tend to become the be-all and end-all.' Streatham's everyday crime was rooted in two polarised contemporary problems: affluence at one end of the division (which mainly meant late-night drunken disorders); and poverty at the other. The affluence tempted the poor to commit crime. There were a number of homes for children in care – mainly black boys – and these youths were responsible for many of the muggings and contributed to the high burglary rate. More than any other, the issue of what should be done about the homes split officers between the 'force' and 'service' camps. An inspector said: 'There are at least two cultures within the division: the "community" approach versus "Adventurers Ltd", who like the excitement and kudos of getting an arrest, and – at the time – don't think of the wider consequences. They rush in with adrenaline pumping.'

A detective explained the dilemma: 'It may not be good politics to target ethnic minority kids in care, but burglaries are running fifty per cent higher in that sector than elsewhere in the division.' He understood what made the boys delinquent and was, like most policemen, sympathetic to young people who 'had never had a chance'. But from his practical perspective, the boys were contaminating one another, and the local community was at unjustifiable risk. He said: 'They are learning much more than if they were "banged up". Inside they have a theoretical education; putting these little buggers together in homes, they get practical experience.' Some of these boys were indefatigable rogues: one, held overnight in a Gipsy Hill cell, robbed his fellow prisoner of £190. The theft was not discovered until his victim went to court, was fined, and realised to his horror that his money had gone. The boy, meanwhile, had been on a clothes shopping spree. The detective agreed that someone should be 'diverting' these kids from crime, but argued vehemently that it was not a police responsibility. But Mr Street was loath to stigmatise the boys and anxious to tread softly: a mismanaged arrest at such a home could set back police/community relations months. The police were not alone in struggling with the dilemma presented by the children's homes. A liberal resident was dismayed to discover that the major impetus behind a campaign for a neighbourhood watch scheme was fear of the homes. 'The traffic in the area is far more dangerous than all the kids who ever lived in these houses,' he said despairingly.

The cornerstone of Mr Street's approach is the belief that successful policing is invariably built on an unwritten contract. 'People's willingness to co-operate is related to the benefits they think they'll derive. People who feel that the police are there to serve them will co-operate. The opposite perception is that the police are there to harass the community and stop people living their own lives. That's the Iron Curtain model. It is up to us to demonstrate that is not the fact. It is only when there is a wide consensus in the ethnic minority community that what the police do benefits their lives that they will have confidence in the police,' he said in one of the conversations that punctuated my time at Streatham. He continued: 'Most young policemen come from outside London. They have no integration with the community and no roots. It is easy for them, without realising it, to suffer from a "fortress" mentality, to feel that their backs are against the wall, to become, in effect, an "occupying army".' An experienced PC said: 'It's tempting to get in your car at the end of the day and drive home with your stereo on, and forget that their problems are your problems.' One officer estimated that only four or five of his Streatham colleagues (out of 260) lived within the divisional boundaries.

Mr Street said: 'When you have responsibility for running a division, you have got to have a clear idea of what you are about, or else you get into a reactive spiral. You'll get by, but what are you achieving? How are you really helping the people of your division? I have a model in my mind of what we should be doing, which I hold dear and which influences my decision-making.' He added that the only way that a police force earns its legitimacy is by working at community relations. 'That is seeking to respond to what the public wants, dealing with the "substance". PR is "hiding", concerned chiefly with image and putting a gloss on what we do,' he said.

Streatham police station was opened in 1912 on the site of a station originally built in 1865. Throughout the time I was there, the front part of the building was being gutted and rebuilt, with the result that PCs worked in appalling squalor. The interior of the station was dull, a place of grey and dun (no one has ever risked a bright splash in a police station). Streatham's other station at Gipsy Hill, was, if anything, yet more gloomy: interminable construction work to install a computer system left a permanent film of dust over everything. The division suffered, according to several officers, from being close to Brixton, which, with its inflammable history and potential volatility, leached resources from its neighbours. Staff turnover was as rapid at the bottom as at the top: during 1988, one third of the police constables left and were replaced. It was routine for all ranks to deplore the regular departure of experienced officers from the division, but the arrival of fresh blood meant that Streatham was not overburdened with cynical old sweats. Men and women with four or five years' service were the backbone of the division. Long-in-the-tooth coppers, who have remained throughout their service tied to the diurnal round of routine policing, not only can be desperate bores, but, predictably, they resist change and are antagonistic towards its implications. They are a dead weight on the force.

I met several older officers of this school, at Streatham and elsewhere, who seldom looked much beyond the sports pages of the *Sun* for intellectual refreshment. I became familiar with the old timers' lament for yesteryear: 'The only way to learn the job is on your own. If you make your own mistakes, you never make them again. The job has gone downhill since the introduction of PRs [personal radios]. They radio in now: "I'm out on the street, Sarge; which foot should I put forward?" Fresh-faced youngsters are brainwashed into following the system. That's how we lost the respect of the public. I'd be in the shit if I went back on the streets because of the changes in society. *They* know their rights. "What's your number?" they ask. You can't get away with the old threats. Everything's got to be done down the line, as per the book. It's not always a good thing to make youngsters aware of their rights and wrongs. Make them aware of the wrongs – yeah. In my day no one took the monkey out of the old Bill. I saw a PC walking down the road last week and being goaded by three coloureds. They're not frightened of the law any more. The bosses want innocent police on the streets, and they teach them how to say "sorry". In happier days justice was dispensed on the streets.'

Most senior officers would like something done about policemen who have lost their enthusiasm. Men nearing the end of their service count off the years like long-term gaolbirds looking towards release. A chief inspector said: 'Tenure's too secure. When the point is arrived at that a man and the force should part company, it is not easy to achieve. The present technique is to kick someone's arse. You let him know: "You are earning a good salary – all of us are: if you're too lazy, the job will say goodbye to you." I know that there are a lot of officers drawing these salaries who do not justify them. The theory is that pressure (not victimisation) will eventually mean that he either gets it together and starts working, or he says "Sod this, I'm going to give my ticket in." There are, however, devious officers who do just enough; they walk a tightrope and never fall off.' He wanted to see a formalised system, under which a written warning would follow a verbal one, and then the force could say: 'Thank you very much for your services.' The Association of Chief Police Officers and the Home Office equally want an efficient system for clearing the dead wood;

however, the Police Federation argues that the problem is poor management, not incompetent cops. A Federation spokesman said: 'The number of officers who fall into the sackable category is minute; no service has a better system of getting rid of bad employees.'

The slack attitude of mind that is fostered by security of tenure is reinforced by the overtime system by which policemen below the rank of superintendent are paid. Clock-watching is endemic. Overtime jobs that pay well and demand relatively little effort – like guarding prison overspill inmates in police cells – are seductive distractions from the hard graft of divisional work. During the miners' strike, some PCs were said to be earning up to £2,000 a month in overtime: 'They were in the supertax bracket,' said an inspector. Overtime payments both corrupt the spirit and create an unattractive, grudging outlook on life. Some officers, while happily pocketing considerably more than teachers or probation officers, retain the hard-done-by demeanour of sweat-shop workers. The Police Federation inevitably opposes the incorporation of overtime into basic salaries. The removal of the overtime principle, they argue, would leave officers open to exploitation by unscrupulous managers. One London Federation rep said: ' "Open-ended" would mean just that. We would be theirs whenever they wanted us, at the beck and call of draconian chief inspectors. People who were after promotion would be here morning, noon and night. You could spend twenty-four hours a day and still not be on top of some jobs; if you put in that kind of commitment, you should be paid for it.' He added: 'However pleasant his face, inside every chief superintendent I have known there has lurked a small or large dictator. I have no faith that people who are that career-orientated will look after the welfare of their men.'

Getting efficiency right is only half the battle to regain lost public confidence. What has soured relations between police and policed more than anything is the attitudes of individual officers. A man who has made a study of the Met said: 'Until fifteen years ago, there was endemic corruption: that has gone. That does not mean that there are not individual policemen who are corrupt, but, if they are caught, they are regarded no differently from anyone else who is corrupt. They are dealt with. Officers who smack prisoners – "handymen" – are strongly disapproved of by their colleagues. There is generally a new climate. However, police officers remain verbally aggressive, abusive, too free with their tongues.'

Such arrogance is notoriously worse in London than in the provinces. London officers are similar people to their out-of-town colleagues – indeed, over two thirds of London's police are recruited from outside the capital – but the culture of the Met (and of a big city) rapidly affects their common outlook. In private most Met officers are little different from the rest of us; collectively they become hardened. During a radio interview, Sir Peter Imbert both denied and confirmed the phenomenon: 'I don't think that it is a general perception that the Met is an aggressive force. If one is working in a country area, where you know the people you are working with, and you can have a daily contact and liaison, inevitably there is going to be a much better relationship. [In London] you cannot have daily contact. The demands on the police are enormously different from demands in other parts of the country.'

Because the London force is by far the biggest – nearly five times the size of the next largest in England and Wales – the overweening bearing of some of its men damages the standing of the police across the country. A senior provincial officer recalled policing 'mods and rockers' disturbances in the 1960s. 'We were keeping the youths on the move, not allowing numbers to build up, but when more bikes started arriving in town, the Mets were sent in. Things started going bloody wrong from the moment they arrived – big punch-ups.' Having once worked in London, this officer was able to analyse some of what he called the 'cultural-based' causes of the Met aggression. 'In the counties we don't know we're born. Don't be taken in by the "lager louts"; that was a press ploy. Small parts of provincial towns are like inner London, but what is missing is the relentless concentration. The Met's problems are to some extent a consequence of deprivation and poverty, and there are criminal families, some bad buggers. Add to that racial implications, and you're starting to get a cocktail for trouble. The Mets, therefore, have to police hard. You have to develop a policy of positive policing – get in and sort it out. This creates the culture: "We are an active force; we don't muck about." '

However, he blamed senior officers for too much tolerance towards these attitudes. 'The Mets are always in numbers, and therefore more likely to act out of character and forcefully because they know that blokes are backing them up. In the counties you have to talk your way out.' He had recently been in charge of a public order occasion. 'I was ground commander, and my prayer was that we didn't bring in the Met. We only wanted the Met – the "grief" – as a last resort. The blokes would say: "Oh Christ, the Met's coming in; things will start to liven up." There's an arrogance amongst Met officers – "We're the biggest force in the country; we police the biggest city." For years they thought they were the only force worth anything. The Mets suffer from a pride which goes beyond pride; they were the untouchables, the experts – the murder squad, the flying squad, the "Sweeney"; it all fed the arrogance, the ego. County police were "straw-chewing, country bumpkins". But they haven't got the right to regard us as amateurs. County forces have discovered that the Met are no better than anyone else.' He said that Met officers who transferred to county forces stand out like a sore thumb when they first arrive. 'They swagger, and take an abrasive approach. In time they mellow.' He said: 'There are punchy, arrogant people in all forces, a leopard doesn't change his spots. But the nature of the Met tends to mould an officer into the sort I have been describing.'

In his own force, the telephone directory containing all the key numbers is no thicker than a weekly magazine; in the Met it runs to several fat, looseleaf volumes, and is permanently out of date because of the high staff turnover and the reorganisations that rumble beneath London's police like a permanent earth tremor. The very senior officers in the county can be brought together round a coffee table. Eighty people are entitled to attend a gathering of the Met hierarchy: if each were to speak for five minutes, their meeting would take a minimum of six hours. But what is more important than any logistics is the tighter control that is possible in a small force, where it is far easier to ensure that the policies and attitudes devised and desired at the top reach the men on the beat without dilution or subversion. 'The newly appointed probationer must be in no doubt that if he speaks to a member of the public in an arrogant way, he'll be on report. He must be aware of what will not be tolerated, and know that, if he steps out of line, he will be chopped. The best intentions are wrecked if there is a weak link in the chain,' said the provincial officer.

2

'Puppy-Walking the New Toys'

'As a police officer, sooner of later you're bound to encounter abuse, threats, provocation, even physical violence. Be careful how you respond. Lose your temper and you could lose your job . . . we need people who can cope. People who are tough, tender, sensitive, strong and disciplined, all at the same time'
– Police recruiting advertisement

These words, under the headline 'COULD YOU TURN THE OTHER CHEEK?', appeared alongside the photograph used on the cover of this book. It shows an unshaven yob wearing an earring spitting in the face of a square-jawed, clean-shaven young cop, who looks at his assailant with a steadfast gaze. Picture and text were part of a major recruitment campaign run by the Metropolitan Police in newspaper colour supplements in 1988 and 1989. In each case a dramatic photograph, taken by Don McCullin who made his substantial reputation covering wars, was accompanied by more words than a copywriter aiming his message at people with a basic education would normally dare employ. Would-be recruits were drawn to the ads by the impact of the McCullin images: a young man smoking a reefer; rival football supporters separated by a fence and a shirt-sleeved copper; a series of people exhibiting stress, who might or might not be lying; a dead child under a blanket. Then they were challenged by provocative headlines and bold cross-headings to read on.

Those persistent enough to reach the end read: 'We're looking for mature, fit people aged between 18½ and 45, especially from the ethnic minorities. You should be at least 172 cms tall if you are a man, and 162 if you're a woman.

Ideally you should have some 'O' level passes or their equivalents, but we value your personal qualities more.' Each year slightly over 10,000 people answer these and other advertisements, one in five of whom will eventually swear: 'I solemnly and sincerely declare and affirm that I will well and truly serve our Sovereign Lady the Queen in the Office of Constable without favour or affection, malice or ill-will, and that I will, to the best of my power, cause the peace to be kept and preserved . . .'

Twenty-one weeks after uttering these words, during which they had completed their basic training, eight young people, seven men and a woman, sat rather nervously in the Chief Superintendent's office on the top floor of Streatham police station. Roger Street was away, and his place was taken by Superintendent Ian Buchan. This was the trainee police officers' first day on the job, and Mr Buchan's task was to welcome them to what one recent commissioner described as 'more a cause than a job'. The eight typified the majority of Met recruits in that they all came from outside London and were to live at first in a 'section house', essentially a hall of residence attached to a police station. The transformation from civilian to police officer – the induction into the tribe – was about to gather pace. They had learned already, they said, to avoid certain pubs where off-duty police stuck out like sore thumbs and were not welcome.

Mr Buchan is a relaxed, approachable man, a far cry from the popular image of the unbending senior Mr Plod. He sat, he told me later, behind rather than in front of the desk because he represented rank, but he spoke to the recruits as an uncle might talk rather than as a very powerful member of a uniformed, disciplined force. His enthusiasm for policing, his Scottish lack of 'side', his darting technique – hopping from one topic to another and back again like a bird in search of juicy grubs – and his occasional air of ruminating aloud surprised the recruits, who had been expecting something more formal and austere.

'In Streatham you'll find everything in relation to policing. I would have loved to have come here as a young copper. It is a busy inner London area with very high robbery and burglary problems. We can't cope with those and we can't cope with our traffic problem. It hasn't got quite the political sensitivity of Brixton, but it borders Brixton and we suffer because some of their villains come to our ground to get rich pickings. We've got a vice problem, very historical – not sure what we're going to do with that, not sure what you can actually do with prostitution. We have a vice squad, but the women come from all over the country despite publicity about Aids.'

He raised immediately the fraught issue of local politics. 'Some of you may have preconceptions about what Lambeth Council is like, a leftie council and all that. It may be politically, but professionally we find we get very good co-operation. Unfortunately everything is political, and they have a police committee that controls liaison with the local police. They're not hard left. We tend to group together these left-wing councils as being very anti-police. They're not. What we tend to forget when we come into London among the great big mass of people is that out there, they are just small communities. In the main they are pro-police; over ninety per cent of our arrests come from information from members of the public.' From politics it was but a quick hop to the closely related issue of race. 'Young blacks sometimes get labelled; they are often in fact born in Lambeth, second generation. There is tremendous co-operation from most of them; only a very small percentage commit robberies and burglaries. You need to sift out how you are going to communicate with these people, because communicate is what you've got to do. You've got to learn people skills. You will have seen hyped-up stuff on TV, where in an hour we can solve anything (although if you're Inspector Morse on Saturday night, it takes two hours!). Life is not like that. Life in the police force is dealing with people. If you ask me what makes a successful CID officer, it ain't the macho bit, it's the ability to sit down and talk. You've got to find a level on which you can talk to villains, so that you can get information from them. You don't do that by being the all-powerful person. It's exactly the same skill as you have got to learn when you're dealing with a six foot-four yob, who's slightly high on cannabis and very anti-you and has committed all sorts of criminal damage.'

Mr Buchan told them that there would be times – facing hostility, dealing with public order, handling a traffic snarl-up – when they would need to exert their authority. 'But one of the things you ought to do while you're out there getting the feel of the uniform is throw a "good morning, sir" or "good morning, madam". They'll give you a smile back, because people want to feel security. Sometimes we're not very good at that. If you adopt a positive attitude, you'll find this a very rewarding job.' He was, he said, going to put stickers on all the police station phones, telling officers to say 'Can I help you?' when they answer. 'If somebody answers the phone like that, you immediately feel as if you're wanted. When people come to the front counter, throw a smile: "Good morning, can I help you?" If they've begun to get an anti-police feeling, you can actually redress that. You're going to be pushed to the emotional limits of your patience. There are some awful people out there as well, and we do come across them. That's when you've really got to keep cool, calm and collected.'

He told them to be smart and fit; enthusiastic and punctual. 'You've come to an alive station, and you're going to be busy.' He explained how the division was accountable to local people: 'They tell us what they want us to do; we don't impose on them. We listen, because if we don't, we're actually policing without the community. Now we can't do that.' He admonished them to work hard and pass their exams, and, when in doubt, to seek advice, and he concluded with a practical homily, advising them to invest their rent allowance in bricks and mortar. 'You are paid a lot of money these days, and it is a temptation to get a super-duper car and go on lovely holidays. But I would just watch that a little bit. You can find one-bedroomed flats in this area for around £48/50,000. And you can afford that mortgage, frightening though it might seem.' As well as being sound business, he said, buying their own homes would get them away from what can become the claustrophobic embrace of the police force. 'There is nothing worse than getting into this thing we call the canteen culture. You've actually got to get away from that, to live out there the same as other people. You'll find it difficult to resist the canteen culture because you are joining an organisation in which you've got to be accepted. But it's a mistake after eight hours on the job to go back to a section house and socialise with police people. There's a balance. You'll find tremendous camaraderie, two families in life, your family and the police family who will give you a lot of support and companionship.' He concluded: 'It's a cracking job; I'm as enthusiastic now and as keen as when I first joined it.'

The eight recruits listening to Mr Buchan ranged in age from nineteen (two ex-police cadets) to their mid-twenties. I first met them while they were still training at Hendon Police College. Senior officers constantly say that the standard of recruit intake has never been higher, and certainly I had no problem with the idea of any of these eight pounding the beat past my front door. When I said as much to another officer, he replied that he thought one of them was 'left wing', and he darkly suspected the young man was a 'plant', though by whom and for what purpose, he did not add. There were two graduates – one of whom was an Asian – the woman, and an ex-soldier. Two of the recruits had been turned down by other forces before applying to the Met, and a couple had had chequered employment records. One had lasted two days on a business degree course; one had embarked on teacher training, but had flunked. There are growing numbers of ex-teachers in police ranks. Ironically, given the supposed stresses of policing, several I met said that they could cope with life on the beat as they had never been able to handle life in the classroom. One recruit had worked in an office and been a sales rep; one had been a supermarket manager.

They already appreciated that there was more to life as a police officer than racing about with blue lights flashing. One grumbled that the ads miss out the paperwork – 'You don't see the half of it; the four and a half hours filling in forms, or the thirty-six pieces of paper you have to carry with you.' They realised that their friends were likely to be concentrated amongst their colleagues, and were becoming slightly self-conscious, feeling that they stood out from other people, even in casual clothes. Two had recently been to a nightclub, where the bouncer came across to explain to them why he had thrown some people out. 'We didn't say anything, but I'm sure he thought we were plain-clothes police,' said one.

When I asked whether their fellow recruits had represented a 'cross-section' of society, one replied sharply: 'The police are not looking for a cross-section, but for special people with character.' But another was more circumspect, saying there were some 'dodgy characters' at Hendon. For most, police pay had been a major attraction, though one young man from Kent, more aware than the others of the cost of living in the south-east, was less impressed. The former trainee teacher reflected on the life he had quit – 'in a fleapit bedsit, working long hours' – and shuddered slightly. Another said that he was already better paid than friends who were army subalterns.

I met them again one night in their section house a few weeks after they had started at Streatham, and I sensed that the barriers were rapidly going up between them and the wider society. They were, said one, already picking up police expressions; a second added: 'I prefer anyway sticking to people I know.' At night they liked to switch off. 'We earn our bread out on the streets,' said one, meaning that they resented being asked to perform an off-duty peace-keeping role. It could have been an old police lag talking. They gravitated towards each other in a local pub, up to eighteen of them bunched round the same tables. 'We stick out like a sore thumb,' said one. A hostile hand had written 'Death to the Pigs' over the pub dartboard. 'That doesn't give you a very nice feeling,' said one. Another shrugged: 'There's scrotes everywhere.' That was not a word he would have used two weeks earlier.

Police recruits quite often come from service families. One of the Streatham intake said: 'I had thought of joining

the army like my father, but the army is always training to
kill people – something they hope will never happen. A
policeman is constantly on active duty, something more
positive than training to kill.' He added: 'It is also a practical way of doing good for the community.' An ex-soldier,
also at Streatham, said that in the army he had been frustrated by always being told exactly what to do; he enjoyed
the greater autonomy of being a PC. Several of the recruits
cited the attraction of 'job security'. One said: 'There are
not many jobs that will be around in thirty years', a remark
which raised a paradox. Many recruits become police officers to get away from humdrum jobs, yet they are joining
an organisation that will tend to their every need and
guarantees them a comfortable pension while they are still
in middle life. A perceptive inspector said: 'The Japanese
corporation didn't invent cradle-to-grave security; the
Metropolitan Police did.'

The Streatham division took the training of recruits seriously, setting them a ten-week course which included 'street
duties', attachments to specialities like the CID, and visits
to courts, mortuaries, battered women refuges. Training
was run by a sergeant and PC, and other senior PCs also
acted as instructors. Recruits who had been assigned to
other divisions were often, said the Streatham intake,
simply thrown in at the deep end. The recruits had been
nervous about the reception they might get on division, but
had been pleasantly surprised. One said: 'Most PCs are
friendly and curious about how training had changed,
though there are a few real dickheads around. Only one
has taken the piss out of me so far. Most are more than
happy to help; we're new toys to look at and play with.'

It is lore among senior officers that people join the police
from a wide range of backgrounds – 'The children of lords
and ladies, of Scottish farmers, of Durham miners, of business people,' said one. Undoubtedly, scions of all these
categories are to be found wearing police uniforms, but the
police are predominantly drawn from the aspiring working
and lower middle classes. I deal in a later chapter with what
kind of people mature police officers are and what attitudes

they have but the feeling I got from trainee police was that they 'knew their place' in the scheme of things. They have little experience of either the upper middle or the lower working class, and feel themselves out of place in both environments. Several told me that they were deeply shocked by the conditions in which some problem families live; one woman officer said she found it hard even to accept a cup of tea in some homes. All police tend to equate 'good' property with well-behaved citizens who merit their respect, while in poor areas there is often a presumption that criminality and loose morals lurk beneath the surface.

There are inescapable pitfalls in generalising about a profession with 130,000 officers, but what I was told by a psychologist with thirty years' direct involvement with the police reflected something I had half perceived. Despite the superficial appearance of self-confidence and authority, many police are essentially unsure of themselves, and need the structure of the force and the visible accoutrements, such as uniform, to give themselves resolution and dignity. The psychologist said: 'Many police are conformist personalities, devalued as children in the child/parent relationship. Being a police officer gives them value.' It is hard when making such judgements to avoid being blindingly obvious or desperately unfair. But clearly some personalities are attracted to the notion of belonging to a powerful uniformed organisation.

The tone set by the PC instructors is less idealised and more down-to-earth than Mr Buchan's oration. Advising recruits never to take anything for granted, one instructor told of a young PC who had been attached to a drugs squad that was constantly arresting the same man. This man's technique was to hide his drugs up his anus in a plastic container attached to a piece of string. This inevitably made him walk in an odd manner. A few days later the young officer saw a Chinese man stepping gingerly along the street: he arrested him, took him to the police station, and – sure enough – there was what appeared to be a piece of string hanging from his bottom. He gave the 'string' a great tug, expecting the drugs container to fall out. Instead the Chinaman nearly hit the roof of the charge room: he had recently had an operation for piles, and the young PC had pulled the end of his stitches. With such homely examples are embryo cops introduced to the mysteries of their trade.

Shortly before the end of each Hendon course, the divisional instructors spend an evening at the college to meet the recruits who will be coming to their divisions. (A chief inspector, giving the instructors a short pep talk, exhorted them not to tell recruits 'to forget all the crap you learned at training school'.) The meeting between the two constable instructors from Streatham and their eight recruits began with a very fierce warning from one Streatham PC about the dangers of hepatitis. He told with some relish of a sergeant who had died after being spat in the eye at a soccer match. 'They push Aids at you, but this is far more contagious. You are in an "at risk" occupation,' he said, adding that at least two of Streatham's 'toms' (prostitutes) suffered from hepatitis and a third from Aids. Their first arrests, he said, would be confronting shoplifters in local stores. He was determinedly forthright. He explained that the front office was an 'absolute joke'. The best idea, he suggested, would be to build a bus shelter outside to keep people dry while they waited – 'only we haven't got the money for a bus shelter'. Relations with Lambeth Council, according to him at least, were 'poor', and the council was 'anti-police'; he had personal experience of a refusal by the health authorities to co-operate simply because the police were involved. The council exacerbated poor living conditions by failing to separate 'problem families' – 'unmarried mothers with fifteen children, each with a different father' – from elderly, vulnerable 'old dears', surviving on meals-on-wheels.

He warned the recruits to be on their guard against the capital's fleshpots. 'I'm not being nasty, but people coming from Scotland, Wales and the north have had money problems. They find themselves in London with more cash than they have ever had previously – and more things to spend it on – gaming clubs, girl friends, boy friends,' he said. One recruit had got into such financial difficulties, he recounted, that his chief superintendent had had to take his chequebook away from him, and only issued a cheque when the PC needed something specific like a new shirt. PCs had put women 'in the pudding club'. 'If you've got any problems affecting your working life, the worst thing for you to do is to bottle them up because they will only get bigger. For Christ's sake tell us. We've been selected because we've got big ears and can listen.'

The recruits were given booklets introducing them to the Streatham division, its people, its geography. Each had already been assigned the identification number that he would wear on his uniform. Each was questioned about education, previous jobs and above all – or so it seemed – about his sporting interests. The instructor spoke enthusiastically about the importance of sport; he told of someone who was alleged to have failed a board because he took part in no sport and was not, therefore, considered a 'team' player. One recruit said he played rugby. 'Good lad,' joked the instructor, 'you've passed your probation.'

The recruits confessed to feeling 'shaky' the first time they confronted members of the public. They are blooded by being taken out to write fixed penalty traffic tickets. After dealing with a couple of drivers, their confidence increased. They quickly realised that most of us are far more apprehensive about them than they are about us. One recruit said: 'This woman was more shaky than I was, which boosted my confidence.' He had been taken aback by the deference shown by another driver. ' "Yes, officer, no, officer" – there was no need for that. He was putting me on a pedestal,' he said.

Recruits are made familiar with street duties by being 'puppy-walked' by 'parent' constables. One afternoon I accompanied Brian Spreadbury, one of Streatham's most experienced PCs and a giant of a man, as he walked a recruit through what is by night the local prostitute area and by day a decorous residential district. A policeman must always know exactly where he is. Spreadbury's technique to ram home this lesson was somewhat melodramatic – the suburban streets of Streatham were suddenly alive with notional gunmen – but effective. After twenty minutes I and the trainee constable both realised just how unobservant we were. 'You'd have been dead by now,' said Spreadbury with some satisfaction when I failed to know the name of the street in which a crazed man armed with a sawn-off shotgun had just 'leapt' from a car. Spreadbury claimed that his record had been to 'kill off' a recruit six times in a two-hour walk. The serious purpose behind the game-playing was to underline that a policeman's radio is virtually useless to call assistance to a heart attack or accident if the officer does not know where he is.

In the next hour the recruit and I failed the Spreadbury test several times, missing a number of landmarks and suspicious circumstances: the obscured entrances to a tennis club and a private school, an open front door. 'Look around and be nosy; look over walls and into alleyways. Don't take anything for granted. These streets are now your "office"; you must know where everything is, just as once you had to know where the files and paperclips were kept,' Spreadbury told the recruit.

He asked the recruit why he was on patrol. 'To prevent crime.' 'No,' replied Spreadbury, 'to detect it.' The police were not employed, he said, to spend thirty years wandering up and down looking decorative. 'We are the most highly paid nosy parkers in London, so be bloody nosy,' and added, 'you might get a bonus – two Dorises stark naked from the waist up.' The recruit obligingly peered over a fence into a garden just as the householder returned from shopping, clearly highly alarmed by the attention his property was receiving. 'Just tell him,' said PC Spreadbury, 'that you're doing your job and making sure that everything is rinky-dinky.' He set the recruit various traps. 'What should you do about that open front door?' he asked, pointing out a door that neither the recruit nor I had noticed. 'Investigate it.' 'No. that's an osteopath's house, where he has his consulting room. The outer door is always open for patients, and anyway, that brown BMW is his car so he's obviously at home and all is well.' Spreadbury had been on this beat for five and a half years, and knew most of the householders. 'Good afternoon, young man,' he greeted a crumbling, red-faced figure in a mohair overcoat. Then to us: 'He's one of the old school; still tips his hat to women.'

Spreadbury mixed practical advice with an entertaining Sherlock Holmes game. Too many officers, said Spreadbury, when they are called to an incident, stand around with their hands in their pockets chatting to each other – 'such burning issues as who's the sergeant bonking? or I had a fucking good holiday'. With a bit of initiative, they could contribute. Go to the corner of the street, he said, from where you can watch two roads, so that you can spot a suspect breaking cover and making a dash for it. Two officers at opposite corners of a block can 'sterilise' an area. Use your local information and become a mini-control centre.

We went onto Tooting Bec Common. Why do people use commons? asked Spreadbury. For three reasons – as a short-cut, to walk the dog, or have a pee. If they are not doing one of these three things, they may be up to no good, probably looking for a 'tom', he suggested. We went to a clearing in the undergrowth, which was littered with smashed sherry bottles and discarded beer cans. 'What sort of people come here?' inquired Spreadbury. 'I assume . . .' began the recruit, tentatively. 'You don't assume anything,' cut in Spreadbury. 'Cases get thrown out of court for assumptions. The poor sods of society come here, not your Mr Averages.' He found a plastic bag containing a yellow substance, and held it up for examination. 'What do you think this is?' Long pause. 'Is it a Durex?' 'It would have to be an elephant's Durex,' replied Spreadbury scornfully. It was, in fact, a glue-sniffer's kit. In the next, much smaller, clearing – a couple of square yards beaten flat round a tree stump – there were dozens of condoms; it was clearly a favourite summer spot for Streatham's prostitutes. 'We're modern archaeologists,' said Spreadbury happily, surveying the sordid evidence.

We stopped outside several houses, and the recruit was asked to divine something about the person who lived in them. Sometimes what he was supposed to look for was

53

obvious, like a doctor's plate on the gate post, but often it was either obscure or more complicated than it appeared at first sight. He correctly identified one house – from ornaments visible through the front windows – as belonging to Asians; he did not see the significance of a lion's head on the wall. According to Spreadbury, this meant that the people must have been east African rather than subcontinental Asians, since there are no lions on the subcontinent. A neighbouring house had a wheelchair ramp to the front door, a point the recruit was advised to take note of in case of emergency. Further down the road a car bore a personalised number plate 'PAT . . .' The recruit, still thinking of the lions, suggested the owner must be Asian – PAT for Patel. In fact, they were Irish.

The next householder might not invite you in, the recruit was told, yet he would not be being rude. What might be his reason? This time the clue lay in what looked like a tiny spring on the edge of the doorframe. It was, said Spreadbury, a Jewish mezuzah – a piece of parchment containing a holy passage – which denoted that the house belonged to an orthodox Jew who would feel that a Gentile crossing his threshold had defiled his home. (In an emergency, Spreadbury told the recruit, he could ignore such sensibilities.) The front door of the next house was wide open. 'All right if I steal your television and video?' Spreadbury called up the stairs, and a very flustered young mother appeared. Two streets further on, the recruit volunteered that Asians lived in a corner house. 'How do you know?' 'There was an Asian woman sitting in a car outside.' The car, however, had nothing to do with the house: the woman was simply waiting while her family went shopping. 'You're feeling a bit inadequate now, aren't you?' said Spreadbury, addressing us both. The recruit admitted that he had 'hated him' for a while.

Spreadbury's sense of theatre was not cultivated for the benefit of the recruits. His size and his past as a streetwise Brixton cop had given him a high profile. I was with him one afternoon in the canteen when a detective rushed in asking him to head a posse to arrest a man wanted for GBH (grievous bodily harm), who was said to be in a pub on Streatham High Road. Spreadbury rounded up all the PCs in the canteen, and over the radio organised a van to take them to the pub. After three minutes on the street corner – which he spent briefing his team with a description of the wanted man and the injunction 'Don't take any chances; don't take any shit' – he gave up waiting for the van, and flagged down a passing coach. To the amazed delight of a group of pensioners on an outing, ten coppers piled on board their coach, and the fairly elderly driver was instructed by Spreadbury to drive hell-for-leather, disregarding traffic lights. At the pub Spreadbury deployed his forces at the various exits, and entered with a small arresting team. The informant pointed out the wanted man; Spreadbury moved swiftly behind the suspect, snatched his glass from his reach, and arrested him before the man knew there was a policeman in the bar. Ten minutes later we were back in the canteen, and Spreadbury was filling in the licensing book, in which every visit a policeman pays to a pub must be recorded. 'You've got to cover your back with paper all the time.'

Despite the wages and the pension, the Metropolitan Police have major problems keeping the force up to strength. Londoners themselves are particularly hard to recruit. Job opportunities are far greater in the south-east than elsewhere in Britain; the salary is not so tempting to a Londoner; and, said one recruiter, 'People in London know what the problems are; they know about street crime and violence, and don't see the job as an attractive proposition. Our activities are far more productive outside London.' A week-long recruiting drive in Hounslow, west London, backed by a local press campaign, drew 20 applicants: a two-day session in Preston, Lancashire, picked up 136. Some provincial forces are overwhelmed by potential policemen. One north-eastern force had 5,000 applications for 150 vacancies. The surplus aspirants are advised to try the Met, which takes just over 2,000 recruits each year out of about 10,000 applicants. 'We are no less selective; no one gets in unless he meets our requirements,' said the Met hastily. This imbalance between supply of and demand for trainee police is the reason why over two-thirds of London's police come from elsewhere.

The Met strategy is to recruit basic coppers rather than high-flyers. The Met recruiter commented: 'If you take in too many well-qualified people, their aspirations for promotion cannot be met, and there will be wastage as disillusion sets in. Forces with a high graduate intake are storing up trouble and will have a great number of unhappy officers in years to come. The basic starting point must be effective and efficient constables.' In spring 1989 there were 1,600 graduates in the Met out of 28,000 officers. There is a highly competitive, nationwide entry scheme for graduate high-flyers, through which a handful of recruits enter the police each year. Twenty-one were accepted in 1988 – including ten for the Met – out of 800 applications. Successful candidates are virtually guaranteed promotion to inspector within five years. Although they are not formally an officer caste – like recruits to Sandhurst or Dartmouth – and they will all have to do two years on the beat, they are expected to rise to at least chief superintendent, with the hope that they will make the ranks of the Association of Chief Police Officers. 'It's a hell of a lift,' said the recruiter. The high-flyers, with their assured promotion prospects, are resented in the canteen culture, which is dominated by officers who never expect to pass beyond the rank of police constable. A constable/instructor told the eight Streatham recruits: 'You can think what you like about it. I know what I think. They [special graduate entrants] whizz around without gaining any street credibility. Some get through without making any blunders; many make horrendous blunders.' A recruiter said judiciously: 'Graduate entrants are wise to keep a low profile during their time on the beat.'

Graduates outside this limited scheme enter on the same basis as other recruits. My sense, confirmed by a chief superintendent, was that they were not usually among the brightest of graduates. In 1988, 7½ per cent of the 2,162 entrants had a degree, about the same number who had no qualifications at all. The vast majority of applicants had left school with five or more O levels (or equivalent) and possibly a couple of A levels. Anyone with fewer than five O levels must sit an entrance exam. There are five tests including simple arithmetic, spelling, the choice of the correct words from given lists to fill blank spaces in sentences. One recruiter – 'many years out of school' – who sat it under exam conditions scored 179 out of 200 (the pass mark is 100), and, as a consequence, was not greatly impressed by what the exam proved. (Older recruits do better than younger ones, a bleak comment on the achievements of the worst of our modern schools.) Certainly police reports are littered with sufficient mis-spellings and grammatical inaccuracies – 'kareer' (career), 'Hide' (Hyde) Park, 'airloom' (heirloom) – to make an English teacher despair.

I spent a morning at the Met recruiting centre at Paddington Green police station. The man in charge was a civilian, Alastair Clague, who, together with a colleague, was briefing a group of senior officers over a cup of coffee about that day's candidates. A formal interview conducted by two officers (selected as good listeners, trained for the task and drawn on rota from the divisions) is the climax to a two-day selection process. The recruits take physical tests, including a mile and a half run which must be completed within a certain time (it is raised for older recruits), and write a short autobiographical essay. About one third of those who answer the ads are invited for interview. Before applicants reach this stage, their lives have been intimately probed through a series of background checks: foreign police forces are contacted if the applicant has lived abroad, school records and job references are sought, homes visited, and relatives interviewed. (A northern headmaster wrote that one applicant was 'sly, deceitful, and given to bullying weaker pupils'. Under 'any other comments' he added: 'Good police material.') The local police officer who visits the home is asked to assess whether he would be happy with the applicant (when trained) on his relief.

The day I was there, the recruits were all women (inevitably elevated to 'young ladies'); there was, apparently, insufficient changing accommodation to mix the sexes. Cramped conditions and the large numbers of would-be recruits – eighty per week – also restricted the assessment possibilities. The Met admitted that their selection processes probably compared unfavourably to those of several provincial forces. One young woman had already blown her chances by being rude to a physical training instructor. 'She was cheeky and offensive, effing and blinding before her gym test. She failed to complete the first lap of the run. If she's like that here, think what a disaster she would be with members of the public,' said Mr Clague's colleague. The young woman would have been sent packing overnight had her behaviour been reported sooner; as it was, the panel was instructed, she was to be rejected however good her interview might prove. (This obviously had the makings of an intriguing confrontation, and I was sorry that it was not one of the interviews through which I later sat.)

Despite the stringent background checks, poorly prepared candidates did reach the interview stage. I was told of applicants who, when asked the unsurprising question of why they wanted to become policemen, answered: 'I couldn't tell you off the cuff.' Some candidates presented themselves scruffily dressed. Women and older candidates give, I was told, the best interviews, because they think through the implications of becoming police officers more thoroughly than do younger men. The bias is now in favour of older candidates, and the average age of Met recruits is creeping up: it was 21 in 1984 and 23½ in 1988. A recruiter said: 'It is a great advantage to have older people on relief: the attitudes of the younger elements – the nineteen- and twenty-year-olds – are the cause of our problems.' The chairman of one of the interview boards said that the best candidate he had seen was a 41-year-old former marine engineer, who had spent twenty years at sea. Some young men simply think 'being a copper sounds like a good idea', said a recruiter, adding, 'The feedback from the boards is that the intake is infinitely better than in the past.' There had been, he said, a bad patch in the 1970s, when 'a number of people came in who should never have joined. We are paying the price for that now, with some appalling people at sergeant and inspector.' I heard that analysis from others: it would seem that while Sir Robert Mark, the crusading commissioner, had been kicking unsuitable senior officers out through the front door, another bunch of people who should never have donned police uniforms were creeping in through the back.

The Met had recently broadened its intake by raising the upper age limit for recruits from 30 to 45, and by early 1989 recruitment had not yet suffered from the declining number of school leavers; in fact the force had reached its establishment level for the first time since 1903. Mr Clague pointed out that, when necessary, the Met could vastly increase the pool of potential recruits simply by reducing the height requirements. (Shortly after the publication of the hardback edition of *The Force*, the Met – largely to recruit more members of ethnic minorities – abolished height minimums entirely.)

One fear the Met has is that provincial applicants may be looking for backdoor entry into their home forces. After training with the Met and a few years' experience, a growing number leave just as they are beginning to repay the investment the Met has made in them. Candidates are quizzed closely on their potential loyalty to the capital and its people. Dr Johnson's aphorism that a man who is tired of London is tired of life applied to a congenial eighteenth-century city with a tiny population. It would be easy enough as a front-line police officer to tire of Peckham or Deptford, Canning Town or Tottenham, and to feel an urge to return to the green grass of home.

I talked to a man who was leaving Streatham for a home counties force. He was young, but experienced, and was an ex-Royal Marine officer who had served in Northern Ireland, just the sort of policeman the Met ought to have been keen to hold. Yet, despite Sir Peter Imbert's highly publicised concern about leakage to the provinces, no attempt had been made to keep this officer in London: no senior officer had taken him on one side for an encouraging pep talk about policing the capital. The departing officer wanted to live where his salary could buy him a three-bedroomed house – property prices in his new county were roughly half those of suburban London; he wanted 'decent' schools for his young family; he was tired of the stresses of everyday London life. It was even dangerous, he said, for a policeman to travel on the London Underground in 'half blues' – usually an anorak or tweed jacket over uniform trousers and shirt. He realised that opportunities for promotion and specialisation would be less good with a county force than in London, but he was happy to trade these for the prospects of a rural home beat – 'panda and wellies'. Even three years ago, he would not have considered the move, but his frustrations had mounted. The provincial force had few twenty-four-hour police stations, he said, so much of his work would be during conventional working hours – another big attraction to a man with a young family. Would anything have kept him in London? 'The opportunity to buy my "job" flat, and if there had been a massive increase in London allowances,' he replied. I don't know how this officer's reputation stood with his superiors, but his relief inspector wrote him a decent reference, and wished him 'Godspeed'. The PC was a reasonably thoughtful observer of policing problems and it seemed wrong that a man like him should be let go without a struggle. He left Streatham the same week that I spent with the recruiting and training departments, observing the cost and difficulty of getting suitable people to police London.

Mr Clague was far from relaxed about the departure of such officers. He said: 'They represent a very significant loss to the Met in terms of investment and expense. Those who go tend to be in the five-to-ten-year service band, the backbone of the reliefs. They are highly attractive to provincial forces.' While about 250 officers leave the Met for the provinces each year, 60 come the other way, usually in search of better career prospects. Some from the north are looking for job opportunities for their children, even though they have to overcome the wide gulf in house prices. A Merseyside inspector had his home on the market for two years without there being a single inquiry.

If the force has problems attracting white Londoners, it finds it virtually impossible to recruit among the capital's ethnic minorities. 'We are very, very anxious to improve the mix within the force,' said Mr Clague. There were, when I met him, 426 black and Asian officers in the Met, 300 of whom had been recruited in the previous five years. Most black recruits come either from outlying areas like Croydon, or from the armed services, rather than from the inner city. 'Ex-servicemen have seen and heard all the racist taunts while they were in the army, and have come to terms with them,' said Mr Clague. The Met conducts drives in areas with high concentrations of ethnic minorities, like Southall in west London, but with little success. 'We work with local authorities, consultative groups and ethnic leaders. By showing we are persistent, there could be a gradual programme of persuasion – "maybe they are serious and do want me". There could be a breakthrough figure, say five hundred. A black looking at the police might feel reassured that he would not necessarily be on his own. I've never yet seen two black officers together in a car,' said Mr Clague. Black and Asian officers are co-opted to take part in recruitment drives – although they tend to be reluctant volunteers – to answer such questions as 'Are the police a bunch of racists?' Advertisements are placed in the ethnic press in foreign languages, and are often aimed at parents who may not feel that their children are aiming high enough by becoming police officers, and who may have brought with them low opinions of the police from their home countries.

Recruiters feel they have probably drained the pool in London. Out of 624 Black and Asian applications in 1988, only 66 were accepted. Both the proportion who are successful and the quality of the applicants are dropping all the time. So the Met is now concentrating on areas of high unemployment and high ethnic population, like Leicester.

Many such areas – the West Midlands, for example – are keen to recruit minority police themselves, and post what amount to 'keep out' signs against London predators. Said Mr Clague: 'We have only tried seriously in the last twelve years, and, given that, we shouldn't be too disheartened. Some might say that the number of black officers there are is quite an achievement. We take the Jesse Jackson line. "It's no good standing outside criticising; the way to improve things is to join and work from the inside." '

The Met has an ethnic minority recruiting working party, which includes the force's senior black officer – a chief inspector from Clapham – and a black race relations adviser to the Home Secretary. The present policy is to be 'flexible' with unsuccessful black candidates who do not meet, but are close to, the formal entry requirements, advising them to try again. The working party is against 'access courses', believing that if blacks were helped to the starting line, once they were in the force they would be seen as second-class citizens, and would struggle to keep up. If in ten years' time they were all stuck at the bottom, that would be bad for them and bad for future recruitment.

Some police have reservations about hard-hitting recruitment ads. Many PCs did not like the picture of the yob spitting in the young constable's face, and a senior officer at the Hendon Training College showed me an alternative advertisement that rejected the high-speed, violent, glamour connotations of policing in favour of messages about serving the community and caring. 'Police who imagine that their job is continuously arresting people are living a lie,' he said. The force was, I was told, planning to project a softer image in its next series of ads. 'There is no need to over-egg the pudding. The job on a day-to-day level is attractive enough to pull in the people we want,' said a recruiter.

I joined a recruitment interview board reaching the end of its morning's work. A chief superintendent and a detective chief inspector were discussing a young woman who had just left the room. She had been of suitable calibre, they decided, but already had a place with another police force, leading them to believe that she had simply thrown a number of cards in the air to see where they fell and that her commitment to London would not be strong. They identified her desire to come to London as the 'Dick Whittington' syndrome: 'She was looking for a break, for an opportunity to come to London, which has an aura about it.' They decided 'not to disturb the situation'. They had already told an eighteen-year-old to go away for two years, and to try again at the end of that time if she was still interested. 'She had potential, but she was not mature enough for the streets of London. There is no such thing as an "L" plate for cops. We could be sending them like little lambs to the slaughter,' said one of the officers.

Their technique was to go through the applicant's record with her, probing in particular what inspired her to wish to be a policewoman, and looking hard at her leisure activities. They questioned each applicant on a topical, relevant issue – that week ID cards for football supporters were being debated in Parliament. The first hopeful to be interviewed after my arrival, a nineteen-year-old with long, curly, high-lighted hair, a cheap grey suit and white silk shirt, apparently made poor use of her spare time. What, she was asked, did she do on Saturdays? 'Lie in, help around the house, shop, go to the pub,' she said rather feebly. In other words, said one of the officers politely, you're 'home-based really'. Her job record was patchy; everywhere she went, the hand of fate seemed to be against her. She had been ostracised in Scotland because she was English, and now was being discriminated against in a London Swiss-owned firm. 'You seem to be unlucky, always falling amongst foreigners,' said the chief superintendent drily. Her school record was ambivalent: 'An able student whose progress was hindered by her negative approach.' She confessed she had not done as well as she might, and blamed her failure on falling into the wrong company. 'You do at that age, don't you?' she asked hopefully. 'I don't know. In my case it was a very long time ago, so I'll have to take your word for it,' said the chief superintendent, in a quite kindly tone. She had claimed that she read as a hobby, but the odd

Mills and Boon exhausted her reading list. When she got round to the papers, she read the *Sun* or the *Daily Mail*. She had once been a barmaid, so was asked her view of 'lager louts' and all-day drinking.

She rallied towards the end of the interview. Asked to comment on why a lot of people disliked the police (a revealing question), she replied calmly that every profession gets criticised. She said she did not subscribe to the notion that policing was glamorous work; she had cherished her ambition since a careers talk at school when she was sixteen; she had, she said, determination, she was caring, fair, willing to learn and ambitious to go up the ladder. It didn't tally with her aimless record, but – rather to my surprise – she was invited to try again in a year. She had twelve months in which to eradicate the deep-seated fecklessness in her nature.

The next young woman had been sent away a year earlier and told to come back. She had used the time to great effect: she had been a member of the Air Training Corps; taken part in the Duke of Edinburgh award scheme; been camping in Scotland and Wales; started flying; she played hockey and netball, and swam competitively. She worked for a building society, but complained that hers was a male-dominated office. The interviewers wanted to know what her peer group might think of her joining the police. Again I was surprised by the sensitivity they showed, probing for pro- and anti-police feedback, almost as if it would be dangerous to recruit anyone contaminated by association with people who found the Old Bill less than perfect. One of this woman's colleagues had said she would never speak to her again because she had a black boy friend who claimed he was constantly harassed by the police. Did she believe that? she was asked. She evaded the question, and received some avuncular advice that there were some 'pretty horrible people out there' and 'some of our customers can be nasty'. She was accepted.

Out of six women they had seen that morning, the panel recommended two, told three to come back in a year and rejected the young woman with the 'Dick Whittington' syndrome. The care with which police are now recruited compared to a few years ago is reflected in the vastly lower drop-out rate during new officers' two-year probation period. Between 1982/83 and 1988, it fell from 26 to 6 per cent.

After further checks – to make sure, for example, that they have not been convicted of a crime since their original application – the successful candidates would be summoned a few weeks later to the Peel Centre at the Hendon Police College for a twenty-week initial training course. They are trained in batches of about two hundred recruits, split into classes of twenty. Early one morning I joined a class that had just arrived – they hadn't yet got their uniforms. What was immediately noticeable about this group was their ages: there was a woman of thirty-nine with two children, a man of thirty-seven, and several others either in their late twenties or early thirties. An historic trend has been reversed – policemen are getting older. These were not the dewy-faced innocents of popular imagination, but in several cases people more worldly-wise than their instructors. A sergeant/instructor said that he was not there to teach these older recruits 'to suck eggs', but to show them how to marry their experience with the skills they would be acquiring to become police officers.

The objective of the first lesson was to warn the new officers against jumping to hasty conclusions. They were asked to imagine that they were members of a plain-clothes burglary squad, relaxing at the end of the day in a cosy old-fashioned bar, divided into curtained booths. They were played a tape recording of an ambiguous conversation between three or four men 'overheard' from the next booth, and told to make their own deductions from it. The conversation concerned a bank, various items of equipment, plans involving the weekend when the bank would be unstaffed, and the division of money from a previous 'job'. The twenty recruits produced six separate sets of answers: six thought that a bank robbery was indeed being planned, six said that the men were painters and decorators, three that they were cleaning contractors, while builders, engineers and fancy-dress party-goers collected one vote each.

The overheard men were in fact decorators, and it was noticeable how accurate the older recruits were. The group discussed the pub conversation and their reactions, one pointing out that in real life the eavesdropping police would not have relied merely on the conversation, but would have taken a look at the men to see whether they were known local criminals, and would have followed them to their cars to check registration numbers. (All role-play training inevitably suffers from a lack of reality.) The instructor introduced the concept of 'frames of reference', which are determined, he said, by 'what you know and what you have experienced'. Younger people, who know little of the world, are more likely than those with *savoir faire* to jump to the more fanciful conclusions. 'We were at a disadvantage,' said one recruit; 'none of us is a bank robber.' He drew a deserved laugh. The sergeant analysed the group reactions: 'The brain does not like empty spaces; it will always seek to make two plus two add up to something.'

In a later session the class was shown pictures that could be interpreted in different ways. Some were visual tricks; others were questions of interpretation. An American study demonstrated that police officers are unusually (if understandably) suspicious. Shown a drawing of a young couple bending over a pram, a high percentage of police will immediately assume the worst, and see in the picture a highly sinister man about to snatch the baby, with a distraught mother standing by; most civilians see a loving mother and father checking that their infant is all right.

I was next taken to an ancient London Transport bus, which is used as a training prop, and asked to play the role of a conductor. Most of the recruits were to be passengers on their way to work, and a WPC was to play the part of a bolshy woman who was attempting to travel further than the distance she had paid for. I, as the conductor, having failed either to make her pay or leave the bus, had to summon two recruits to deal with the situation. (The woman was under strict instructions not to budge.) As the officers attempted to negotiate with the woman, the 'passengers' played their parts with gusto: 'Throw the cow off; I've got to get to work.' Eventually, the two officers decided they had no option but to remove her forcibly, which they started to do somewhat clumsily, hurting her arms.

The instructor, a long-in-service PC addressed as 'staff' by the recruits, halted the game, and assessed the two recruits' efforts. They had done quite well, he said, but should have asked the conductor to produce his fare table; advised the woman how she could complain; and they should not have allowed either the passengers or the conductor as much leeway as they did. 'Take charge,' said the 'staff', adding that they should always remember that in a real situation the event would probably be the biggest thing to happen to the passengers in weeks. They would carry the story to work with them, repeat it in the pub and at home. 'The public will be watching you, and you have got to project an image of professionalism,' said the instructor. He advised them to call the woman 'madam' – not 'love' or 'dear' – and not to rise to insults. 'If someone calls you a "pig", remember it stands for "professionalism, integrity and guts", and say "thank you".' He suggested that they might be able to build on such a situation, by calling later at the bus garage, getting to know the conductor, and through him learning of the regular problems on local buses. 'Make the garage a "teahole", but remember that a "teahole" isn't just a place for having a cup of tea. You go there for information.' Finally, the instructor, having watched the recruits' rather crude attempts to remove the recalcitrant passenger, seized her hand, turned it over behind her back and frog-marched her to the top of the stairs almost as if he were helping rather than forcibly compelling her. 'That arm lock works,' he said with a pleased smile, 'on even the big hairy-chested ones.'

What I was watching were relatively new training methods. Recruits are now expected to do most of their formal learning in the evenings and over the weekends, so that they arrive in class ready to put theory into practice or to discuss it in a practical manner. An inspector/instructor said: 'Recruits' self-awareness, their individuality and their uniqueness are respected. This is not a sausage factory.' He added that there had been vast changes in training since he had passed through the Peel Centre nearly twenty years before. 'It was far more rigid and disciplined; we spent hours and hours learning whole paragraphs by rote,' he said. Practical policing was then learned, he said, in a rather haphazard way on the beat. The deputy commandant of the Peel Centre, Superintendent David Jarvis, said: 'We have shifted from a knowledge base to a skills base. Police need the skills to apply their knowledge in complex social situations, in which the power of arrest is often useless.' To this end there is a lot of role-playing of the sort I took part in, with video recordings and playback. Outsiders are brought in to act the parts of members of the public – youths on YTS schemes and pensioners, among others. A deaf group had been recently, presenting the recruits with problems of both communication and perception. One of the deaf people assumed the role of a thief, but, because he was handicapped, the young officers treated him with kid gloves, never suspecting that he could be capable of villainy.

The Centre employs a full-time manual writing team, who constantly update the material used in training. They aim at a reading age of sixteen – which is the age at which most recruits leave school – and use as many graphics as possible, on the basis that one picture is worth a thousand words. New legislation is reduced to an 'all-the-cop-on-the-beat-needs-know' formula. I asked an instructor how the Centre coped with race and other prejudices. The first essential, he said, is to acknowledge that no one is without prejudice. The vast majority of recruits start by claiming to be prejudice-free, but rapidly change their minds when they are given attitude tests. 'The aim is to keep the lid on prejudice, especially at moments of danger when they've got their backs to the wall and are under stress,' he said. Some recruits were adept, he said, at disguising their true beliefs. 'They appear to toe the party line, but in reality they don't change their attitudes. They only let you see the side they want you to see,' he said.

American research into the political attitudes of policemen found that before enlisting they were marginally more conservative than their peers; during training, they absorbed liberal notions; but, after they were assigned to the streets, they became more conservative than they had been before they joined. British officers told me that this roller-coaster progress of attitudes, observable in Britain also, was quite explicable in terms of the experience police have: 'They get a very distorted view of life through contact with people either in trouble or creating it,' said an inspector.

'The majority of police are middle-class with middle-class values,' he said, 'with little time for minorities.' In practice, the consensus on the relief is to get the job done, rather than to sit about talking politics. 'However, they do bear the brunt of anti-police criticism; often feel under siege from the local population, and under threat from politically hostile local authorities. This creates a feeling of alienation – "them and us". It is easy, therefore, for them to lose their sense of proportion and to start to harden up; easy to feel that everyone is out to attack you and no one is for you – even though it is just not true. In inner London, where most of the recruits will cut their teeth, the perception that they lack public support is understandable.'

On the night before the Streatham 'eight' passed out from Hendon, one of them said: 'It doesn't matter how many people you ask, there are basically three reasons for becoming a police officer: for the pay; out of a sense of adventure; and because it is a worthwhile job.' After six months of asking many young policemen and women why they had joined, I had no quarrel with that analysis.

3

'When the Wheels Come Off'

'Late turn, oh so boring. You hear a pub fight, people getting hurt, glasses in faces, and you think "Yeah!" If you hear a serious disturbance now, that is it; the canteen will clear itself, people climbing over each other to get to it. You never think: "Hang on a minute. What am I trying to do here? Get to a situation where someone may try to put a knife to my head?" '
– WPC

'Come on luv. Move! Oh my God, I don't believe it.' 'Terry', a PC recently returned from the advanced driving school and on his first stint as driver of the 'area' or fast response car, was, as ever that week, in a hurry. Ahead of us, an elderly woman driver, oblivious to the blaring two-tone siren and the flashing blue light, hugged the middle of the road at a steady 25 mph. Her driving mirror was redundant. Eventually, we squeezed by, accelerating to 75 as other cars and pedestrians took evasive action. After a meandering first hour of duty – the topics that day were the previous night's beers and curry – this, at 8 a.m., was the first 999 call of the early shift. Commuters making for Streatham railway station broke from their private reveries as the two-litre MG – 'one owner, 338 crazy drivers' – cut across the packed oncoming traffic on the High Road and jinked through the narrow space between parked cars into a suburban street that might have either been coming up in the world or going down.

As usual, I had failed to understand the crackling radio message, and had to ask the radio operator, 'Peter', to repeat it. Two teenaged boys were fighting, he said, and the call had been made by their frantic mother. A middle-aged black man let us in, and the area car crew sprinted up the poorly carpeted stairs. The recently alarmed mother, who was waiting at the top, said that the emergency was over and she was sorry to have bothered the police. Her sons had been fighting over whose turn it was to have the stereo system in his bedroom and had now resolved the dispute. Terry knocked at a scuffed white door, and a black youth with a hangdog air eventually opened it a crack. The other boy joined his mother. Satisfied that no one was hurt and that the argument was indeed over, Terry admonished the mother: 'Keep them apart, there's a love.' Adding to the boys. 'And no more fighting.'

Half an hour later we had a rendezvous with detectives who were hoping to arrest a suspected burglar. The wanted man was known to be physically big and the two detectives were quite small; they felt vulnerable in their sharp grey suits and shiny black shoes, so had asked for some uniformed help. 'What's the matter?' asked 'Bill', an extra PC who was being given a lift by the two-man area car crew. 'He's a bit large, that's all,' replied one of the detectives, sheepishly. 'The old blue serge has to dive in and save the day again,' said Bill, happily asserting the mythical primacy of the uniformed PC. 'Chummy' wasn't at home, or if he was he wasn't answering the door to five policemen. Back in the car for another hour of criss-crossing the division. For a while Terry remained in buoyant mood, regaling everyone we encountered with his small part in an armed robbery the previous day, a good tale that grew with the telling. There was another emergency call, and the adrenaline started pumping again: 'Do you think the blue light is there just to play with?' muttered Terry. 'Come on, get out of the way.' Before we reached the address, the call was cancelled. 'No further assistance required.' It was shaping as one of those days of damp squibs and false alarms. A woman had run a battered Ford into a yellow sand box, and the car now wouldn't start. She appeared to be a social worker transporting a mentally handicapped small boy. He was terribly upset, and wept and clung to the nearest leg when the police rolled the car down the hill to start it. The engine died again, and the woman was directed to a garage.

And that, for six hours, was it. The radio appeared dead. The citizens of the Streatham division were at harmony with one another. For anyone but police officers charged with 'keeping the peace', that might have been considered a satisfactory morning. But we were like fishermen when nothing was rising, aggrieved and dispirited. We had a fast car, a blue light, even a shield in the boot, and no one to nick. Terry eventually acknowledged that we might do better to save the Met's petrol. Much of the rest of the shift was passed in Gipsy Hill police station where Terry had to fill out property forms, the ultimate bane of a police officer's life. He had at least as much trouble with his forms as the social worker had had with her car.

Finally – joy, oh joy – a call in the dying minutes of the shift to a bank where a young man was apparently trying to pass a duff cheque. Terry and Peter disappeared into an interview room with an assistant manager and the suspected youth. A second area car from a neighbouring division arrived, and two more police dashed in; a small crowd gathered, presuming there had been a bank robbery. 'I saw a couple of blacks,' said a sixtyish man in a raincoat. 'Was it them? They don't know the world they're living in. They're all crooks now.' After twenty minutes the four officers emerged; the youth had simply been overdrawn. A disappointed huddle of bored citizens dispersed, and two bored policemen returned to Streatham nick to sign off.

A few days spent with a police force's front-line troops are a powerful corrective to the popular portrayal of policing as a series of tidy jobs with beginnings, middles and ends, and no time wasted in between. The notion that police work is always directed to a purposeful and achievable conclusion is as fallacious as is the idea that there is a scoop on the line every time a news editor's phone rings. The police often refer to themselves as a 'Band-aid' or 'Elastoplast' service. An inspector said: 'Essentially we're like the firms we call when someone has a smashed window; we're a "boarding up" team.' Terry gave the view from the front seat: 'The trouble with our job is that we do too much. People with burst pipes ring the police.'

On another day our first call was to a school where parents were reported to be fighting; same irate language from Terry, same rather scary driving. We burst up the steps into the school office, where genteel middle-aged women in tweed skirts and Shetland sweaters eyed us as if we were something slightly unpleasant that had fallen from space. Wrong school. Terry swore none too softly: 'If they gave us the **** right location, we'd find the **** right place.' A few radio calls later, we did reach the right school. A separated mother and father had arrived simultaneously to pick up a child, and for a moment it had seemed that they might come to blows. However, by the time we got there, they had departed. Another anti-climactic day was shaping. Terry explained their mission: 'To stop crime and keep the traffic moving.' We certainly kept moving, round and round the division; sometimes Terry would accelerate to 50; on a call we might touch 90. Terry explained the technique – taught at Hendon – as 'dominating the road', much as a policeman is taught to dominate disputes to which he is called. The car with its manual gear change and 91,000 miles on the clock would not have lasted long against a thoroughbred.

Driving the area car, said Terry, was the 'pinnacle': 'It's enjoyable to be left alone to do your own thing, driving the streets looking for stuff. You don't want to be chased all the time.' We passed through Streatham's prostitute area; although it was only five o'clock, two young women in short, tight leather skirts wiggled their way along a sub-urban street. 'Just going home, are you?' 'Yes.' The speaker was spotty with frazzled hair, and antagonistic. I saw many prostitutes while I was in Streatham; 'good time' girls they were not. But they were all streetwise and often funny. This pair recognised the area car, and knew that its crew could not afford to get tied down arresting them. Unlikely though it may seem, there is business to be done at 5.00 p.m. in streets of otherwise Edwardian gentility. The 'tom' squad would start its patrols in an hour: then the girls

would go skittering down the roads as fast as their con-
stricted legs could carry them.

The crew – radio call-sign 'Lima Five' – had two sources
of instant information: Streatham division personal radios,
linked to the local communications room and carried, when
there were enough sets, by all Streatham and Gipsy Hill
officers; and a radio main set. This was tuned to pick up
999 calls for Three and Four Areas of the Metropolitan
Police, covering eighteen divisions, a vast swathe of south
and south-east London from the Thames to the Surrey and
Kent borders. Even when not a mouse stirred in Streatham,
someone, somewhere, in that population of nearly two
million people, needed the police urgently. Every time the
controller came on air, a life was falling apart. 'Alleged
drunk-in-charge'; a man fighting a woman; a 'male' becoming violent with his daughter – all within five minutes.
Across the nation in a thousand area cars the Terrys and
Peters, in varying states of boredom or tension, waited to
respond.

Our next call was to a small, new council house. Several
bangs on the door drew no reply. Terry was just going to
check with a neighbour, when a window opened on the
first floor and a tousle-haired, black woman in a low-cut
nightdress stuck her head out, and told us to go away.
What had apparently been a lovers' tiff, violent enough for
her to call the police a few minutes earlier, had given way
to resumed passion. Terry and Peter demanded to see both
partners, who came grudgingly to the downstairs hall,
stuffing themselves into jeans and shirts, to make sure
neither lover was injured.

Just before six, there was finally action worthy of the
area car: a call to a housing estate where a teenaged tearaway
had apparently smashed in his parents' front door. A panda
car was already there, and the youth, drunk and covered
with an unlikely amount of blood, had been arrested. He
was taken away, and a WPC was sent to examine the
damage to his parents' house. Suddenly the radio burst into
jabbering life, and we rushed to the house. The tearaway's
father, a West Indian, was lying in a chair hovering, it

seemed, between Gipsy Hill and the next world. He had what appeared to be a deep hole in his left temple and a stabbed arm. On the floor was a screwdriver and a knife. An ambulance had been called, and the injured man held a bandage – taken from the area car's first-aid kit – to his head. 'Oh my God, I've got pain in my arm; this pain is killing me,' he moaned. 'Never you mind. He's been nicked. You just get yourself to hospital,' said a PC consolingly. A smashed pot plant lay near the injured man's feet. Next to the door a framed prayer mocked the scene: 'Bless this house/Oh Lord we pray/Make it safe/By night and day.' On the wall a picture of the family united for the camera in happier times hung somewhat incongruously next to a 'Charles 'n' Di' souvenir wedding plate; a prayer book lay open at Psalm 112: 'Blessed is the man that feareth the Lord . . . his seed shall be mighty upon earth: the generation of the faithful shall be blessed.' Later, the son denied everything, claimed that the father had attacked him, and must have fallen over. A successful prosecution would depend on whether the parents were prepared to give evidence against their son.

Police officers have a phrase, 'when the wheels come off', which is used often enough to achieve the in-house status of a cliché. It covers all those occasions when order succumbs to chaos, and is all-embracing enough to include most turmoil from a pub fracas to community rioting. The work of a police division is based on the notion of 'response'. The majority of police are walking the beat, driving a car, sitting in the canteen, waiting for the call that tells them that somewhere the wheels have come off. A member of the public has a problem; there is a burglary; a car crash; a child is lost; a shopper is 'mugged'; a householder is locked out; a husband hits a wife; and the police respond. In large measure they are judged by the speed of that response, and their attitude when they arrive. Many burglary victims are adequately happy if the police come quickly and are sympathetic; they have been conditioned to understand that the arrest of the burglar or the recovery of their property is improbable.

By the time I had been out several times in area cars, I no longer felt quite my original alarm as we zipped along the wrong side of a central reservation towards oncoming traffic. When there are no 999 calls to hare after, the area car crew back up the pandas, running errands and making themselves useful. One night a rather low-key search for a 'suspect' was interrupted by a call from the relief inspector to bring him a Breathalyser kit. The inspector and his sergeant, travelling in an unmarked car, had found themselves following a small Datsun being driven incredibly slowly by a young woman, whom they at first suspected of not having a full licence. But, when they stopped the car, they smelt drink and sent for the Breathalyser. The woman failed the roadside check, and the area car took her to Gipsy Hill where the test that establishes guilt or innocence would be conducted. 'You've had a few too many then?' said Bill. 'Probably one too many,' she told him. She was rational and certainly not drunk, and spoke of her job at an estate agency. Later she failed the test. Not all policemen like Breathalysing people. There, but for the grace of God, go many of them. I have certainly drunk with officers who later drove and for whose chances of passing a B-test I would not have given a great deal. My companions were running big risks: failing the Breathalyser is potentially catastrophic for a policeman, and in London will usually result in dismissal. Several Met officers from other divisions have been sacked while I have been writing this book. One officer complained: 'Up until now, if you got bagged you could expect a rocket at worst, although it wouldn't do your promotion prospects much good. People never got sacked unless there were aggravating circumstances.' Since a Yard 'crackdown', there now have to be mitigating circumstances for someone not to be dismissed – rushing a sick child to hospital perhaps. Anti-drink-driving campaigners would like to see Scotland Yard's tough policy extended to all police forces. They suspect that many police officers escape prosecution because other police are inevitably reluctant to breath-test them. A West Midlands detective was quoted as saying: 'If you're in the force, the chances of getting picked up and charged are remote. Being able to get away with it is almost a perk.'

Police reluctance to Breathalyse colleagues extends in some cases to a reluctance to test other 'respectable' citizens, unless the motorist concerned is clearly drunk. One PC told me that, when he had served with a county force, he would only Breathalyse people who were visibly unfit to drive, and would take keys away from others who had simply been drinking. He would hand the keys in at the station as lost property, and tell the drivers that they should claim them in the morning. My companions in the area car were made of sterner stuff. Shortly after we had dropped the young woman at Gipsy Hill, we came across a car with its rear fog light on. On the back window someone had drawn in lipstick a heart with an arrow through it, with the names 'Jeff' and 'Karen' above and below. The driver had obviously been to a wedding and, as it was now past midnight, was likely to have been drinking. He was flagged down on the basis that a fog light can be 'very dazzling', which seemed to me as near as dammit to a random stop. He smelt of drink, and was tested, but the meter showed orange rather than red, which meant he was below the limit. He was, it turned out, both the groom's brother and best man, so had been remarkably abstemious in the circumstances. His car, he told us, had been cleaned that morning, and someone must have inadvertently pushed the fog light button; on such a casual act his licence and even perhaps his job might have depended. After we had gone our separate ways, a minor argument broke out between my companions about whether they should have applied the test; one clearly felt they had harassed the driver unduly. There had been no sign of erratic driving.

If the police are ambivalent about drinking drivers, they are united in their detestation of the other alcoholic phenomenon of our times – the drunken yob. Shortly after the area car crew had sent the best man on his way, a nightly ritual was played out on Streatham High Road as the Studio night club closed. The pavements were crowded and the central reservation festooned with drunk teenagers.

As we cruised by, our driver, 'Tony', heard one large youth sing out: 'Harry Roberts is a friend; he kills coppers.' (Roberts was convicted in 1967 of shooting three policemen at Shepherd's Bush.) We drove past and parked the car across the pavement to intercept this young man. Tony – even larger than the youth – towered over him, inviting him to repeat the sentiments of his ditty. The youth, soft and drunk, backed down, losing face with his companions, which had been Tony's aim. As we drove off, Tony said with sarcastic satisfaction: 'He's well hard; I wonder if he's got any more carol-singing to do.' Tony had once served in a provincial force, where night patrolling was more systematic than it appeared to be in London, where the crew's brief, he said, was to look for motor crime and keep an eye on commercial property. In several days in the area car, I never discerned a logic to the routes we followed. Police car crews, however, have finely attuned eyesight and lateral vision; even at night at high speeds my companions were able to take in significant details of people, vehicles and houses. Tony had a miraculous ability to read and memorise number plates. Checking the numbers with the police computer is a major strategy, not only when looking for stolen cars, but also for keeping track of known or suspected criminals. For example, the ownership of a car seen parked outside a suspected drug dealer's house can first be verified on the computer, and later the car can be stopped many miles away, ostensibly for a traffic infringement, without the driver making the connection between the stop and the visit he made.

Only once when I was with the area car was it called to a situation that, for an instant at least, threatened danger. An off-duty detective spotted a car being driven erratically and at high speed, and Lima Five was called to intercept it. We saw it coming down a hill towards traffic lights and swung out in front of it, nose to nose. Bill went to the driver's door; suddenly he was shouting 'Get out, get out.' As the young driver, smartly dressed and neatly coiffed, stepped from the car, Bill made a dive under the front seat and came up holding what looked like a genuine Browning automatic. The excitement was short-lived. Bill, an author-ised firearms officer [AFO], realised that it was a sophisti-cated replica. The driver, a trainee estate agent, claimed that he had it for self-protection, having been twice mugged. After some deliberation Tony and Bill decided simply to remove the gun and send the youth on his way. The next call was to a housing estate where two men had been robbed after leaving a drinking club. The victims were pie-eyed with drink, and didn't elicit much sympathy from my companions: 'People who get pissed and show off their money have got it coming to them.' An ancient Ford Escort turned out ahead of us, showing no lights. 'What a wally!' He was 'pulled' and the car meticulously examined. There was no tax, and one tyre looked as if it had had the tread ironed out of it. 'You look at it, pal. This is well bald, isn't it?' The details of ownership checked out with the computer, and a slightly fortunate citizen departed with a warning rather than a ticket.

After a day's 'fast response', I would return the following day full of 'what happened next?' questions – 'Was the arrested man bailed?' 'Did the victim live?' – but seldom got any answer without several inquiries. At first I took this as evidence of lack of curiosity by police officers, but, after a few days, I realised that a continuous tide of new events inexorably bore away yesterday's happenings. A few minutes after taking part in an arrest, a relief officer may be off for four days, returning for a week of nights when he would be unlikely to hear what had happened at court. It is understandable, but inefficient and possibly even dangerous; it is clearly important for the fast response offi-cers to know, for example, whether a man who has carried out a stabbing is back in the community or behind bars.

Like everyone who has watched police cars racing through crowded traffic, I had from time to time wondered whether such speed was necessary. 'It must be their lunch break,' said a man waiting at a zebra crossing as a police Ford Sierra flashed by. Advanced police drivers are impres-sively skilled, and my perception of the danger we posed as we roared through suburban south London was that of a staid private motorist. But very few of the 'shouts' we answered merited any risk. A senior officer said: 'Police officers do not have a God-given right to break traffic regulations. A driver should resist temptations; there is nothing more dangerous than when the adrenaline rises. No call is so urgent as to justify an accident. Too often young lads think it will never happen to them, but, of course, no driver is fireproof.' He added that he understood the temptations: 'It's rather nice on a summer's day, when the young ladies are about, to thrash through a town with everything going.'

Shortly after I had this conversation, there was a rash of highly publicised accidents in which police car chases led to the deaths of innocent drivers and passengers. Several of the crashes were almost carbon copies of each other. A police car pursued a suspected stolen car – driven, as they usually are, by a teenager without a licence – and the fleeing car crashed into another vehicle, killing its occupants. None of the accidents resulted from the hot pursuit of such 'dangerous' criminals as bank robbers, and the public perception was that the thrill of the chase was distorting police drivers' judgements. One night when I was with the Streatham area car, the crew told me of an incident they had been involved in twenty-four hours earlier. They had been following a motorcycle at a steady 30 mph, when suddenly the bike, which had a pillion passenger as well as the rider, nipped behind a taxi, and shot off. Lima Five, supported by other area cars, gave chase at speeds of up to 90 mph. Finally, the bike crashed at a roundabout, seriously injuring the two young men on it. Fortunately, no one else was involved. The rider was marginally above the legal drink/drive limit, and had panicked when he was followed. The enormous publicity generated by the fatal crashes – in one, three members of a football team were killed, and in others the victims were babies and children – led to tougher guidelines. Police drivers were told that, where the suspected offence was minor, such as a stolen car, they should follow at a distance rather than give hot pursuit. It was better to have criminals escape than to put lives at risk. But similar accidents continued.

An accident involving a police car is known as a 'polac', and is investigated 'independently' by the area traffic department rather than by the division to which the driver belongs. I did not have an opportunity to follow such an investigation, but I spoke to a woman who witnessed a crash which she believed was caused by dangerous police driving. She was visited several times by investigating officers, and from them she formed the strong impression that the police were rallying round their own man. She did not hear the outcome of the inquiry, and was never called as a witness, but she contrasted the time and attention given to the accident with what she regarded as skimpy inquiries into a recent burglary at her home. A senior police officer, to whom I related this account, said that he would presume that the painstaking effort by the accident investigators showed the police were trying to 'do' their driver rather than to exonerate him.

The lack of consistency inherent in the fast-in, fast-out reaction to crises, highlighted by the driving of the area car, also mars the more considered police response to longer term problems. I went with a beat officer to the home of a distraught foster mother, who had in her care a girl she genuinely believed might be murdered. Our visit followed what the woman described as 'copious' abortive phone calls to the police station. The girl, aged fifteen, was on bail for several offences, and had a relationship with a pimp with a criminal record for drugs, guns and living off immoral earnings. Under his influence, the girl broke her bail curfew virtually every night. She claimed to be pregnant by the pimp, which seemed to the foster mother to be prima facie evidence on which to base a charge against him of having sexual relations with an under-age child. When the girl did return home, she had often been severely battered. The foster mother was visibly under stress, pulling at the neck of her pullover and chain-smoking. She had been driven to distraction trying to find someone who would help her sustain her responsibility. The local authority had done 'sod all', and, when there had been a warrant out for the girl's arrest, Gipsy Hill police station could not find it. The woman said: 'If every time the girl broke her conditions of bail, she was picked up, she would learn. What it really needs is a policeman to take some interest in her.' She appreciated that the police were short of resources, but felt that, if they tried, they could find the girl within ten minutes. As she poured out her story, I thought of the hours I had spent in the area car doing not much more than killing time. The truth was that this was exactly the sort of case the police run a mile to avoid. It involved a juvenile who was in the care of the distrusted local authority; the outcome was likely to be messy and imprecise. Like a rubber ball, responsibility for the girl would come bouncing back to them. The foster mother was left with her despair: 'This kid is going through the net, and no one is doing a damned thing to help her. I just have a feeling that she is going to end up being murdered; she is so vulnerable, so at risk. There would then be an inquiry which would find that everyone had fallen down on the job.' The PC listened sympathetically. He would, he said, make a further note in the station 'missing persons' book, so that it would be taken 'seriously', and he would make a report to the CID about the possible unlawful, under-age sex.

At about that time a conference was held concerning a fourteen-year-old boy who had been missing for eighteen months. He was the son of a prostitute who had disowned him at birth, and he had been absent for four months before his step-parents even reported him missing. The case had fallen through the abundant cracks in the system both because of the recent fast turnover of senior officers at Streatham, and because there was no insistent family clamouring for action. Everyone at the conference was conscious of the contrast between the dilatory inquiries about this boy and the effort and manpower put into the then recent disappearance of middle-class estate agent Suzy Lamplugh. Superintendent Buchan, who chaired the conference, said: 'We have been pussyfooting around for the last twelve months. He could be on the "rent boy" circuit; his body could turn up anywhere. I feel very uneasy. We have got to get to the bottom of this.' A teacher from the child's school said that no one any longer remembered the boy. The boy's brother was a 'rent boy' in the West End, but there was no record of the boy himself at the 'juvenile protection bureau'. The most profitable avenue for inquiry appeared to lie in the missing child's love of circuses (on a previous occasion he had run away to join one). The general assessment was that the boy was alive and well, and living on his wits. The police realised that he wouldn't thank anyone who found him, brought him 'home' and returned him to school. However, it was decided to re-open the inquiry. 'If we spend a bit of money on loose ends, maybe he is just below the surface,' said Inspector Don Broadbery, the community liaison officer. Four months later there was still no news; the case was passed to the Area Major Investigations Pool (AMIP), who were up to their necks in murders.

The biggest operation mounted during my time in Streatham was a drugs raid involving seventy-five officers on a large house that had been taken over by squatters. The house had been targeted as the result of information from the local home beat officer, John Fogg-Elliott. So sensitive was the operation that I was excluded from a criminal intelligence meeting at which it was discussed. The argument was that, if the squatters were tipped off, I, as the only non-police officer present, would have come under suspicion. Fogg-Elliott's information was that the house (once a prosperous home, now awaiting either demolition or redevelopment), was being used for drug-dealing, especially during parties on Friday and Saturday nights, and that at least one serious dealer was involved. Over the next few weeks, preparatory work – surveillance from a nearby flat, the following of vehicles, the checking of convictions of people living and visiting the house – was entrusted fitfully to a number of police units, including the Territorial Support Group (TSG), Streatham CID, and 'A' relief (to which Fogg-Elliott belonged). What news there was from this intermittent attention confirmed the initial intelligence; all that remained was to pick the right time and the right troops for a raid, which promised to net several substantial drug pushers and a lot of users. There were also peripheral criminal activities, such as the illegal sale of booze and a shady secondhand car lot operated from what once had been the garden. It was, in the words of one officer, 'a lovely address'.

For weeks nothing was done. Was it, I asked Fogg-Elliott one day, on the back burner? 'It's in the fridge,' he replied. The subject arose sporadically at 'morning prayers'. Two teenaged girls had provided information that Rastafarians were selling tickets to Saturday night 'acid house' parties at which drugs were being traded, and that alcohol was being sold. A senior officer told me: 'It will be Fogg-Elliott's operation. He will set up the OP [observation post], and will virtually have twenty PCs at his disposal to raid the place.' He explained the new horizons opening up for PCs. 'We're trying to enhance the status of the PC on the beat, and we're not very good at it. We have got to get the guys doing the job actually to make the decisions; they will work far more enthusiastically than if the decisions have been imposed from above.' He said that Fogg-Elliott was right to feel frustrated, because action should have been taken six weeks earlier. 'I was furious. A PC had proposed the raid; it had been accepted, and we, as management, have done nothing about it. We have let him down, and I feel bad about it.'

Something had to be done, it was agreed by all, but nothing was. The *mea culpa* theme played for several more weeks. It would have been unsafe, it seemed, to rely on the report provided by the two girls, since they were untested as informants. More observation and tailing were required, since the worst option would have been to blunder blindly into the house. For the raid to succeed, there had to be first-rate intelligence: the raiding party had to know exactly what and whom they were looking for, the layout, the exits. They had to go in numbers sufficient to deter anyone from being tempted to resist them – the minimum ratio was two officers to each party-goer. (That month there had been a minor riot after a raid on an acid house party in Sevenoaks, Kent. Senior officers were concerned that, in the more

combustible environment of inner London, a wheel didn't
come off.)

The raiding party would need specialist assistance: manpower from the TSG; drug-sniffing dogs; drugs officers to
identify suspect substances; vehicle examiners; a licensing
inspector. They required equipment; hydraulic jacks to
'pop' open doors without alerting the occupants; axes and
sledgehammers for tackling other locked doors; 'dragon'
lights – powerful hand-held torches – in case someone threw
the mains switch; plastic bags for collecting and identifying
evidence. Finally, police would need the utmost speed and
surprise. A drugs raid is useless if the end result is a throng
of people knee-deep in discarded drugs, none of which can
be accurately connected with individuals. 'A' relief resumed
surveillance, setting themselves several weeks to gather the
detailed information that would be needed. However, no
sooner had they begun the work than the raid was suddenly
brought forward. It was to be 'go go' in forty-eight hours.
PC Fogg-Elliott was on holiday!

The rush almost inevitably meant that the raid would be
flawed. As one of the officers who was counselling delay
said: 'To fail to prepare is to prepare to fail.' It was decided
to strike on a Friday rather than a Saturday night. Saturday
would have been the optimum night with the highest chance
of the 'main men' and the maximum number of drug users
being there, but the police feared they might be outnum-
bered on a Saturday. In the countdown hours, those in the
know assumed a spirit of jocular despair. Many of those
complaining had the luxury of knowing that they had no
responsibility. It is difficult to pull together the disparate
elements required for a successful raid, and hit the perfect
moment to go in. I had asked a senior officer several weeks
earlier why plain-clothed officers were not sent in, disguised
as party-goers. It was dangerous, I was told, and might
have blown the operation. In the absence of decent intelligence from within the house, there was a strong whiff of
fiasco in the air, and circumspect officers were distancing
themselves from the outcome long before the raid got off
the ground: 'I can live with the knowledge that this was

not my doing,' said one. There was no guarantee that the key suspects would be there.

There are a whole host of reasons why it is difficult to mount a full-scale raid. The officer in charge must always be conscious of the potential volatility of a confrontation between large numbers of police and possibly drug- or drink-inflamed partygoers. The units involved only come together at the last minute. The police have only one shot: if by ill chance (for them) the chosen night proves a poor one for the operation, no repeat is possible. The briefing for the Streatham raid took place at 10.30 p.m. in the snooker room at Gipsy Hill. Even this did not go entirely to plan; the crime squad, a dozen or so plain-clothes officers, went to the wrong location. The objectives were clearly set forth; plans of the house, obtained from the local authority, were handed out; tasks were assigned. Downstairs, preparations were made for receiving prisoners; extra tables were set up in the custody suite, and sergeants and inspectors brought in to handle the paperwork. The cells were cleared. A pimply youth was led out handcuffed to a black WPC: 'Getting married, are you?' asked a PC, and drew a blank, unhappy stare from his colleague.

The troops were loaded into transit vans and green police buses, where they dined on southern fried chicken and mild hysteria. The officer in charge waited for news to be radioed from the front by a PC hiding in a tree opposite the house. At midnight the PC reported there were only fourteen or fifteen 'guests' at the party; another eight drifted in at 12.10; a further half-dozen five minutes later. With seventy-five men at his disposal, the senior officer was getting close to his 2–1 ratio, and he was becoming concerned that the activity in and around the police station might jeopardise the raid. 'If I think that I'm under pressure, I wonder what Eisenhower felt like. I'm in no physical danger, and I'm not putting anyone else in real physical danger,' he said.

The rest of us boarded the buses and drove to within two streets of the target. The order to go was immediate, and the officers struggled from the vehicles and sprinted towards the house. As we ran, a piercing shriek rang out from the next road; a man in a stocking mask was battering a woman over the head. The crime squad rushed to the spot and quickly discovered the would-be rapist hiding in a garden shed. Our arrival was a coincidence, and the arrest by far the most significant of the night; it might, a senior detective said later, have prevented a murder.

At the house, I charged through the nearest door which happened to lead upstairs, where bemused squatters – rather sad middle-aged men – were being roused from mattresses on the floor. Cans of Guinness and saucers full of cigarette ends littered the rooms. The men were nothing to do with the more exotic drugs party below, and, had the police intelligence been better, that part of the house could have been safely ignored. When I got downstairs, a number of handcuffed party-goers were lying face-down on the floor. The walls were painted black, decorated with red and green fluorescent paint – 'dream zone', read one slogan; the DJ had let off the smoke machine; a neon bulb cast mauve light on a Stygian scene; an imitation flashing blue police lamp decorated the bar.

One uniformed PC was in heated confrontation with a handcuffed young man. 'I've got nothing on me, nothing. You can't fucking arrest me,' the man protested vehemently. The officer was pushing him about, and being fairly heavy. He prevented the young man's girl friend giving him a cigarette. As he led him away, he slipped something into the suspect's top pocket. 'You put that in my pocket; you can't nick me for that. You fucking put it there,' shouted the youth. 'I see, ' said a senior officer entering the room at that moment, 'we have the first allegation of planting.' I had not seen the beginning of this confrontation. However, some days later I was told by another PC who had been there that the youth had thrown something to the floor as the police burst in. What the officer I saw did was restore the discarded object to its rightful owner. This was not, volunteered the second PC, 'in order', but nonetheless understandable, as the evidence (presuming that what had been picked up was a drug), would clearly be stronger if the drug were in the accused man's pocket rather than on the floor. In the officer's eyes, what he had done was, I suppose, designed to ensure that 'justice' was done.

In a back room half a dozen handcuffed and prostrate men littered the floor. As each was removed, he had to be helped to his feet; it is hard to get up when your arms are pinioned behind your back. A PC leading a man to a van said: 'You'd better remember before we get back to the station, or you'll be in more trouble than possession.' The words could obviously have been construed as a threat, but, again not having seen the start of the altercation, I could make no judgement. A curtain had been slung across a door, and behind it WPCs were searching women. Party-goers were both black, including Rastafarians, and white, but most of those arrested were white. The tension eased perceptibly once it was obvious that what remained for the police was essentially a mopping up operation. A young woman appeared from behind the curtain. 'No drugs?' asked a PC. 'You *are* a big disappointment to me.' The black DJ, removing his equipment, was asked by a PC whether he had been paid. 'No, I'm waiting for you guys to sort me out.' 'Didn't you get my tip-off?' joked the PC. Officers carried away trays of lager and a bottle or two of spirits. A detective came out with a plastic bag: 'A bit of resin, some herbal stuff and forty quid – small-time dealer,' he said. Other small amounts of drugs, including 'crack' and LSD, were also found.

Outside, where no one appeared to have the spirit to do anything about the secondhand cars, PCs were assessing the night's achievement. Several were offended that such a fine house had been reduced to a venue for drugs parties: 'Someone spent a lot of money building this house, and look at the state of it,' said one. The consensus among the troops was that there would be few 'bodies' in court; none of the key suspects had been present. However, the night had not been the utter fiasco some of them had been cheer-fully forecasting. There had been arrests, and, with luck, the raid might teach the organisers not to do it again, though the more cynical suggested that the main movers, having escaped the net, would simply open up for business elsewhere.

A short post-mortem was conducted at the police station. A TSG inspector was vociferous. He complained that because of poor intelligence they had lost vital evidence. Undercover partygoers could have pinpointed the bar as the centre of the drug-dealing. 'Whoever was doing the OP should have been able to say the people inside were mainly white; a chap and a woman could have gone in there as easy as anything,' he said. He complained also that the house plan had been inaccurate. A sergeant added: 'If we had gone in, we would have known to forget the rest of the building. Unfortunately the raid was put together at rather short notice. We had to go with what we had, which wasn't enough.' The officer in charge told the TSG inspector that he looked a bit down in the mouth. 'I thoroughly enjoyed it,' replied the inspector. 'But I don't want you to go home too happy, guv'nor. You haven't got the bill yet.'

Officers concerned with the raid continued to mumble for some days. The general opinion was that, had the intelligence been more accurate, better results could have been achieved with half the numbers of police. As it was, even some offences that were uncovered, such as the illegal sale of alcohol, were never followed through. The canteen, I suspected, was as happy as if the raid had been a roaring success. The guv'nors, they said as they ordered their chips, had blown it; and they rolled their eyes in a familiar gesture of despair towards the canteen ceiling and the unseen powers above.

As the raid receded slowly into station mythology, routine policing re-occupied the centre of the stage. As well as covering shifts, each Streatham relief has territorial responsibility for two of the division's eight 'sectors'. Run-of-the-mill matters are passed to the relevant relief inspector, and dealt with as other priorities and the shift pattern allow. Organising responsibility in this way does not make for systematic response to the public's needs, and causes, I suspect, much of the dissatisfaction that so colours the public's perception of the police. The co-ordinator of a neighbourhood watch scheme on a council estate found a stack of discarded cardboard boxes that had once contained television sets. Suspecting that he had stumbled on evidence of a robbery, he called the CID, only to be told that the home beat officer was off and would be asked to look into the report two days later when he returned. Chief Superintendent Street, to whom the co-ordinator complained, was furious. But shuffling responsibility onto absent colleagues is inescapable when reliefs are conditioned to think of only one quarter of the division as 'theirs'.

Mr Street was working on a plan to reduce reliefs to the minimum required for instant response, re-allocating the majority of his uniformed staff on a permanent geographic basis. Reliefs were, he had decided, 'an expensive luxury'. Thinking aloud, he said: 'Reliefs are essentially fire brigades. When a call comes, they all go rushing off. It's not their fault, there's no malice in it. It's just that they want to work. But it is a myth to assume that they are a means of patrolling an area.' If reliefs became slimmed-down response teams, 120 officers would be available for permanent attachment to neighbourhood sectors. Under the control of sergeants, they could patrol on a consistent basis, responding to the sort of calls that have in the past been set on one side. Shifts would then be organised to match coverage to demand. 'You would achieve two things: recognise the reliefs for what they are, and restore local patrolling,' said Mr Street. 'Until we allocate the resources we've got as efficiently as we can, I don't think we can complain too much about being under-resourced.'

4

'A Game of Odds'

'We don't get promotion out of feeling collars. The public says, "You'll get made, sergeant, for this arrest", but it's not true. All you get out of arresting people is aggravation. If I don't arrest anybody at all, I get no trouble. I may be completely non-productive, but, as long as I'm always early, the job says I'm a nice boy who never gets complaints.' – Detective Sergeant

A veteran PC, with twenty-five years' service, told me that when he started his career it was quite usual to spend two hours with a burglary victim. In that more tranquil age, the police officer did not leave the scene until he was sure the victim had overcome his initial shock, had made contact with a friend or relative, and had enough money for his immediate needs. Today, said the PC, police are little more than a recording service. Officers frequently do not bother even with the bare minimum of inquiries – calling on neighbours to ask whether they saw or heard anything.

Whatever else the police may do, from controlling football crowds to stopping motorists, there is one irreducible responsibility by which they will always be judged: the prevention and detection of crime. In many respects it is an unjust yardstick, in that most of what makes for crime lies far beyond the control or influence of the police. But, until better criteria are devised, crime figures will remain the stick with which the police will be most often beaten. Of all the dissatisfactions I heard voiced with police performance, none was more bitter than those of victims who felt that the police response to their losses was unprofessional or inadequate. Burglary is widespread enough for all of us to know such victims, and their unhappiness does more to shape our opinions of the police than do the most sensational stories of corruption and 'rotten apples'.

According to a senior detective, the reality is that at a local level only murder and rape are adequately investigated. 'There are,' he said, 'usually ten to twelve detectives on a straightforward pub murder, which will be easier to solve than the average burglary. Whereas one detective constable will be given a list of a dozen burglaries, and told to go out and investigate them.' It is public opinion which sets these priorities, and it is the public who suffer when minor crimes are not properly pursued. A chief superintendent said: 'We are told to use our money to the best effect. But we might get a missing child, and, although we know in our hearts that she is dead, hundreds of police officers will be tasked to find her body. Child murder is seen by the public as the most serious crime. We respond, therefore, to public pressure. Catching robbers and burglars has to be put on one side while we hunt for a corpse. We do not control our resources.'

Streatham's senior detective was Detective Chief Inspector John Walsh, a chunky, dark-haired man who wore comfortable, rather than smart, lounge suits, and usually, like most senior officers in plain clothes, a police or club tie. He became a friend, and on several occasions called me in the middle of the night to tell me of breaking investigations. He had served virtually all his twenty-four-year career in the CID, much of it in specialist squads at Scotland Yard. He is, I was told by someone who had followed his achievements, a first-rate 'thief-taker', an estimation that I could well believe. However, at Streatham his designation was 'Divisional Crime Manager', and his job was essentially to keep an often creaking show on the road. On several days after 'morning prayers' I joined him in his cubby-hole of an office, the floor of which was usually covered with cardboard boxes containing a backlog of cases. We often just had time to stir our coffees when the phone would ring, and AMIP (Area Major Investigations Pool) would be on the line trying to poach Streatham detectives for major crimes elsewhere. Mr Walsh would turn despairingly to his pinboard, and run through the names of those detectives not already committed. (Once he was down to three out of a nominal twenty-two full-time officers.) 'We're running with four officers, could you try elsewhere? You know I would help you if I could,' he would begin, but usually ended by agreeing to one more officer being pulled off local burglaries and street robberies to join a murder squad. At one stage, over half the divisional detectives across London were assigned to AMIPs. 'I'd like him back by such-and-such a date,' Mr Walsh would conclude hopefully, and run his pen through another name on the wall.

His other millstone was the still fairly recent civilianisation of the prosecution system. The handing over of court prosecution to the Crown Prosecution Service (CPS) had been matched by the creation of crime support groups (CSG) within divisions. The notion was that police would be spared the bureaucracy required to prepare cases for court and therefore have more time for investigations. However, the level of pay for the new civilians was so derisible and the training so inadequate (there was none for the first two years) that the CSG could not cope. A legal secretary with a firm of West End solicitors could earn almost twice the salary of a CSG clerk. Cases were being thrown out of court because the paperwork was inadequate, incomplete or even lost. One detective suggested that CSG and CPS clerks – not at Streatham – were being 'got at' by criminals and induced or persuaded to 'lose' files, much in the way that juries are sometimes nobbled.

Twenty years ago virtually every crime would have been investigated by a detective, but the soaring rate of reported offences forced the police to ration the attention given to individual crimes. A formal points system which was employed when I was at Streatham was abandoned because of public dissatisfaction, but it remains common sense to assign genuine effort only to those cases that are the most likely to be solved. When assessing a burglary, the value of the property taken is of less consequence than the quality of the evidence, such as a description of a suspect. However, because the well-off are more likely than the poor to possess either identifiable objects or to have marked them, higher value crimes are the most likely to be vigorously pursued. There is a greater chance of recovering eighteenth-century porcelain figures, for example, than video recorders.

Streatham, where the points system operates, screened in about 30 per cent of crimes, almost twice what had been anticipated when it was launched. Detectives were not automatically sent to burglaries, though personally Mr Walsh felt strongly about a crime that amounted to a plague in an area of bedsits and transient people. He argued that house-breaking – now often dismissed as a relatively minor offence against property – was tantamount to an act of violence, and that the courts are too lenient with burglars: 'I would give everyone one chance, but the second time they really should learn from a deterrent sentence. The crimes have gone up and up and up because the yobs think that we've made them socially acceptable.' He told of offenders who gave the police 'V' signs after they had received non-custodial sentences. 'If they're not locked up, they say, "Yes, we got away with it." We criminalise people by being soft.' And he cited the case of an offender on bail from eight courts simultaneously. 'He has only got the way he is because, having been arrested time after time, he eventually believed that nothing would ever happen to him. The police force has got to be backed by effective sanctions in court, which I don't think we are getting at the moment. The average guy won't be incarcerated until he has been convicted four or five times, and – unless he is extremely unlucky – that will mean he has committed nearer forty or fifty crimes.' Mr Walsh favoured the 'short, sharp shock', to which much political lip-service has been paid, but which many police contend has never been properly implemented.

The majority of police I met believed wholeheartedly in the deterrent value of heavy (or even brutal) punishment. A detective sergeant (DS) said: 'A good percentage of hooligans are cowards, and it's proved through history that a person will bully if he knows that he is not going to be hit back.' He said that his father, a professional soldier, had shared a barrack room with a man who had been given twelve strokes of the cat for armed robbery. 'This man said he never, ever wanted that to happen to him again. He may have been mentally marked, but if he's mentally marked so that he doesn't commit offences again, that can't be bad, can it?' By contrast, a chief superintendent, who had watched offenders come back time and again to the courts, believed most sentences were futile. 'For example, what is the point of fining someone who has no money?' he asked. Whenever possible, he said, offenders should be cautioned rather than prosecuted.

I came across several young 'professional' criminals, with one of whom I talked at great length as I report later in this chapter. They were often, as Mr Walsh suggested, committing crime morning, noon and night, frequently to feed a drug addiction. (The arrest of one youth will sometimes stop a crime wave in its tracks.) They were rarely either contrite or frightened of the consequences. A few months before I went to Streatham, I spent a week at a young offender institution in the north of England. Although the 'prison' ran a positive regime and the young men were serving very long sentences, I met very few who thought they were being either rehabilitated or deterred by the experience.

I went to court with a detective sergeant and two detective constables, who were hoping that a remand prisoner might be returned to police custody so that he could help 'clear up' about seventy crimes for which they were sure he was responsible. On arrest, the young man had said that he would be happy to co-operate, but he had, the police believed, been 'got at', either by a solicitor or by his fellow remand prisoners. He was a heroin addict, who most afternoons had jemmied his way through patio windows in streets close to where he had been brought up. The streets, backing on to a series of alleys that allowed burglars a quick getaway, were highly vulnerable. A nearby network of otherwise similar suburban roads had not been touched because they afforded a housebreaker almost no cover. The

95

DS estimated that, because of the youth's desperate need for cash and the speed with which he got rid of the proceeds ('knocking the gear out'), the young burglar seldom received more than a trifling percentage of the value of what he stole. Irreplaceable family treasures were sold to 'fences' for a song.

The DS talked to the burglar through a judas hole in a blue cell door. The youth wore a green cardigan, and had unkempt hair and the feckless demeanour of many persistent young offenders. At the sight of the DS he stirred from the bunk on which he had been lying, and pressed his wan face to the small aperture between us. 'You're coming with us for a few days,' said the DS. 'No, I'm not,' said the youth simply. And that basically was that, though the DS did make a formal application in court. The burglar's solicitor argued: 'He might admit to things that were not down to him. He has indicated to me that he no longer wishes to co-operate with the police.' The DS riposted: 'This man has admitted many further burglaries in a general way. We are not seeking to clear up all the crime in Streatham, but to take him to burglaries in a very small area clearly done by one person.' The magistrate made a practical judgement: 'If he won't co-operate, then there is no value in him being in police custody.' The youth, who had spent his few minutes in the dock nodding and winking to an acquaintance in the public gallery, returned to his remand centre. What aggravates the police about such a situation is that, while the rights of the offender have been scrupulously protected, the 'rights' of his victims – most of those burglaries would now never be 'cleared up' – appear not to concern the courts.

This perceived imbalance between 'rights' and 'justice' makes police cynical about the court process, while some critics of the police, like the writer Ludovic Kennedy, say it can tempt officers to 'strengthen' the evidence against suspects they 'know' to be guilty. It upsets police officers that the term 'miscarriage of justice' is used exclusively for the wrongful conviction of the innocent, and not for the far more frequent, as they believe, wrongful acquittal of the guilty. As with most suggestions of police malpractice, the rank and file response is that indeed there has been abuse in the past, but, for whatever reason – in this case the safeguards in the 1984 Police and Criminal Evidence Act (PACE) – there no longer is. However, while I was writing this, allegations were made in the Midlands that detectives had added extra pages containing fabricated admissions to already signed statements. A Streatham detective, speaking hypothetically, said that if he saw a 'guilty' man acquitted three times, he would be sorely tempted to 'fit him up'. He admitted that he had been 'swift' in his time, but added that he had never been 'corrupt'. He said: 'I have never taken a brass farthing, and I have been plenty of places where I could, believe you me. And I'll tell you why I didn't. I didn't want to wind up in a little stone box for seven years.'

Although PACE gave the police some extra powers, it also restricted their freedom of action. It lays down precisely what is and is not permissible throughout the process of investigation. Detectives who could once roam the wide seas now set sail with their courses marked. A DS referred to the 'good old days', when a prisoner could be held for seventy-two hours before being taken to court. 'Three days were perfect. You took one day to soften your man up – I don't mean hitting him, I mean just having him.' What critics saw as abuse of the Judges' Rules (which had previously determined the treatment of prisoners and the admissibility of evidence), many police defended as necessary flexibility. A DCI said: 'For years police officers proceeded almost by stealth to achieve the results society expected of them. We sustained such severe criticism that along came the Royal Commission that brought in PACE. The Act is a clear statement by society about what conduct they expect from us, and we're professional enough to say "Sod it, if that's what they want, if they want people to walk free because we can't apply a bit more pressure, then that's what they'll get." ' He added: 'It's in nobody's interest to get an innocent man convicted, because if you do you've still got the villain walking free. That's the thing that annoys me about Ludovic Kennedy; his attitude is almost that we preconceive the idea that a man is guilty.'

I have explained how I was never likely to be intimate enough with a case to see malpractice, though I am as sure as I possibly can be that none happened while I was at Streatham. But the natural tendency of the police, especially when under pressure, to get a 'result', to presume that the right man has been arrested, even if some of the evidence does not quite fit, clearly is a threat to the process. This was, of course, the contention of those who campaigned for a decade for the release and exoneration of the 'Guildford Four'. One of the major operations I witnessed (at least partially) was the hunt for an arsonist who had been active in and around Streatham High Road. It was a high-priority inquiry – one fire nearly cost a life – and the crime squad, a team of a dozen tyro detectives, was deployed during the dark hours of the weekend, when the arsonist habitually struck. One night the police were summoned to a house divided into bedsits, where one resident had pushed burning paper under the door of another. The culprit, an ex-mental patient, was immediately suspected of being *the* arsonist, and was held in police custody for several days while he was taken to the sites of other fires to see whether he would admit to any of them. The suspect knew the streets where the fires had been lit, and could even describe one of the derelict houses where the arsonist had struck. He told police that he sometimes wandered abroad, not absolutely sure what he was doing. A detective, close to the case, felt that the suspect was the right man but was not owning up because he feared being sent to prison (rather than back to a mental hospital). One very senior officer was convinced they had the guilty man, and that he would eventually 'remember' the other fires. The next weekend, the 'real' arsonist struck again.

The familiar charge that police 'fit up' professional criminals, a separate issue from mistaken zeal – was refuted, albeit rather obliquely, by an experienced detective chief inspector. 'There are five thousand armed robberies a year, and that's keeping me quite busy enough. Why should I need to go out and fabricate evidence against anyone else? There are plenty of real robbers, there are plenty of real burglars . . . more than we can deal with.' He had worked on Scotland Yard specialist squads, where, he said, it would have been very easy – to 'go swimming' for three months instead of keeping surveillance on criminals, and then plant evidence on the suspects. 'It is still alleged that we do, but that sort of defence is run less than it used to be. I really think that juries are getting fed up with that. We must have had a tremendous arsenal of sawn-off shotguns ready for planting.' The detective's task, he said, is to arrest with the best evidence, but before anyone gets hurt. 'That's the pig. I'm patient on that sort of thing. If you can afford the luxury of good quality surveillance, you're going to prove yourself right the correct way.' But juries, less inclined than they were to accept the police word for anything, require more convincing than they did. 'You really need to let a conspiracy go quite a long way to obtain a conviction these days,' said the DCI. 'Twenty years ago, if you stopped three or four guys in stolen cars, with sawn-off shotguns and balaclavas, you'd have had no trouble in securing a conviction. Now they run all sorts of monstrous defences. I feel very sorry for juries. Without doubt there is intimidation. They just get a phone call, or word through the guy in the corner shop, that it would be a great shame if Fred Bloggs were to be convicted and their pretty young daughter disfigured. The average juryman doesn't want to be there in the first place, so why the hell should be put his family at risk?'

The Ludovic Kennedy solution to the question of fabricated prosecution evidence is that Britain should move to the French system of a *juge d'instruction*, whose interest lies in determining what happened rather than in securing the best case for the prosecution. Partly because Kennedy bases his argument on examples of miscarriages of justice resulting from police manipulation, and partly because police already resent the civilian CPS, most officers oppose a reform that would, paradoxically, greatly diminish the chances of 'guilty' men walking free. In the French higher courts the conviction rate is more than 90 per cent, while in contested cases in Britain it is about 50 per cent. Detectives argue that the French system would emasculate them because the further they are distanced from running investigations, the weaker become their sources of criminal intelligence. A suspect is at his lowest ebb just before he goes into the dock, and may then be prepared to do deals – names in return for a good word to the judge. When police handled prosecutions, that was the crucial moment when they made contact with potential informants.

The relationship between detectives and informants provides opportunities both for the gathering of vital intelligence and for potential police wrong-doing. The present rules, formulated in the aftermath of Sir Robert Mark's drive against CID corruption in the early 1970s, require that all informants are listed on a register; that supervising officers are told about all meetings; that informants are shared by at least two detectives. Many older detectives complain that their hands are now tied; some I met were even prepared to defend (up to a point, at least) corrupt detectives who were convicted and sacked admidst a blaze of publicity during the Mark purge. One said: 'There is always a danger of imposing current standards of morality historically. At that time, they needed to be there in the underworld. They were expected to use the pubs and clubs, and encouraged to meet with criminals. It was a way of life, and they would have been criticised if they had not. Once we had been prevented from mixing, our sources of information dried up; the baby was thrown out with the bath water. They gained a lot of information and made a lot of arrests. That episode was blasted out of all proportion.'

He then put the canteen case against the exposure of most police malpractice. 'Publicising every incident of corruption has been counter-productive. The public now believes that all police are corrupt, with the result that the jury system has become a game, not due process. There is a gap between factual and legal guilt. If a case turns on one police officer's account, you are very fortunate even to get that officer's evidence accepted, never mind a conviction. Because we have on occasion been shown to be liars, the notion has been implanted that every policeman is a liar. People with vested interests would dearly like to undermine public confidence in the police.' A trainee detective put the stereotyping complaint thus: 'If you went to get your TV set repaired, and the shop was rude and inefficient, you would not deduce from that that all TV shops are rude and inefficient. Yet that is exactly the way in which people judge the police.' Officers seldom add that the opposite process often works in their favour; after the police have been in the news for some heroic or tragic reason, individual police will be stopped by strangers and thanked, commiserated with or congratulated.

I spent a day at the Hendon Police College watching newly appointed detectives being trained in interview techniques. They were all men (women are still grossly underrepresented in the CID) with an average of ten years' service. They wore shirtsleeves – white and striped shirts were favoured – and sat in low, comfortable chairs. Each clasped a large blue file of course papers, which had been assiduously highlighted before the lesson. An instructor said: 'We provide them with a set of golf clubs, as it were, and show them how to use them. It will be up to them to choose the best ones for the job,' and added, 'within the rules of the game, of course. There is no point in being disqualified in court.' The emphasis was on practical work, both in class and in interview rooms equipped with video cameras and tape-recorders. 'Fifteen years ago,' said one instructor, 'they simply pinned your ears back for ten weeks. Now we work on the principle "If you tell me, I'll forget. If you show me, I'll remember. If you involve me, I'll understand." '

The trainees were told that before an interview a detective should learn as much as he can about the crime and the suspect. If possible, he should visit the scene; if not, at least study a map. He should talk to other officers who have arrested the same suspect, study the man's criminal record and learn what he can from divisional intelligence. 'If you haven't done your homework, that's when credibility starts flying out of the window, and that's what we don't need. A simple error can destroy everything that goes thereafter. For too long we have launched into interviews without taking everything relevant into consideration,' they were told by their instructor, DS Brian Crouch, a thickset, bearded man, acknowledged as one of the Met's most accomplished interrogators.

He advised the trainees to spend time 'rapport-building', perhaps a whole interview devoted simply to getting to know a suspect and to studying his 'non-verbal behaviour'. In simple terms, if the suspect sweats, bites his nails, and taps his feet as a matter of course, the interviewing detective cannot put much significance on those mannerisms when the questioning hots up. On the other hand, if a previously calm man becomes flustered as soon as the crime is mentioned, it is likely that he knows something about it. Most people, said Mr Crouch, know when their own children are not telling the truth because the children are so familiar; when a detective begins an interview he has no prior knowledge. 'Try to make it seem as if you've got a common aim, and are moving towards the same goal. There's nothing wrong with being friendly. "A trouble shared is a trouble halved",' he said. Mr Crouch told of one rather cynical trainee detective who put rapport-building to the test, and was amazed when a criminal – well known for his antagonism to the police – signed a statement under caution for the first time in his deviant career.

Trainees were urged to pay attention to such details as preparing the layout of the interview room. 'It is important that you have firm objectives in mind. Your interview will be an official document which will be examined by all sorts of people,' he said. They were exhorted to remember that their mission was to arrive at 'the truth, the facts'. At one end of the scale, the suspect may have planned and carried out the crime, and disposed of the loot single-handed; at the other, he may have nothing whatsoever to do with the crime. 'We must not lose sight of the fact that we do arrest innocent people. They must be let go as soon as possible, because it means you have a guilty man still running round the streets,' said Mr Crouch. But he added later: 'Sometimes you know it is him, but you haven't got the evidence for a conviction. We all know the difference.'

He set what proved to be a humbling test of our abilities to distinguish truth from lies. Three DCs who had served together were each to present us – twelve trainee detectives and myself – with separate versions of the same arrest. We were then allowed one question each, and on the basis of their initial accounts and their answers we had to decide which of the three had actually carried out the arrest and was telling the truth. Not one of us got it right. The genuine arresting officer appeared hesitant and indecisive; in fact he was racking his brains to remember accurately an arson case which had happened many months previously, while his plausible companions were simply reeling off the first thoughts that came into their heads. 'First assumptions,' said Mr Crouch, clearly delighted by our collective failure, 'may lead you up the garden path.'

The detectives were tutored in the 'halo/horn' theory, which holds that our reactions to people are heavily influenced by entirely illogical preconceptions. Maybe we don't like certain names, or – more likely – certain groups of people. You may, Mr Crouch said, have had a row with someone called Simon, and therefore believe that a suspect called Simon is guilty. 'It's that silly.' Men like women more than they like men, and are therefore more inclined to believe them, he said. He emphasised the potential of psychological approaches, telling the trainees about techniques to create dependency in prisoners. One police officer, suggested Mr Crouch, should cater for all a suspect's needs – food, drink, exercise, phone calls – so that the prisoner becomes reliant on that officer, building a relationship that might in due course lead to the suspect confiding in the officer.

The final exercise of the day involved splitting the detectives into groups to study real crimes at the point at which suspects had been identified and arrested. The detectives' task was first to prepare themselves for questioning the suspects, and later to 'role-play' the interrogation in front of video cameras. The police are having to learn new skills for interviewing on tape; most officers are convinced that they, rather than suspects, will gain credibility from the spontaneity of tape-recorded interviews. The existing system, which requires officers to write down painstakingly every question and answer, allows suspects an inordinate amount of thinking time. What particularly pleases detectives is that on tape the validity of all the old clichés – 'You've got me bang to rights, guv' – which criminals do use, but which juries no longer believe, will be re-established. One cited the remark of a robber arrested 'live' on the TV series *Flying Squad*; when asked whether he wanted a solicitor, he replied: 'I think I'll want God here; I'm really knackered, aren't I?' A detective said, 'If we'd put that in evidence, we'd have been laughed out of court.'

Many detectives believe the public and the media are ambivalent about when and where the police should take the gloves off. The public want people arrested, but they also want policemen to stay within the rules. An old-style DCI almost spat out his tea when I mentioned the former Commissioner, Robert Mark. 'You don't catch tough inner city villains by employing lilywhite coppers; for ten years after Mark we could scarcely touch an informant,' he said. 'To some people, the very idea of police doing deals with criminals smacks of corruption, but we need the information.' Another DCI said that the attitude of most people he knew socially was: 'If you know he's done it, bloody well get him convicted. Yet they want different rules to apply when we deal with "Joe Public".'

A young PC said: 'We never seem to get it right. If you stop a motorist, he complains that you should be out chasing muggers. You arrest a burglar, and he wants to know why you're not devoting your resources to armed robberies. If you stop a black, he says you've picked on him because of his colour; if you stop a white, he accuses you of being afraid of blacks.' A senior detective argued that the police's primary function was to secure convictions: 'If guilty people are seen to be walking free, then you are going to have vigilante groups springing up and saying, "Well, what's the point of going through with the legal process? Let's go and do it ourselves." ' A detective sergeant said that whether pressure on suspects and the cutting of corners are acceptable depends on whether the police have the right man.

Solicitors feature alongside the media in police demonology, and they in turn often have low opinions of the police. One solicitor said that he had never been able to put his finger on specific police malpractice, but that he often caught the whiff of tainted procedures. That suspicious attitude is reciprocated when police talk about 'briefs'. Under PACE, all accused must be advised immediately they arrive at police stations of their right to a solicitor; the solicitor's first act is often to tell his client to say nothing, creating an inescapable tension. A DCI said: 'I'm all for the protection of people who are perhaps being arrested for the first time, and who may not be in their normal frame of mind, but should we really go as far as to protect guys who have been arrested on many occasions before, and know exactly what the score is? Do they need a solicitor to say "My client doesn't wish to make a reply"? If you believe he has done it, you've got to try to prove it, and one of the methods is interrogation.' However, he recognised that, since the CPS and the courts now seldom accept uncorroborated admissions made without the presence of a solicitor, such confessions are not worth obtaining. Police officers themselves, when they discuss what they would do if they were arrested, usually say, 'Send for a brief and shut up.' One detective said: 'You could question me for three hours, and I wouldn't say anything.' A small minority of solicitors are suspected by police of being in the pockets of criminal clients, and prepared to impede inquiries by, for example, tipping off the associates of an arrested man. Detectives also allege that there are barristers who, for the right money, will run defences they know to have been concocted. I watched an experienced detective and a solicitor spar warily. Both were civil, though the solicitor was somewhat supercilious and the policeman elaborately polite, but neither was frank. Under the British adversarial system of 'justice', their interests were inimical.

On this occasion it seemed to me that it was the detective, rather than the lawyer, who was trying to serve the public interest, but on another day, no doubt, the lawyer would be on the side of the angels.

Detectives complain almost as bitterly about the CPS as they do about defence solicitors. Not only do they believe that cases are lost through incompetence, but they accuse the CPS of being over-cautious and of often failing to send suspects for trial, even when, according to the police, there is a good chance of conviction. What is worse, argue detectives who in their early careers prosecuted minor offenders themselves, officers no longer cut their teeth in the lower courts, so they are unpractised when they have to go into the witness box in important trials. A detective sergeant said: 'The CPS has devastated the ability of young police officers to give evidence. These kids might be courageous on the streets, but they are terrified in front of a judge.' He alleged that the quality of service offered by CPS lawyers was so poor – as I write, there are vacancies for 413 solicitors and barristers, a shortfall of 23 per cent – that defence counsels 'get away with outrageous things without anyone taking them to task'.

But detectives' chief bugbear in the criminal justice system is, without doubt, the jury, widely considered to be alternatively erratic and bloody-minded. A DS said: 'I've looked in the dock and then at the jury, and wondered if they are the right way round. Go and look at juries taking the oath; some of them can't read it. The Bible's of no more importance to them than a Hank Jansen thriller. Are these people capable of judging their peers?' Another DS told a story, which he swore was true, of a friend who overheard the deliberations of a jury through an open window. The jury, so the tale went, agreed quickly and unanimously on the accused's guilt, but decided that they ought not to return to court too quickly. Twenty minutes later, they had talked themselves into acquitting him.

One of Graham Greene's cynical police chiefs orders: 'Round up the usual suspects.' In practice when a crime has been committed, that is sound advice. But the term 'suspect' is an elastic one. There can clearly be specific suspects for specific crimes – a burglar, for example, whose 'MO' (*modus operandi*) matches the methods employed in a house-break. But there can also be more general categories of suspects. Shortly before Christmas 1988, the Streatham division, together with the fifteen other London divisions with the worst records for street robbery, was given a £16,000 overtime float to mount a campaign against 'muggers'. The task, code-named 'Operation Turpin', was handed over to the crime squad, augmented by a few officers from the reliefs. The crime squad consists of about a dozen PCs and WPCs ambitious to become full-blown detectives. They are a division's storm-troopers, mobilised for the aftermath of a major crime such as murder and for specific campaigns such as a drive against burglary.

They operated out of a cosy, if ramshackle, temporary hut in one corner of the station yard. A water boiler was always on the go, and the walls were decorated with maps bristling with pins which indicated the locations of whatever crime was being targeted, and with pictures of relevant suspects. What inevitably struck the newcomer was that every face, bar one, of the known street robbers was black. This was a statistically accurate reflection of the youths who were snatching handbags and jewellery in the High Road, but it led inevitably to a concentration of police activity on black youths in general, certainly those congregating in shopping areas. A detective said: 'Ninety-five per cent of robberies are committed by blacks, so targeting them means you are concentrating on a potential ninety-five per cent of the crimes: it's a game of odds.'

A chief inspector said: 'Most criminals are aged fifteen to twenty-one. It is therefore wasteful of effort to be chasing after middle-aged men and women. So we chase juveniles and young men, and in certain categories we chase young blacks rather than young whites. If it's a "snatch", we're almost certainly looking for a young black; house-breakers, generally speaking, are white. Of course, whites snatch handbags and blacks burgle, but that doesn't alter our shorthand priorities.' A chief superintendent said: 'The truth is that only a comparatively small number of blacks commit these robberies, but a large proportion of young blacks are stopped in connection with them. As a consequence, relations between young police officers and young blacks are not good.' Another said that in the interests of good community relations the police had to develop a more sophisticated way of identifying potential street robbers than simply by the colour of their skin. To carry on as at present was to criminalise large numbers of young blacks.

The robbery campaign strategy was for the squad to set out in unmarked vehicles, including the battered red builder's van, with blacked out rear windows and spy holes, known as a 'nondy' (nondescript), and keep observation in the High Road. The officers were under specific instructions not to be 'swift', but to go for substantive offences while at the same time protecting the victims. The problem they faced was a microcosm of the difficulties that confront armed police pursuing bank robbers. The crime had to be committed for there to be evidence – the now abandoned 'sus' laws discredited pre-emptive strikes – yet if a 'mugging' were allowed to take place, it both endangered the public and quite possibly meant that a fast-moving youth would escape before the police could pounce. The action usually began when a group of black teenagers were spotted, who immediately became, for identification purposes – 'suspects', referred to over the radio as 'I/C Threes', the racial designation for blacks (whites are 'I/C Ones', Asians 'I/C Fours', and so forth.) They would then be tailed, sometimes for hours, as they meandered up and down the shopping streets, buying fast food and playing football with Coke cans.

After publicity in local papers and a number of arrests, word about the squad's activities got out, and the daily chase became a game of cat and mouse. One night a 'suspect' approached our unmarked car and rapped on the window. 'Can you tell me the way to Streatham nick?' he asked with a broad leer. The next day eleven officers in four vehicles followed one suspect back and forth to Croydon three or four times. The youth would board a bus, travel three stops, dismount, cross the road, and ride back in the opposite direction; occasionally he would disappear down side roads or into shops, before leaping on another bus. At his heels would always be one of the two or three officers wearing 'covert' radios, while the cars and van would take it in turns to follow any bus he might board. The objective was to sustain 'eyeball' – i.e. keep the suspect in view – and to be close enough to nab him if he did make a snatch.

The patience of both parties was remarkable. It was a horrid wet December day, and by mid-afternoon a deep gloom had fallen across south London; the shoppers looked depressed and the goods in the shop windows, tricked out with tawdry decorations, were uninviting. In our car, one of the PCs kept up a running commentary over the radio: 'It's off, off, off' as the bus bearing the suspect started up; a minute later, 'It's stop, stop, stop.' The police lost him briefly in Croydon, until he re-emerged among a largish group of youths who were jostling shoppers waiting at bus stops. 'Contact, contact, contact,' came the cry. There was fear in the eyes of the shoppers as they hunched against the driving sleet and the youths surged around them. After several hours, during which one of the police cars broke down, our youth – without so much as having dropped a sweet paper – returned home, 'housed' in police parlance. He was, his tailing posse then realised, one of the suspects whose picture graced the wall of the crime squad hut. 'If only these little urchins knew the money that was wasted as they sit there playing with their little cans,' said a WPC.

The next night when a thick fog, orange under the sodium vapour lights, threaded its way between Streatham's Victorian houses, a woman was mugged while we were pursuing another set of youths on their inconsequential High Road progress. When we arrived, the victim, a sec- retary in her mid-twenties, was still clutching the strap of her bag, which had been tugged from her as she returned from work burdened by shopping. Her attacker had been black, young and about six feet tall, but beyond that she could not easily go: 'He looked like so many people you see about Streatham.' We drove around the streets for a while, but on a cold night there were few people about. The woman, who had lost not only her money and credit cards but also her glasses and house keys, sat in the front room of a neighbour's flat and sobbed intermittently, gasping 'Oh my God' while she told her story. Between sobs, she counted small mercies: 'I was lucky he didn't stab me; I should be grateful for that.' 'It was,' she said bleakly as we departed, 'one of those disasters.'

Arresting burglars is yet more fraught than catching street robbers, requiring inexhaustible reserves of patience for nightly surveillance on hard-hit streets and the discreet tailing of suspects. Some police estimate the odds against detection for a 'good' burglar at about 40–1, which makes thieving an attractive temptation for a certain type of lackadaisical youth, whose appetite for the good life outstrips his capacity or energy to earn it lawfully.

I visited one such young man, who lived in a squalid DHSS bedsit with his mother. He had been described by a detective as a 'good class' thief, which made it hard to visualise how a 'poor class' burglar might live. 'Charlie', then aged twenty, had an ethereal air about him, and I was not surprised to learn that he had an O level in art, and had worked briefly for a design firm. But for the previous three years, interrupted by one short period in prison, he had, by his own account, flourished as a burglar. 'I get bored with things very quickly,' he said. 'I like a change. I don't really like working for people. I look at it as them earning money off me. It may sound stupid, but those are my principles. Working for someone, you're like a robot. I want it all now.' He rocked back on his heels and smiled as he spoke.

He got, he claimed, a 'buzz' out of thieving. 'I suppose it's all part of the fun; your adrenaline's pumping and all that. People make a hundred quid a week; I could make that in a second. I don't think I could live on one hundred pounds a week.' He saw me glancing round the threadbare room. 'I enjoy going out. I never have any money; most criminals don't. I blow it in an afternoon. I go to a club and spend

110

a grand on champagne and come home skint.' Charlie had been in trouble with the police since he was eight. 'I'm not sorry for my life-style,' he said, 'otherwise I wouldn't do it. I'm only sorry when it involves my mum. It's not very nice, but it's the way I am. If I want something I have to go out and get it; no one's going to give it to me.' His mother asked him whether he would return property if he discovered that the victim were destitute. 'Not if it was going to incriminate me.' 'Have you actually got a conscience?' she asked despairingly. Charlie had not enjoyed prison, but he had survived it, and looked on the prospect of returning with relative equanimity. 'You're learning something every day – useful skills for the outside; you learn your trade in there. There's not much else to do, so you talk about crime. You come out and you've got to start all over again; you've got to get money. I was scared and I thought about prison, but it all comes down to money. I get pissed off, getting bored on the dole. I would do anything to stop going back inside . . . except stopping crime.'

Charlie continued to get arrested and bailed, bringing inexorably nearer the day that he would draw a long prison sentence. Streatham householders continued to suffer a pestilence of burglaries. A detective sergeant, speaking generally, said: 'There isn't any law and order. To get law and order, you've got to take the rights away from the offenders and give them to the victims. Why should a mugger who mugs an old lady have exactly the same rights as the old lady? In fact he's got more rights. She'll go to court and be attacked by the defence counsel, and he'll get every bit of help. He's got to have the benefit of the doubt, because that's what law and order says.'

I thought of Charlie as I visited victims. Mrs 'Edwards', an elderly woman, very deaf without her hearing aid, had been burgled while she slept, and someone she took to be the same thief – 'that animal' – had returned a few nights later, trying to smash his way through a stained glass window. 'Can you imagine what it is like to wake and find that that bastard has been in my room prowling around? If he comes round again and I have the opportunity, I will

111

kill him with my bare hands. I am consumed with righteous indignation. I feel violated. Burglars have no wish to work, and I shake when I think that we are at the mercy of lazy, indolent bastards. We take protection. We tried to make our house a fortress. He must have taken an iron bar to my beautiful window, just to get his hands on our possessions. We're pensioners, not flash. Now I feel disgusted and sickened when I go to bed at night. I abhor bluebottles. When I find one in the kitchen, I pursue it and crush it to death. I would kill that burglar now with no more compunction than I would kill a bluebottle.'

The burglar had taken both a ring given to her by her mother on her sixteenth birthday and her golden wedding ring. But the loss that had hurt most – of irreplaceable photographs of her children – was the result, not of the burglary itself, but of a staggering piece of police incompetence. The photos, which had been in Mrs Edwards' bag when it was stolen from beside her bed, were returned by the thief a few days later through the post. Mr Edwards had taken them to the police station in case they might have had fingerprints on them, and left them at the front office. From there they had vanished. In a letter to the police, Mr Edwards wrote: 'It may sound very trivial, but these photos of my children – taken some forty years ago – were very precious to my wife. They were of great sentimental value, and the family will be upset to know that the police have lost them.' He had had great difficulty either to find the right person to speak to at the police station or to get an answer to his telephone calls. 'I would have thought out of courtesy the CID office could have replied to my inquiries.' It was a letter written in sorrow, not anger, but his wife pulled no punches: 'What happened to my photos epitomises what happens in Streatham,' she said. 'The police don't know what they are doing. They are a waste of time – totally incompetent.' So upset were the couple – they told a senior officer, 'We have been robbed of our peace' – that they were thinking of leaving London. Senior Streatham officers were almost as upset as the Edwards. It was they who put me in touch with the couple, a gesture which – in the light of what Mrs Edwards had to say – amounted to an act of contrition.

The police also told me about 'Nigel Vance', a young professional man who, having been burgled many times in a year, had had ample opportunity to watch the police at work, and was not impressed. He had remained fairly placid the first two times, but after the third break-in he began to develop a nose for police inadequacies. 'The full extent of the officers' "exhaustive" inquiries was to ask a slightly drug-crazed twerp from the squatters next door whether he had seen anything,' he said. Having conducted his own inquiries, he claimed that the police had not knocked on any other doors. 'A burglary with no intruder is pretty much at the bottom of police priorities,' he said, but he was determined that the crime should not just be written off. Despite his calls, 'Bugger all was done. No point of contact was established. I don't give a monkey's when I have been burgled about how stretched they are elsewhere. I need to rely on them to protect *me*; by protecting me, they protect other people,' he said. A detective told him what he considered a tired story about lack of resources. Mr Vance said: 'I felt rather like I was an irate granny, who complains that youths torment her cat, and the police put on a great show. Essentially I was just fobbed off. "It's not a particularly important burglary . . . we're after much bigger fish . . . we've got murders going on . . . we've got rape . . . your problem, though to be deplored, is not worth wasting police resources on. You've lost your stuff, shrug your shoulders and carry on." ' Mr Vance asked: 'Why have I never seen a single bobby on the beat? The only time I've seen policemen round here is when I've been burgled and when a neighbour found an intruder in his house. Then you couldn't move for policemen swarming over everything. The police generally appear to be reasonably incompetent. Individually, they're tremendous people trying to do their best, very devoted and all the rest of it. But collectively, lines get crossed and things go wrong. When you need them, they don't actually come up with the goods.' It took nearly an hour for the police to respond to a 999 call following his fifth burglary, when most of the goods bought to replace those stolen in the earlier burglaries were taken. Again, the police took refuge in their lack of resources, which, as Mr Vance said, 'is not something you can combat when you're dealing with the PC on the desk.' Mr Vance's conclusion was that the police have either been stunned or conditioned into accepting an intolerable level of crime. He said: 'They know that it's bad, but they don't do anything about it. "That's the way the world goes round, guv; there's not a lot we can do to stop them." They're dulled; their sensitivity's dulled. Maybe they're bored to death with the statistics thrown at them, or they've just learnt to accept the fact that they're always going to be losing their battles.'

Nothing excuses the failure to make elementary inquiries, but the truth is, as one senior detective said, that the vast majority of crime cannot be solved by 'detection'. Luck, in the form of a member of the public who not only sees something suspicious but is prepared to act, is usually what leads to arrests. The arrest of three thirteen-year-olds who had mugged an elderly woman was entirely due to another boy, who knew the names of the offenders and saw the attack, and who called the police. So swift was his action that the money was recovered, a rare outcome for a street robbery.

Ambitious detectives try to spend as much of their careers as possible in specialist Scotland Yard squads. There is more glamour chasing a gang of 'blaggers' or 'pavement artists' who lift several hundred thousand pounds at gun-point from banks than in trying to arrest 'scrotes' who snatch handbags. And, broadly speaking, the more serious the crime, the better the chance of solving it, and therefore the greater the professional satisfaction. Tackling divisional crime is like playing a lottery. A DCI, about to become 'crime manager' for an inner London residential division, admitted that he hoped the appointment would only be for a year, because he was anxious to get back to the Yard. He had recently worked on some of the most 'celebrated/notorious' crimes, like the Brinks Matt robbery at Heathrow

Airport, and felt rather out of touch with 'fish and chip' crime. 'Burglars are different, and it's going to be difficult for someone like me to adjust; in divisional work, you're really looking for a needle in a haystack.' But he did say that he thought it right that he should be judged on whether local crime went up or down during his stewardship. 'I don't mind being held responsible. With selective targeting and with a crime squad, you can have an impact. You can reduce the crime rate.'

Every burglary victim, he said, should have at least one visit from a detective. He added: 'The Commissioner said that it was time that we stopped telling lies to the public. Householders know that when you go to a burglary the chances of solving it are pretty slim. But they do appreciate a visit. I know it's a bit of a PR exercise.' Then he continued rhetorically: 'How many PCs who get called to a burglary now knock on the neighbours' doors? The "uniform" who go to burglaries now will tell you that they're too busy.' He agreed that clock-watching and overtime bedevil routine policing. 'They can be totally inflexible. It's certainly true of the CID nowadays as well. No one seems prepared to give anything to the job any more,' he said. He recalled an operation to arrest a 'hole-in-the-wall' gang, who burrowed their way between shops. At a crucial stage a TSG surveillance team had pulled out because their overtime budget was exhausted. 'It's an amazing situation really, but that's the world we live in,' he said.

It is in part because it is so hard to catch offenders that police are punitive in their attitudes towards them. A DS said: 'The most frustrating thing is the type of sentence courts hand out to bad transgressors, the people who go out and cripple, violate and desecrate someone's home.' He told how when he had been a PC he arrested a burglar who had defecated in the middle of his victim's bed. 'I was so angry and incensed that I put his face in it. That guy should really have been punished for that. Do you know what happened to him? Conditional discharge. He is now doing life for murder. I wonder how different it might have been if that man could have had shock treatment early . . .' But, whatever the courts do, for most detectives the thrill of the chase never palls. This DS said: 'Routine bores me. It's not very good for the family, but I like being called out in the middle of the night to a murder. I like sitting in observation posts. It's an exciting job; anyone who tells you that it isn't is talking nonsense. It's exciting even after nearly twenty years. In what other profession, apart from being a soldier – and he's not fighting wars very often these days – could you have the adrenaline running to such a point?

'Take an armed robbery. You're armed and waiting for the team to arrive. You know they're coming; the information is good. The actual hyped situation there is unbelievable. When you think that a policeman goes over the top sometimes at the time of arrest, you've got to have been in that situation to understand. I've seen officers – when there have been fourteen or fifteen of us and three robbers on the pavement, handcuffed, with guns to their heads – actually smash the villains' car to pieces. They've got so much tension that they release it on the villains' car, which, anyway, was probably stolen. You're supposed to be above that.'

A former inner city officer said that any policeman 'earning' his salary in such an area draws complaints. 'I was very, very active. I teamed up with a mate, and we got involved in everything that moved.' He catalogued theft, criminal damage, assault, ponces, offensive weapons, drugs. 'You name it, we were hunting it.' As relations with the local community deteriorated – these were the years just before the 1981 riots – so the job became tougher. When he started, he said, two officers could walk into a blues club and arrest someone without 'aggro', even though there might be fifty or sixty people there; by the time he left, such an operation would have taken twenty men. 'If a policeman got beaten up, we would retaliate. We would get a fistful of warrants and hit them for a month, and the status quo was re-established. A folklore developed. All officers were tarred with the same brush – that they would fit up the evidence at the drop of a hat,' he said. West Indians required street credibility; if they were arrested, they gained status by claiming to have been beaten up, he said, which is what would have happened to them back home. Finally, overwhelmed by outstanding complaints, he left the inner city division 'bitter and annoyed'.

A DCI recalled 'the only time I've ever hit anyone in this job', and added that over twenty years later he had still not forgiven himself. He was fingerprinting a man who had beaten a four-year-old to death. The man just referred to the dead child as a 'thing'. The then young detective punched him in the stomach. 'He never complained. Nothing more was said. But I learned a lot. I was cross with myself that the emotion came out in that way.' This detective said he had once been offered a massive bribe to say that he had seen an accused criminal somewhere else at the time of a major robbery. The offer was relayed to him through a junior officer, who was immediately suspended.

'Corruption will always go on, regrettably. Some people will say that it once bordered on the endemic. Temptation is always there, and we have got twenty-eight thousand officers, but there's no way it's endemic now. In my earlier days I noticed two or three things that I felt at the time were extremely strange. Looking back, I've no doubt that some naughty things occurred.'

5

'A Nasty Case of Death'

It was 3.30 on a December morning. I had been doing some hard pounding in the area car and was looking forward to spaghetti bolognese in the Streatham canteen – a pre-Christmas treat cooked by 'A' relief. We were returning from trying to placate a Spanish restaurateur who had been woken by rowdies, when on the steps of Gipsy Hill police station I encountered the unlikely (for that hour) figure of Detective Chief Inspector John Walsh, arrayed in a garish blue-and-white pullover. 'I've just called your home,' he said. 'I think we've got a murder on our hands.' It was not pleasant, he added, the body had lain undiscovered for at least a week, and the putrefaction was dire.

For a moment I thought he was pulling my leg, since the area car is automatically dispatched to reports of major crime, and I had been a passenger in it for several hours. The crew had been busy, but with nothing that could not have been dropped for a murder. But murder, and a particularly unpleasant one, it proved to be. Late the previous evening, after the pubs had closed, an Irish mother and several of her sons, having fortified themselves with Dutch courage, called the police to say that they were concerned about their daughter/sister, 'Mary', whom they had not seen for a month. She was not on the phone, her flat was locked, and they had failed to get an answer despite several visits. The police sent a probationer PC, who smashed a kitchen window with his truncheon and was nearly knocked back out again by an horrific stench. He found Mary lying face-down in her living room; three round marks were visible on her back in a gap between her pullover and her trousers, and the PC, suspecting foul play,

118

prevented the family from touching her – or anything else in the room. According to his own statement: 'The family of the deceased was led into the kitchen and comforted.' It is acts like this that senior officers have in mind when they wax almost sentimental about the job done by young constables. This PC, a quiet, reserved young man, was only a few months out of training school. He had acted decisively, shrewdly and compassionately, and was still on the front door guarding the scene many hours later. The PC called the CID, and a detective constable, uncertain whether the marks were signs of decomposition or of violence, summoned Mr Walsh from his bed.

A doctor had certified the inescapable fact that the woman was dead, and had told the detective that decomposition usually started with slits in the skin, rather than with round holes. Rapid research in the collator's office had established that Mary had a minor criminal record. The flat, one floor of what had once been a prosperous Edwardian family home, had been blighted by a succession of uncaring tenants and by traffic trundling incessantly past the front door. The front garden was neglected, the house shabby and down-at-heel, and the glass in the street door crudely boarded up. But what set it apart that morning from tens of thousands of similar houses was the smell that began at street level and grew in power as we ascended the stairs. If you obtained half a dozen ungutted herring, shut them in the fridge, unplugged the machine, and then returned a week later, you might have some idea of the final stench that assailed us. It clung to our hair and to our clothing and lodged in the back of our throats for the rest of the day.

Its source was a petite figure, looking more like a waxwork dummy than a human body, sprawled on a dirty pink carpet. She was dressed in thin, cheap black trousers, a grey-patterned sweater and black espadrilles. The round marks in her back could be seen from the door, but the most macabre initial sight was the dead woman's right hand which, resting beside her head, was black and dried almost to the bone. The expert opinion of those familiar with

119

sudden death was that if there had been central heating, the body would have virtually disintegrated.

The large room presented a surreal picture of horror and normality: there were fragments of a smashed whisky bottle across a wide area near the door; blood was spattered on the wall and on a coffee table, beneath which there was an upturned ashtray; the carpet under the body was black with dried blood, and there was what proved to be a human nail on the red sofa; an empty can of Holsten Pils lay near the desiccated hand, and an abandoned Guinness can at the dead woman's feet; blackened fruit had decomposed in a glass bowl; jeans had been hung over an unplugged radiator to dry. Next to a single bed, neatly made with a duvet, the dead woman's glasses and handbag rested on a chair. As well as these expected feminine touches, there was evidence of male habitation – a pair of shiny black men's moccasins behind the door and a shaving kit in the bathroom. On the dressing table there was a copy of the *Sun*, which was dated 18 November: it was now the early hours of Monday, 19 December.

We returned to Gipsy Hill, and Mr Walsh began to pull together a team to handle the initial stages of the murder inquiry. A pathologist, a detective sergeant, and a photographer were called from their beds. The Detective Chief Superintendent in charge of AMIP was alerted. Since Mr Walsh's responsibilities as the divisional 'crime manager' prevented him running inquiries, the investigation would be assigned to a detective superintendent. From some well-guarded hidey-hole, a detective produced a whisky bottle, and two or three of those who had viewed the body and inhaled the stench poured themselves large slugs. Mr Walsh's mood alternated between horror at what we had seen, pleasure in having such good reason to call people so early, and exasperation that the Gipsy Hill contact list was chronically out of date and about as much use in this emergency as a Swahili telephone book. 'It appears,' he told those he woke, 'that the young lady has not been with us for four or five weeks.' Hastily arriving detectives indulged in some cop-type grumbles: 'Just what you want at Christmas, all this aggravation,' said one. 'Jesus, guv,' said another, opening his wage slip which had been put on his desk overnight, 'I can't live on this; you'll have to give me more overtime.'

The pathologist, whom I had previously met arrayed in a dapper dark suit, appeared at 5.30 in dirty jeans and a pullover. He had spent much of the previous weeks carrying out post mortems on the victims of the Clapham train disaster. We returned to the murder flat, where a pretty woman photographer, prudently wearing a face mask, was taking pictures. 'She's a bit of all right, she could take my picture anytime,' said a uniformed PC outside the door. Five weeks earlier the dead Mary had drawn that sort of comment: life went on. Inside, the pathologist turned the body over, and maggots stirred on the blackened carpet. What looked even to my unpractised eye like a series of knife wounds disfigured the corpse, which was matted with dark, dried blood. 'Maggots,' said a detective knowingly, 'don't start for three weeks.' A large plastic sheet was laid out, and Mr Walsh and I retreated before the full horror of the awful corpse was stretched out. A few minutes later the pathologist joined us. 'You can fairly safely say she has been stabbed to death,' he said, and he spread his hands in an all-embracing gesture across his own midriff to demonstrate the extent of the wounds. It was, in John Walsh's words, 'a nasty case of death'.

The post mortem revealed a total of twenty-five stab wounds, most of them on the victim's lefthand side. There were cuts on her left arm showing that she had tried to defend herself. At least four of the stabbings would have been fatal – one in the aorta, two in the kidneys and one in the liver. Her neck had been virtually severed, though – as far as the pathologist could tell from the comparative lack of blood – it seemed that this additional gruesome brutality had almost certainly been carried out after death. The murder weapon, the pathologist told the police, was probably a kitchen knife with a five- or six-inch blade and a single sharp edge.

The professional view was that, ghastly though the murder might be, it would not require the talents of Hercule Poirot to solve it. 'I don't see this being a great problem. At the end of the day it has got to be domestic,' said Mr Walsh. There was no sign of forcible entry; the killer had let himself out and double-locked Mary's front door behind him. At Gipsy Hill, Brendan Gibb-Gray, the AMIP detective superintendent assigned to take charge of the murder, had arrived. He had been jogging when the call was first made to his house, and he was thin and fit (a bottle of Perrier sat on his desk throughout the inquiry), a contrast to many senior detectives. He usually wore a well-cut grey flannel suit, and carried his files in a small sports bag. His first task was to assemble a murder squad without stripping Streatham CID of too many detectives. AMIP was already heavily committed, and a few hours later there was to be another, much publicised, murder a few miles away. Because of these demands on detectives, Mr Gibb-Gray had what would normally be considered a very small team for a murder. It comprised his own 'bag carrier', Mickey Wright, a cheery, middle-aged detective sergeant, with a passion for horse-racing; Brian George, the Gipsy Hill detective inspector, whose skill was to keep his colleagues' feet planted firmly on the ground; DS Colin Waldron, an occasionally inspired Streatham stalwart, who leapt from notion to notion like a mountain goat; two 'indexers' – jobs which appeared to be reserved for women – who kept the card file cross-reference system up to date (computers do now exist, but their use is limited to especially complex cases); and five or six detective constables.

A large basement room was set aside for the inquiry. One wall was covered by a white board, on which the proven facts were entered; like the leader board at a golf tournament, it gave an instant picture of the state of play. The first, simple entry was Mary's full name, together with her date of birth and criminal record number; the evil she had done, such as it was, lived after her. Tables were arranged in a horseshoe; British Telecom was summoned to install direct lines; an answering machine was purchased (the operation of this proved to be at the margin of the team's technical ability); a carousel for the card indexes and a photocopier were ordered; and the battle to get a typist, which was to last the duration of the inquiry, was joined.

If Mary's family had already had a few drinks when her body was discovered, by mid-morning they were, according to a detective who had visited them, roaring like Caliban's companions. They were due to come to Gipsy Hill, and Mr Gibb-Gray was apprehensive: 'Tell them to come in sober; we're not going to be fucked about by them. If they are drunk, or close to it, don't take any statements. Be quite ruthless. Kick them out, and tell them to come back when they have sobered up.' A PC from the front office put his head round the incident room door: 'The "O'Callaghans" are here,' he said, smiling broadly. They were indeed. The mother was screaming: 'You've just got to find the bastard who murdered my daughter; I know the bastard.' Later one of the brothers head-butted a door. But their immense distress was evident. Some refuge was necessary from the horror they had witnessed that morning, and it was not surprising that they had been drinking. The police decided to go ahead with the interviews and to take 'elimination' fingerprints. A close friend of the family, who had known Mary for ten years – his face purple with the ravages of drink – struggled for the right words. Mary, he told a detective, had been a severe alcoholic. It was a salient feature of the case.

Mary had come to London from Dublin twelve years earlier. At first she had been a high-class 'escort' girl, earning up to £3,000 per night from wealthy Arabs. Once she had submitted topless pictures of herself to the *Sun* in the hope she might become a 'Page Three' girl, but had been rejected. When the police held a press conference about the murder, that rejected snap was carried by the *Sun* on Page Nine. What had not been achieved in life was almost achieved in death. The strain of being an escort had, according to a friend, driven her increasingly to drink; the drink reduced her desirability and lessened her price. She was thirty-three when she died and had been living for about four years in the flat where she was murdered. Her rent was paid by the DHSS, and she drew £50 every fortnight in benefit, which was habitually blown on booze. She earned extra money sporadically as a barmaid.

The most vital information produced by the shocked family was that Mary had been having a tempestuous affair with a man called 'Ali', an Arab who was married with a small child. The police rapidly established that this man had vanished at about the date on which Mary had been murdered. A stabbed woman and a vanished lover appeared to add up to an open-and-shut case. Yet, even if Ali walked into Gipsy Hill, would it have been possible to charge him? Mr Gibb-Gray was not convinced. There was no weapon, and no bloodstained clothing. But there was also no rush. 'Domestic' killers, once their passion is spent, are seldom a danger to anyone else. Mr Gibb-Gray considered it prudent and safe to leave the hunt for Ali while his team concentrated on the case against him.

The detectives' efforts were to be divided between recreating the milieu in which Mary lived, and finding out as much as possible about Ali. The system of investigation had been used by Scotland Yard murder squads for at least a quarter of a century. 'It has never let us down', said Mr Gibb-Gray. He did not mean that all murders were solved, but that there had been no horrendous blunders, like those that allowed the Yorkshire Ripper to remain free for so long. Each fresh piece of information led to an 'action', which was numbered by Mickey Wright. If urgent, it was assigned to a suitable detective; if not, it was 'referred' for future consideration. At the same time, the information was indexed and cross-referenced. In theory, any fact, name, telephone number, rumour, address could be instantly accessed. If all the detectives were suddenly reassigned, a new team should have been able to pick up where they had left off. Before each statement was filed, it was checked for fresh information, which then led to fresh 'actions' and further cross-referencing. It was Mr Gibb-Gray's task to ensure that the officers' efforts were effectively concentrated, that morale did not flag, and that, when necessary, they cut their losses.

The team met twice a day; each member gave an account

of his activities since the previous meeting. Like a judge presiding over a trial, Mr Gibb-Gray kept his own record of the inquiry in a large red manuscript book. Christmas presented him with practical problems. Police officers love office lunches, the profession's tribal feasts. The crime squad, who initially helped the murder team with door-to-door inquiries and an abortive search for the murder weapon, wanted to know whether they could go ahead with their Christmas lunch, to which the answer was first, 'Yes, so long as you don't all get absolutely out of the game,' then, once it was clear that there was little more than the squad could do, 'Yes, even if you do.' Gibb-Gray had to juggle his budget against the urgency of the inquiry, and, continuing to believe that Ali – by now the 'wanted' man – was not dangerous, stood the whole squad down over Christmas. 'Most of the people we want to see,' he said resignedly, 'are going to be on the "hit and miss" anyway.'

The cost of the inquiry was always on his mind. Every murder investigation is *sui generis*, and cannot be judged by normal yardsticks of cost effectiveness. However, there must be cash limits and detectives cannot simply spend like shore-leave sailors. The longer the hunt for Mary's killer took, the longer south London divisions were deprived of detectives sorely needed for 'routine' crime. 'The public,' said Mr Gibb-Gray, 'is never aware of the hidden price they are paying for a murder inquiry.' He kept a tight rein on expenditure – 'This is going to be the year of the auditor,' he told his detectives – and aimed to return his officers to their divisions as quickly as he could. 'There will come a time in a week or two when we have done everything we can; at that point another hundred thousand pounds will not get us significantly further,' he said.

Sitting in the inquiry room, occasionally going out with the detectives, and talking with Mr Gibb-Gray was like being a spectator on the edge of a stage. As the statements began to accumulate in the black clip-file next to Mickey Wright's desk, the lives led by Mary and Ali were slowly laid bare, and with them a metropolitan sub-world about which few Londoners have an inkling. There is no more thorough investigation than a murder inquiry; nothing is off limits, and the normal human inhibition not to probe beyond the point of intrusion is suspended. Murders expose the milieux in which they happen, and present intimate portraits of human beings under stress which the most searching profile of the living can never match.

There is in Britain a substantial underclass, who are so poorly housed and educated that they are excluded both from the opportunities that most people take for granted and from bourgeois standards to which increasing numbers aspire. Within this underclass there are sub-cultures, and it was to one of these that Mary's alcoholic coterie belonged. Her associates formed a community of rootless exiles, not one of whom had been born in England, let alone London. They owned little more than the cheap clothes they stood up in; they lived in the worst inner city housing. Almost no one worked; if they did, it was either at menial, poorly paid tasks, such as hotel skivvying, or as self-employed scrap dealers, scavenging amongst the detritus of an affluent society. They did not drive cars. Almost their sole pleasure lay in drinking.

One of this milieu, 'Bridie', a woman of Mary's age and a previous lover of Ali's, was the oldest of a family of thirteen half-brothers and -sisters. She had no idea who her father was; when she was born, her mother had been below the age of consent, and Bridie had been brought up by her grandparents believing that her mother was her sister. 'Eva', a middle-aged German who traded scrap, lived among a Hogarthian cast of winos, who went by such nicknames as 'Mad Albert', 'Edward the Confessor', and 'Tiny Tim'. When one was interviewed by detectives, he said candidly: 'I have an alcoholic problem, and do have a bad memory, and during drinking I have spells when I can't remember anything.' Such people did not make the most reliable witnesses. Mary herself was both alcoholic and promiscuous. Her long dark hair and slim figure attracted men, who passed through her life and her bed like trains through a commuter station. She had had several abortions; had been treated regularly for depression; and been diagnosed as a deeply disturbed personality. At the best of times her life was a disaster, and a calamity was always on the cards. But she was, said her friends, two people: when sober, 'a very sweet kid', charming, presentable and full of vitality; and when drunk, a raging, unpredictable slut. Most of the men who fell for the sober Mary were rapidly disgusted by the drunk alter ego. A few months before her death, Mary met a young woman called 'Susan', and invited her to share the flat. Susan told detectives: 'Mary rarely had much money, and when her Giro cheque came, she would go out on a drinking spree. I often wouldn't see her for two days, and she would come back broke.'

Ali had arrived in London at about the same time as Mary. He was the bright child of Middle Eastern peasant farmers, and had won a British Council scholarship to study electronics in England. Side-tracked by Western hedonism, he did not fulfil his promise, and, leaving college without qualifications, he earned his living as an electrician. Like Mary, he was promiscuous. Given the slightest opening, he would proposition his friends' girls – his wife believed he slept with her sister while she was giving birth to their son. He carried condoms on his professional house calls and invited lovers to spend the night in his home when his wife was away visiting her parents. Unlike those Lotharios who take a relaxed attitude towards their conquests, Ali was regularly consumed with jealous rage. Yet he was, by unlikely contrast, a steady and reliable worker, who had been employed by one company for three years, and had worked at weekends in a chain of fast food shops. His firm gave him a bright red van, and his two occupations – with the opportunities they gave him to meet people – meant that he was known to a wide circle of people.

Although a Muslim, Ali was attracted by heavy-drinking women who seemed happy to have affairs with a man who splashed his money about. The source of his wealth remained a mystery; he only earned £7,000 a year, but when he disappeared it was discovered that he had over £11,000 in deposit accounts. Ali himself had boasted that he had rich relatives who sent him money. However unlikely this was, it added to his glamour and earned him the nickname of 'the Sheikh'. When the police dug into his past, they discovered that he had shown a previous capacity for wild and verbally aggressive jealousy. Bridie told detectives that on the break-up of their two-year relationship, he had begged and cajoled her to return: 'He tried everything, proposed marriage, threatened to shoot me, although I never took the idea seriously.' On the rebound he married a woman from Inverness whom he had made pregnant. He was not happy to be tied down, and proved a poor father and husband. Darting about in his van, the Sheikh soon resumed the life that had been interrupted by matrimony, calling occasionally on Eva to let her know about opportunities for scrap. It was in her den of drinkers that he met Mary. One witness said later: 'He appeared to be immediately besotted by her, and started to show off to her about money. She reacted favourably towards him. They hit it off, and the whole conversation was between them. He offered to buy her a flat.' The pattern for what was to be a short, stormy relationship was quickly set. Ali took Mary to a restaurant, where, largely owing to her gargantuan thirst, the bill came to £120. Back at her flat, the by then very drunk Mary reared up at Ali, called him a 'black bastard', said she didn't trust him, didn't want to have sex with him, and threw him out. Despite this unpropitious start to the relationship, Ali moved in with Mary, bribing her with munificent gifts, including a washing machine and a television. Mary herself was far from infatuated (she told a girl friend that she and Ali had never had intercourse), but she did see in him possibilities for rich pickings. When asked by a friend how things were going, she replied, 'Magic; I've got another Arab.' Susan told the police: 'At first their relationship seemed to work well, but soon they were for ever arguing. Sometimes it seemed to last all night.' Ali boasted that his house was worth £180,000 and Mary told him to sell it and get the money. Mary would slap him, but, although he raised his hand, he never hit her. Susan continued: 'He did say "I will kill you". It was an expression he used quite a lot when they rowed, more often than was normal. Sometimes when Mary was not there, he would tell me that he would kill her; this was because he thought that she was going with other men.' Ali told Mary: 'Now that I have left my wife, my home, for you, I will kill you if I ever come back here from work and you've changed the lock and got someone else and tell me to piss off.' Mary had laughed. In company his jealousy was absolute, and he would scarcely allow Mary to speak with anyone else.

Mary's last night alive passed in a familiar pattern. An all-night drinking session ended at breakfast time at the flat of Edward the Confessor. Ali was sober, Mary half-cut, and Ali had been disgusted when she sat on the Confessor's knee, kissed him and called him 'darling'. He wanted, he told Eva later in the day, to vomit because of the filthy state of the place. He could not bear to see the woman with whom he was so passionately in love fondling a semi-vagrant. Ali departed for work, which, as it was Saturday, should have been at the fast food shop. But he never arrived.

He was next seen by Eva, when he turned up in an utterly distressed state late that afternoon. He was sobbing, and unsuccessfully implored Eva to come with him to Mary's flat. Ali said: 'If you don't come, you might never see me again.' She asked him about his job. 'I'm not worried about my job. I told my boss that I had woman problems. I've left my wife and picked up with rubbish and I'm desperately in love with a piece of rubbish.' He appears to have returned to the flat and to have been waiting for Mary when Susan, who had been evicted by the 'lovers', arrived to collect her possessions. Susan told the police: 'He said that he was going to kill her when she came home, because he was upset at the way she treated him. He said he gave her money, and what more could he do, but that she stays out and doesn't come home. All she wants me for is my money.' He was shouting that he loved Mary. He demanded Susan's keys, so he had in his possession, whether he realised it or not, all the keys to the flat except those carried by Mary herself. Nothing further is known about what

129

happened inside the flat until the young PC broke in with his truncheon four weeks later. The presumption must be that Mary was murdered within an hour or so of the meeting between Ali and Susan.

Ali's movements over the following twenty-four hours were chronicled up to a point, though there remain crucial gaps. In the early evening he returned to his wife to show her how the central heating worked, as he would not, he said, be coming back. His wife said: 'You had better hurry, your girl friend will be waiting.' He replied: 'I haven't got a girl friend. I'm finished. I'm in pain all over.' She asked: 'Have you got Aids or something?' 'No,' he replied, adding: 'When I go away, don't call the police. I'll be arrested. People are after me.' He claimed that he had tried to commit suicide three times in three weeks.

He was next seen at 1.00 a.m. by his boss, who heard a car, and looked out to see Ali getting into a cream-coloured or brown Datsun. The red van was parked outside, and the keys together with a note from Ali resigning his job had been pushed through the door. The writing was shaky, his boss said, as if Ali had been drinking.

Four hours later, Ali's wife was woken by an insistent ringing on the doorbell. A Datsun was in the middle of the road with two men in it. Ali himself was in a collapsed condition, 'wet with lying in vomit'. (His wife had never seen him drunk before.) He demanded a doctor, but she called an ambulance, and the crew carried him to the kitchen and laid him out on the floor. He told his wife that he was scared, and asked her to stay with him. When he fell asleep, she went through his pockets, where she found a note. It read:

I AM GOING TO KILL MYSELF
BECAUSE I LOVED MARY SO MUCH
I CANNOT LIVE WITHOUT HER.

Then on the other side:

PLEASE TO THE BRITISH LAW

NEITHER MY FAMILY NOR MY
FIRM IS INVOLVED IN THIS MATTER
ONLY EVIL . . . PEOPLE WHO ARE ENGLISH
AND IRISH.

At lunchtime Ali ordered a minicab to take him to Streatham. Twice he asked the driver to stop so that he could
be sick. The driver felt that Ali was not merely ill, but that
he was 'acting strange' and giving off 'funny vibes'. Later
Ali returned home to bed, asking his wife to wake him at
five and to call another minicab. The second taxi driver,
who knew Ali, found him perfectly normal during the jour-
ney, which was to an address in Streatham. Ali asked the
driver to wait, and then waved from the front window,
indicating that he no longer needed the car. When the
murder hunt began, the owner of this house was out of the
country; the police had hoped that he might know where
Ali went next. However, on his return, this man said that
Ali had merely come to collect £100 which he was owed
and had only been in the house for a few minutes. There,
effectively, the trail ended.

Normally in a murder of this sort, the killer is either
found fairly rapidly or, in remorse, commits suicide. What
perplexed the police in this case was that Ali's actions were
wholly inconsistent. He had, it is clear, two distinct and
opposing character traits. He was the punctual, conscientious worker, greatly valued by his employers; he was the
tempestuous, erratic lover, given to threats of murder and
suicide. In the hours after Mary's death, the rational in him
was hard at work: he returned his employer's van and wrote
a note resigning his job; if he did kill her, he had been
level-headed enough to dispose of the weapon and any
bloodstained clothes he might have been wearing; he had
double-locked the door to the flat; he went home to show
his wife how the central heating worked; he had been concerned enough about his own health to call a doctor; he
visited a friend to collect money. All these were the acts of
a man apparently concerned about the future. At the same
time, the passionate in him was stirred: he threatened

murder; he spoke wildly of being 'finished'; he wrote a suicide note; and he gave a stranger 'bad vibes'.

The dilemma that faced the police was that in his first state of mind Ali appeared quite capable of planning a competent getaway; in his second he seemed likely to rush off and kill himself. Throughout the inquiry, which lasted about a month in earnest, Mr Gibb-Gray's team veered between the two theories. At first, suicide seemed highly likely, and all unidentified bodies were checked. Ali had over £11,000 instantly available in various accounts, yet had not touched it as he would surely have done had he been alive; he had a vehicle in which he could have driven to a port or airport, yet had returned it. Perhaps, with a dreadful symmetry, Ali was lying dead in some undiscovered flat, his body putrefying. Yet he was a flamboyant man, given to histrionics. If he did kill Mary, and wished to die himself, he might have been expected to return and die beside her, a Romeo beside his Juliet. He would, surely, at least have killed himself in such a way that all the world would have known his grief. It is very difficult to commit suicide and dispose of one's own body simultaneously (which is why many people believe that Lord Lucan is still alive). 'He could hardly throw himself into the concrete foundations of a motorway without being noticed,' said a detective later.

An 'all ports' warning was issued, and airline passenger lists to Ali's part of the Middle East were checked. Mr Gibb-Gray decided against interviewing airline crews, which would have been time-consuming and indecisive. Ali's picture and details were circulated to police throughout the country, and every 'action' not specifically directed at 'eliminating' Ali was 'referred'. The physical evidence was stored in a grey cupboard at one end of the incident room, as day by day detectives recovered clothes and documents. One potentially significant forensic clue, a blood-stained shirt stuffed down a leg of a pair of jeans hanging in Mary's cupboard, was somehow not discovered during the initial search. By the time it was, the blood on it was so 'gungy' that it was of little direct evidential help. However, by then the circumstantial evidence was sufficiently overwhelming for Mr Gibb-Gray to believe the police had a case on which a jury would convict.

Ali's wife, having reported him missing to her local police station a week after he had disappeared, had returned to her parents, and a detective was to fly to interview her. In order to get authorisation for the ticket, Mr Gibb-Gray had to break from the inquiry and write a submission to the relevant Yard department – 'a bureaucratic nonsense', as he put it. It was Day Three of the inquiry, and the whole operation ground to a halt while Mr Gibb-Gray satisfied an official that it was necessary to interview a murder suspect's wife. Documents had to be faxed, and inevitably ended up in the wrong bit of the Yard. While all this went on, the detective nearly lost the last seat on the flight.

Not all the witnesses were keen to help. One of Ali's friends told detectives that he hoped Ali had got away. Mr Gibb-Gray threatened to 'arrest' several recalcitrant or elusive witnesses. 'I know it's Christmas, may the spirit of goodwill be with you and all that, but she's getting to be a bit of a nuisance,' he said of one key witness who was permanently on an alcoholic cloud. The police faced two practical problems. Most of Mary's associates were so regularly drunk and lived so erratically that it was hard to track them down and to make sense of what they knew; most of Ali's associates were to some degree antagonistic. There was a double skin between the detectives and the immigrant population. The first was cultural: the police had difficulty with names, relationships and the immigrant way of life. The second was one of attitude: some people trust the police so little that they drag their feet even when asked for help on a murder inquiry. I went one day with two detectives to visit a family who knew Ali well. Their displeasure at our arrival was very evident; they treated the police with hostility and perhaps also a trace of contempt. There was no reason to suppose they were not telling the truth, but they clearly were not going to put themselves out to help. It was 'us against them', and Ali was 'us' and the police were 'them'.

The team were so frustrated at one stage that they considered calling in the immigration service, who are more accustomed than the police to the culture and traditions of immigrant groups. A thorough investigation of the legal status of some of Ali's associates might, they reasoned, 'wind a few people up' and flush out more information about him. They also tried to 'gee up' witnesses who, they felt, had been less co-operative than they might have been. Several of the team said that, given the solidarity of small immigrant groups and their hostility to the police, it was far easier for a wanted immigrant to go to ground than it would be for a native Briton.

When it became clear that Ali was not simply going to fall into police hands, Mr Gibb-Gray held a press conference at Scotland Yard. He calculated that the case might command some space in the slack news period between Christmas and the New Year, but the press conference was a low-key occasion, with crime reporters in frivolous Christmas-week mood. It was an occasion of police euphemisms and press circumlocutions. 'We suspect this man [Ali] is concerned in the death,' said Mr Gibb-Gray (i.e. 'We believe he did it.'). Had Mary, asked a reporter, been 'a lady of the night?' (I thought the phrase had vanished from the English vernacular at about the time that George Orwell was lamenting the decline of the English murder.) The press conference achieved little, except to give the *Sun* a chance to run the 'Page Three' picture they had spurned a decade before. A later airing of the case on *Crimewatch UK* produced sixty reported 'sightings', mainly in a provincial city pinpointed by the programme as one of the places in which Ali might have sought refuge. Streatham detectives visited the city, but drew a blank.

Public interest in a murder depends very largely on the status of the victim and/or the killer. The press devoted acres of space to the simultaneous murder inquiry into the death of a pretty photographer's assistant, strangled and raped near Wimbledon. A doughty campaigner like Diana Lamplugh, who kept her daughter Suzy's disappearance in the headlines for months, can create interest and therefore extend an inquiry that might otherwise fizzle out. An upper-crust murder, like the Lucan killing, will hold the public imagination almost indefinitely. In this league table, the squalid murder of an alcoholic former 'lady of the night' by an Arab immigrant ranks low. The distinctions of class and value that label us in life, dog us in death.

There were two possible sightings of Ali locally. A man who knew him well said that he saw him on or shortly after the day that Ali disappeared. Ali had looked dishevelled and unshaven, and had not responded when the friend tooted his car horn. Eva met a mutual friend on a bus, who had told her that Ali was alive. In great excitement Eva persuaded him to come home with her. She left him at her flat while she tried to phone the police from a call box, but she failed to reach anyone who knew anything about the case, and by the time she returned the man had gone. At night the incident room was unmanned, and the 999 switchboard, not knowing specifically which murder squad was which, had called several numbers in vain. The man who was going to 'meet' Ali may well have been another of the confused alcoholics, but he may have had genuine information. So much painstaking care went into the inquiry that it seemed wrong that there was no way an informant could get in touch with a knowledgeable detective after five o'clock in the evening. For want of a shoe, the horse was lost . . .

After five weeks the inquiry reached the point in Mr Gibb-Gray's equation at which further expenditure could not be justified. 'We are,' he told the team, 'running out of places to look.' Having at one stage been convinced that Ali had killed himself, most of the squad finally felt he was alive and abroad, and that he was unlikely ever to be brought to 'justice'. Ali had friends who, the police were convinced, would have dissuaded him from committing suicide, and given him practical help. 'You can hear them saying "Don't do it",' said one detective. Ali's wife believed that he knew people with the means and contacts to spirit him out of the country. There were clearly others who might have been able to help the police. The night that

135

Mary died, Ali was in the company of two men, who picked him up outside his employer's home after he had dropped the van; who must have been with him while he drank himself to the point of collapse; and who, four hours later, delivered him covered in vomit to his wife. They have never come forward.

Mr Gibb-Gray returned to an administrative inquiry he had been conducting at the Yard, and the detectives began to drift back to their divisions. Detective Inspector George prepared case papers for the Crown Prosecution Service. There was an end-of-term feeling in the murder room, where the exhibits were being packed for dispatch to a warehouse in Cricklewood. A murder inquiry is never 'closed', and in that warehouse, together with the index cards so carefully filled in by the WPCs, the sad evidence of Mary's blighted life will moulder gently down the years. I took a final look through the statements, and there was still not one by someone born in England. Two exiled cultures had come briefly together in a violent tragedy.

Once the coroner had been informed that the murder hunt had run into the sand, he released Mary's body for burial. On a wet cold winter's day, Mary was laid to rest in a south London cemetery. A robin with ruffled feathers hopped onto the neighbouring headstone of Edward Colman, 'departed this life September 27th 1874'. One mourner's toes peeped through holes in her cheap plastic shoes. One by one, Mary's relatives, their eyes puffed with grief, stepped to the graveside to scatter holy water over the coffin enclosing her mutilated mortal remains. Sixty yards away, lurking discreetly behind the Gothic gravestones of Victorian families of substance, a detective surveyed the mourners. Ali, however, was not among those present.

6
Softly, Softly

It would be an hour at least until the light failed on a grey October afternoon, but 'Doris Peters' was already preparing for bed. She had pulled a chipped kitchen chair bearing an ancient black and white television set close to where she would lie through her solitary evening. In the hall, a heavy table stood ready to be pushed against the inside of her double-locked and double-chained door. She wore a woollen hat that could have served as a cosy for a large teapot, and was muffled in a voluminous cardigan. On the mantelpiece was a photograph from 1940 of a small family group: the husband in RAF uniform, a pretty daughter in a beret, and an elegant woman wearing a trilby pulled low across one eye. Now it was hard to detect even the outline of that finely boned face in Mrs Peters' anxious, withered octogenarian features. She could, she said, have been a model; from the picture it was easy to believe that claim.

Happy that she had an audience for a few minutes, Mrs Peters took us on a tour of her tiny flat – 'Daddy,' she said, referring to her husband who had died eight years before, 'was doing it so nice.' She plunged into drawers to retrieve the meagre treasures of her life: a bas-relief of York Minster – 'my beloved York'; more photos, each with a story. As the familiar faces from her collection passed under her gaze, she repeated. 'They have parted from me, but they are at peace now.' It was a remark made not so much in sorrow, but rather in envy. At the age of eighty-four Mrs Peters was far from being at peace. Marooned on the fourth floor of a block of council flats on a fast deteriorating estate where Streatham meets Brixton, her world had become a small prison. On the ground floor a man with a string of criminal convictions presided over a Fagin's kitchen, where a dozen child thieves met to plan their crimes and dispose of their loot. Next door, squatters staged all-night parties, the noise from which kept Mrs Peters, and several elderly neighbours, awake in unholy terror. On the floor above lived a 91-year-old woman who had been burgled three times, the last when she was in hospital recovering from a mugging.

'Why are we being tormented like this? How could they do this to us? It is agonising for us, it is awful. Would all those people in power like it?' she asked. She recalled the early days on the estate, when it had been a showpiece: 'How lovely the flats used to be, so residential, so clean.' Now the downstairs neighbours smashed the lights, urinated in the lift, tormented her cat. 'Have we,' she asked despairingly, 'got to be intimidated?' The question was directed at my companion, PC Chris Birkitt, the home beat officer for the St Martin's estate. It was an awkward inquiry, for it flew to the heart of a fraught subject – community policing. By calling regularly on Mrs Peters, and other isolated and vulnerable pensioners, PC Birkitt was certainly fulfilling part of what most people would believe to be his mandate. But what could, or ought, he to do about the turmoil and lawlessness that created Mrs Peters' deep apprehension? 'Unless I get a formal complaint, there is really nothing much I can do,' he said, acknowledging that most of the extreme anti-social behaviour that blights so many lives lies at the margin of the law.

In the atmosphere of terror that pervaded the estate, a formal complaint was as unlikely as a peaceful night. As I got to know St Martin's better, I met many far younger and more resilient residents than Mrs Peters who would not have dreamt of reporting even serious criminality to the police. To have done so would have been to invite certain abuse, and possibly a brick through the window, the slashing of their car tyres, or even – and it happened to one man – the petrol-bombing of their homes. There was no point, said PC Birkitt, in even having words with Mrs Peters' principal torturer as the man would only be offensive, and might well take it out on the old woman. He would, however, try to speak with a local housing officer, though this would have to be done surreptitiously since Lambeth was not enthusiastic about co-operation between their officers and the police. Birkitt and some of the housing staff had made a 'tit-for-tat' accommodation. Despite politics and the often mutually hostile attitudes of their organisations, home beat and housing officers have common cause in seeking to make inner city estates fit for human habitation.

Through PC Birkitt I got to know several elderly residents, each an island in a sea of lawlessness. The din from a squat beneath one woman, a cancer victim, had been so enervating that she had contemplated suicide. 'I never closed my eyes for five weeks, and I ended up in hospital,' she said. The noise was not simply that of an overloud television, but of sound systems designed for discothèques, which played at 'rent' parties (parties where guests are charged for entry and drinks are sold illegally) – many nights until dawn. What was being destroyed was not just her, but her previous capacity to help others. 'They used to call me "nurse" Edith; not any more, I'm half dead myself. I'm terrified. I only go out shopping, and then I lock myself in.' Another woman regularly called on by Birkitt worked as a school dinner lady: 'I still have something to get up for each day.' She also barricaded herself in at nights. She said: 'I don't feel that I should have to live in fear, but I've seen how easily they kick in doors. It doesn't matter how many locks you have. I would never have believed that life could have become like this. If you say anything, you get a mouthful of abuse. They call pensioners "old cows".' This woman had recently provided information that helped PC Birkitt arrest a burglar, and he was concerned that she might suffer reprisals. He warned the suspect: 'If anything happens to that old lady or her flat, you'll be the first one pulled in for it.'

A few hours later as we walked the estate, PC Birkitt and I heard the crash of breaking glass. Birkitt thought someone was breaking into a car and we dashed towards the noise. At the sight of a rapidly approaching policeman, two youths crossed the road away from us. 'Oy, come here,' bellowed PC Birkitt. The boys continued retreating. 'Oy! Yes, you two.' Both stopped, and one shuffled a few reluctant paces towards us. 'It weren't fucking me; it were fucking 'im,' he said truculently, indicating the other youth who had started to slide away again. The cause of the noise that had caught our attention was apparent: a pint beer mug lay shattered on the pavement. Further shouts – 'Come 'ere when I tell you' – and the other youth dragged himself towards us, muttering a rather half-hearted admission. PC Birkitt lectured him: 'I don't live here, you do. What about the old ladies who have to walk along here? What about' – with a sudden flash of inspiration he produced the name of the leader of the local hooligans – ' "Norman's" dog?' Slowly and without grace, the youth picked up the worst of the jagged bits of glass and placed them over a low wall. 'I was taking it back to the pub, wasn't I?' 'Why were you walking in the opposite direction?' 'Because I'd dropped it, hadn't I?' Like a baseline game of tennis, the exchanges were tedious, but Constable Birkitt had taken a minor stand. Next time, conceivably, that youth would pause before committing an act of vandalism. A 'Mrs Peters', peering from behind her curtains, might have been marginally reassured; the forces of law and order were abroad and active.

Articulated public concern about crime is seldom heard from such places as St Martin's. Neither members of committees on law and order nor police officers live there. Areas that, owing to their needs, should command enhanced police attention and resources draw the short straw. A 1988 report published by the National Association for the Care and Resettlement of Offenders (NACRO), 'Policing Housing Estates', found: 'The plight of the residents of run-down, vandalised housing estates, three times more likely to be the victims of certain crimes than the statistical average, does not attract the increase in public expenditure given to the law and order budget.' The report added that crime tends to be concentrated in certain areas and its impact focused 'disproportionately' on particular social groups, chief among whom are 'people living on the poorer housing estates'.

People on these estates feel abandoned. Most of those with skills and decent jobs have gone to owner occupation in London's outer reaches. A teacher, one of the few professionals living on St Martin's, said: 'There used to be a caretaker, Bill, who patrolled with his dog. He had some authority and provided cohesion.' Caretakers, like regular cleaning and prompt maintenance, were victims of a combination of local authority cuts and inefficiency; Lambeth offered its caretakers early retirement, and on St Martin's they took it almost to a man. Lambeth, haemorrhaging from public expenditure cuts, failed dismally to take advantage of what help there was: it was named in 1989 as one of the few inner city authorities not to have participated in the government 'Estate Action Programme'. The caretakers' departure deepened the void. A Catholic priest said: 'When you come to the door, people are suspicious, even of a clergyman. This is the way we live now.' Bang on any door, and a dozen neighbouring dogs, bought not as pets but for protection, bark; tread carefully, for they foul the pavements.

The real victims of criminality are those who live cheek by jowl with the criminals at the bottom of the social heap. There was, at least until recently, a paradox at the heart of the police response. Crime was, they claimed, uniquely a police responsibility. But because inner city victims carry so little clout, places like St Martin's, where by natural justice that responsibility should have weighed most heavily, attracted a fraction of the resources they required. Co-operation with other agencies was fitful, historical animosity and suspicion clouding the relationship. The police are now casting around for fresh, more constructive ways to proceed, and, if they haven't yet found them, the fault is not entirely theirs. The buzz-words are 'inter-agency approach', but past incidents, temperament and politics construct walls between the police, the probation service and local authority professionals like social workers.

141

Despite PC Birkitt's co-operation with housing staff, he had no contact with other 'professionals' on the estate. 'I have never gone out of my way to get in touch with anyone else,' he said. A probation officer said: 'On the ground the multi-agency approach is not in operation. Working together, sharing perceptions on how to handle the problems, only happen at the highest management level; they don't filter down.' Some senior police officers make genuine, if not always sustained, efforts to reach across those walls into other camps and into the community. At the canteen level, however, traditional police prejudices about the 'do-gooder' classes – sometimes simply branded 'left-wingers' – often remain in depressing working order, and the antipathy is reciprocated in town halls.

The evils that afflicted St Martin's fell in the no man's land between the entrenched positions taken up by the mutually suspicious authorities. The police were wary of rent parties. A raid could result in a full-sized punch-up or, if there were allegations of police brutality, a community-wide disturbance. The parties are well organised, advertised on pirate radio stations, and attract large numbers – over one hundred people in quite small homes. A lot of money is made. On one summer's evening, when there had been eight 'outrageously noisy' parties on the division, the police had been forced to close a road where one was still in progress at 9 a.m. An inspector said that, although the police recognise that they have a duty to prevent a breach of the peace (which most rent parties clearly constitute), in practice they can only contemplate 'softly softly' measures, such as trying to remove the booze or the loudspeakers before a party begins. Even such action depended on man-power-intensive observation or accurate information from within. A senior officer said despairingly that once a party had started the police were virtually impotent. 'Yes, we want to act, but give us some money. Saturday nights we're up to our necks in muck and bullets. Often at midnight every single officer is tied up in the custody suite.' A resident said: 'I can see people taking the law into their own hands.'

St Martin's, the fifth biggest estate in the borough of
Lambeth, was built between 1959 and 1970, and has passed
through the ownership of three local authorities – the LCC,
the GLC and now Lambeth. When it and 14,000 other
properties were dumped in Lambeth's lap, the borough's
capacity to manage its housing stock efficiently was overwhelmed. St Martin's residents complain that the borough
concentrates its stretched efforts in areas like Brixton,
where crime and social dislocation are more dire than in
Streatham. St Martin's, comprising 1,200 homes and a
population of about 4,000, is a far cry from some of the
walkway-ridden giant estates nearer the centre of London.
It has trees and open spaces, and the old people clearly do
not exaggerate when they claim that, after the slums from
which they had been 'decanted', it was, if not paradise, a
vast improvement. But now it takes an effort of imagination
to conjure up the erstwhile model estate. St Martin's is
blighted by an astounding array of shattered property and
litter. There are mattresses and smashed TV sets at every
turn, abandoned cars, splintered sideboards, split sacks of
rubbish spilling soiled nappies and broken glass onto the
pavements, beer cans, plastic bags and drifting newspapers.
Under some flats the rubbish is piled deep against the walls,
like it is beneath cell blocks after a prison riot. The windows
on the communal stairways gape with jagged holes. Below
the flats, basement rooms that had been designed as laun-
dries have become the sites for innumerable fires. Many
flats are squatted; others are empty – 'voids' in the jargon
of local housing authorities. The liberally provided garden
beds are swamped with beer cans, fast food boxes, rolls of
cardboard, chip papers, soft drink bottles. The windows of
the youth club are bricked up, and the premises defended
by steel doors. Someone had made an effort once; the
outside walls were decorated with a frieze, showing kids
playing various sports. In one corner the artist had added
a fair drawing of the Prince of Wales's three feathers – 'Ich
Dien 1981'. A professional youth leader had recently quit
the club, discouraged by the depredations inflicted on it by
a minority of the estate's youth.

143

Chris Birkitt was a Permanent Beat Officer (PBO), and the system he operated is known as 'sector policing', variations of which are to be found throughout Britain. The Streatham scheme had been introduced three years before my arrival by Sheila Ward, a previous chief superintendent and a strong advocate of neighbourhood policing. Having day-to-day responsibility for a community is not an easy option for PCs – 'It is far harder than popping here and popping there in a panda,' said one inspector. This 'softly, softly' policing had not been welcomed by some officers who dismissed it as an evasion of the force's primary goal, which must (for them) always be to 'nick villains'. A senior officer said: 'One view was that while we were out promoting goodwill, we were being taken to the cleaners on street robberies.' A detective inspector (not at Streatham) looked totally blank when I used the initials 'PBO', which said much about his not untypical attitude towards and knowledge of neighbourhood policing.

St Martin's and its dispiriting problems were Birkitt's principal responsibility, though his sector also contained some older residential streets. He was attached to 'A' relief, and his inspector Ian Hogg kept a supervisory eye on the sector. PC Birkitt, however, worked hours suited to the demands of his beat rather than the rigid shift system. With days off, holidays, paperwork, and frequent calls on him, when the relief was short, he was probably on his territory less than twenty-five hours a week. When 'A' relief was on duty, its 'walkers' were supposed to pay particular attention to the relief's sectors, but St Martin's is a twenty-minute hike from the police station, and it was rare for an officer to reach the estate without being diverted elsewhere. When I was at St Martin's with PC Birkitt, we were often stopped, usually by elderly people, to be told how nice it was to see a policeman on the beat, a compliment which said more about the absence of officers than it did about their presence.

Chris Birkitt was, I assessed, fairly typical of other PBOs in his attitude towards his job. He was keen to make his mark and do his job well, but his ambition lay elsewhere –

in his case to be a detective: 'I enjoy taking statements and investigating.' St Martin's was a stepping stone. Birkitt was preparing, with great enthusiasm, a profile of known St Martin's criminals, as a dowry to take to the crime squad when the time came. He had discussed the pros and cons of the job with other beat officers, and he regarded himself as half volunteer and half pressed man. But it was an indication of how short of experienced officers Streatham was that Birkitt should have been tapped for the vacancy, since, when he started at St Martin's, he was little more than a year out of training school. He had joined the police at the age of twenty-five, after eight years in engineering, and was conscious that, for his age, he was 'short of service'. He therefore wanted to vary his experience, and was anxious not to be typecast. When I met him he had only been on the estate a few months, and, though he had got to know it and its people well, he was still feeling his way towards the right balance as a community police officer.

His technique, he said, was to let wrong-doers know that they were 'out of order'. 'I don't nick them for every stupid little thing they do, otherwise my arrest rate would have gone up horrendously.' Sometimes it was more important to recover stolen property than to arrest the offenders. He had been investigating a burglary at the youth club, from which the fridge, video recorder, television and other equipment, without which the club could scarcely function, had been stolen. 'I've gone to the lads and said that I don't want to know who's done it, but the club needs the property back. If you're forever nicking them, they're not going to trust you. In their own eyes a lot of the things they do are not morally wrong.' It would, in any case, have been impossible to sustain a high arrest rate and keep a high profile on the estate, as further hours would have been eaten up at the station processing the charges. Birkitt was not making personal moral judgements, but tailoring his constable's discretion to the reality of the estate.

Birkitt often felt sorry for the boys he arrested, understanding their inadequate backgrounds. But he said: 'I have a duty to people who have suffered because of them. A lot

145

of PCs would simply say that they are little shits, and that's all there is to it. They get fed up with people who don't appreciate being helped.' Birkitt's priorities were, first, to 'get to know who my villains are'; secondly, to be seen – 'It gives you a lift when an old woman comes up and touches you for reassurance'; thirdly, to be trusted, so that he got information, often through an arrangement like a special phone number designed to protect the anonymity of his contact: 'People will tell a home beat what is happening when they wouldn't tell another policeman.'

Later he became concerned that his relaxed approach was making him too familiar to the estate's youths. 'What I have done is try to befriend them; now they are taking the mickey and I've got to become a policeman again,' he said, resolving to crack down on the hostile, unpleasant language that often greeted him on his rounds. 'Why should I stand there and take all the abuse under the sun? People who would hesitate before insulting someone in a pub in case they got a punch on the nose don't care with a policeman. We can't give the "verbals" back because of the uniform,' he said. He was upset also that the then President of the Association of Chief Police Officers had recently said that the police 'were losing the streets'. 'The yobs,' he said, 'will have their morale boosted; they'll say "we're winning".' A few days later Birkitt's fears were confirmed: he was involved in a fracas – provoked, according to him, when a boy spat at an elderly woman – which led to charges of assault against two youths. Birkitt was off work for several days, as was another PC injured the following day in a related scrap with the same boys. On this second occasion the 'cavalry' was called in, police officers responding in numbers. The aftermath was a series of complaints against the police – a relative of one of the accused youths described the police as 'terrorists in blue' – more charges against the boys, and eventually a new policing strategy for the estate.

The incidents, together with other events, including the 'rescue' of a young prisoner from the back of a police car and a serious affray a few months earlier, produced a series of 'tension indicators', a monitoring tool devised after the Scarman report into the Brixton riots in 1981 to help senior officers detect and pre-empt social unrest that might lead to widespread disturbance. The most serious report concerned 'Norman', the best known of St Martin's criminals. A policeman attending court overheard Norman and another known criminal discussing St Martin's. Norman had allegedly said that there was going to be a fight between rival gangs and/or the police, and that his gang had guns, obtained from robbers on the run from prison. Norman had also warned another police officer that the next time the police came on the estate, they had better come with shields, as 'there'll be fifty of us, and we'll be tooled up'. He added: 'I'll do time for a copper.' Birkitt, who had established a regular dialogue with Norman, put the remarks down to boasting and to an attempt to wind 'Old Bill' up. However, he added: 'Norman is basically stupid and could well do some serious harm.'

A number of meetings were held. For the benefit of senior officers, Birkitt was asked by Superintendent Buchan to analyse the gathering crisis on St Martin's. 'It's a hell of a big estate, and you're at the end of a thin line up there on your own,' said Mr Buchan. Birkitt spoke of the gangs of aimless kids, and of his concern for the old people who suffered abuse and worse. 'If you were sitting in my chair, what would your decision be?' asked Buchan. The consensus was that it had to be demonstrated to the delinquent youths that 'we control the streets, not them'. Birkitt was encouraged to be tough. One senior officer said: 'Wrong is wrong, and we'll investigate and arrest whatever the reverberations. Birkitt may not be the Number One son up there, but he is doing a good job. These yobs have got to be nicked; we can't have a scrote abusing an old woman. Birkitt must keep up the firm policing and bring the rest of the estate with him.' Buchan decided to 'show a bit more uniform'.

In fact, at that stage very little was done. The division was not always efficient at translating decisions into action. Birkitt remained unsupported until further, more serious, trouble a few weeks later led to a much greater police presence on the estate. The catalyst was a fire-bomb attack on a community leader, whose efforts to help his fellow residents had led to his being branded a 'collaborator'. This time, the new strategy was effectively implemented. It was decided that Brixton's mounted officers should exercise their horses daily on St Martin's. Kids who will not normally talk to police will – so the theory goes – approach an officer on horseback, though the ploy does not always work: 'Don't you realise that's a pig on that horse?' said a fifteen-year-old girl pulling her brother away from a mounted officer. In addition, dog handlers were to patrol the estate after dark; special constables were to walk the St Martin's beat at weekends; and Birkitt was to be reinforced by another PBO. Birkitt was torn about whether to accept this assistance: 'It makes it look as if they're winning, but it *would* be nice to have someone else there.' The senior Streatham officers, anxious for long-term improvement on the estate, were conscious that a show of strength alone would simply keep the lid on. Mr Hogg said: 'We've got to get people from St Martin's involved; there is no dialogue at all.' To Birkitt he added: 'You've got to step back sometimes, though I'm not saying that you shouldn't take action when you need to. We can't allow boys to get away with abusing the sheriff. If you are doing your job, you're going to get complaints – there's no two ways about that.' Birkitt was directed to prepare his crime profile of the estate, and Scotland Yard was asked not to dispatch more than two patrol cars to answer 999 calls from the estate. If back-up officers were needed, they were to go to rendezvous points from which they could be deployed under the direction of local officers. These measures appeared to work; St Martin's *was* quieter, though one reason was clearly the coincidental jailing of one of the estate's most disruptive young men. A Streatham inspector said: 'Problems on the estate flutter up and flutter down; when they flutter up, policemen get injured, so we want them to flutter up as little as possible. One incident could trigger off something bigger, which is why we get concerned with events that seem relatively trivial.'

To Streatham's rank and file police on routine vehicle patrol, St Martin's remained bandit country, dubbed the 'Bronx'. It was both the potential site of serious civil disorder and a continuous source of emergency calls. One night, a drinker in a pub rammed a glass into a seventeen-year-old's neck, and missed killing him by a few centimeters. The day after the glass attack, PCs coming on parade were warned that the suspect, who had gone to ground, was 'tasty'. 'He looks like an animal, and probably is one.' It was the wanted man's habit to walk St Martin's with a Rottweiler on a leash. If he is seen, said the inspector, he is to be approached with caution. That was a metaphor for the whole estate.

The system worked by PC Birkitt is essentially a return to the 'bobby on the beat', a phrase with comfortable connotations that conjure up the 1950s era of *Dixon of Dock Green*, when one middle-aged figure in blue serge, proceeding on his rounds, was a reassuring symbol. There were people Dixon policed 'against', but they were a small minority, criminals on whom the full majesty of the law was expected to fall, or misguided youngsters. He had *carte blanche* to keep boys in order with the traditional clip round the ear. That never, as every policeman in middle life tells one incessantly, harmed anyone. The attraction of the *Dixon* formula has grown along with a nostalgia for the age it represented. But, even if our memories were accurate, turning the clock back is clearly impossible. The police have to accept that these are more complex times, and that their authority is now challenged by substantial and significant minorities. Many of these people live in such inner city areas as St Martin's.

Senior officers like Chief Superintendent Street who keep in touch with their communities know that at least part of the answer lies in intensive local policing. In the few places it has been tried, 'success' – measured both statistically and in terms of public satisfaction – has been remarkable. Since 1984 a team of six home beat officers under a sergeant has

149

been dedicated to the Pepys estate in Deptford, also south London; in four years both burglaries and motor thefts halved. The team is so familiar to residents (and therefore unthreatening) that most arrests can be carried out single-handed. The sergeant said: 'It helps if you are on first-name terms. Even if they don't like you, you have a dialogue. When we came down here, it was a pretty grim place to live and people were frightened to go out. It is not a rose garden now, but it has improved a lot.'

St Martin's, like the Pepys estate, is the size of a village. But it is nothing like the village of popular imagination; rather it is a random collection of mainly deprived people – single parent families, pensioners, the unemployed, ethnic minorities – who have little place in the hyped contemporary picture of Britain as a thriving, entrepreneurial community. The majority desperately need the reassurance and protection afforded by good policing, but a minority, sizeable enough to dominate the culture of such estates, actively reject the police, whom they regard as an army of occupation. A larger number, forced to come to terms with the dominance of the lawless and unruly, simply regard the police as irrelevant. A council employee who worked on St Martin's said: 'Police/public relations are seldom convincing; people are not persuaded that the police are their friends. As far as the kids are concerned, they are as much the enemy as the Tories, the middle classes or the blacks. They are seen as agents of the state, the mechanism for Tory law and order.'

In the face of such hostility, senior officers at Streatham ponder a great deal on how they can satisfactorily police St Martin's, but they know that tackling disorder is simply a palliative, and no more sensible as a long-term cure than rushing more doctors to a town polluted by noxious industrial fumes. Police of all ranks claim from time to time that their thin blue line is all that stands between anarchy and order. The truth is that they are constantly treating symptoms rather than causes; the less sensitive often don't recognise or acknowledge that there are causes. 'Too much is expected of the police,' said a crime prevention specialist.

'They are called to fill a huge vacuum. The informal community mechanisms that used to keep young people in line have broken down.' A victim support volunteer, speaking of another Lambeth 'high crime' estate where a survey had discovered that 50 per cent of residents had either seen or heard a crime of violence in the previous years, said: 'We had a dream that we could build trust between victims and their neighbours, create a community that could respond to its own need.' The notion was to be based on a series of 'care watches' among small groups of neighbours, but the researchers found that it took up to ten years for new tenants to become accepted, and that the people whom residents feared most were those very neighbours on whom they were being asked to rely. Sad experience had taught them that if they gave the neighbours a key while they were away, the neighbours were likely to pinch the video recorder. Within months, the 'dream had gone out of the window'. Apathy and distrust won the day. The volunteers were advised not to visit the estates after dark, which was understandable but scarcely the basis on which to build the self-confidence of the local residents.

'Curly' runs a small shop on the edge of St Martin's, which had been broken into the night before we met. A few pounds had been taken, and one intruder had gratuitously poured lemonade over the electric till. Curly said: 'I couldn't be bothered to tell the police; it was a crime done during the dark hours, and there is a limit to what they can do. Policing on the whole is immaterial. What you want really is a copper standing outside your door until you come back again, that would be the only answer. To the police, I am just another problem that happened over the weekend. They'd fill in the appropriate forms and promise to keep a closer eye, but they've got so much bloody work on. It's very manpower-absorbent to send a bloke round. My best approach is to strengthen the door. In the end I'll have strengthened every bloody area in the shop and they can't get in. When people have empty pockets and they're on the dole, you can understand them wanting to go out and get what they see on TV.' Curly sees a great deal of the St

Martin's youth (a small boy had opened his flies and peed in the shop a few days earlier – 'He did it for kicks, shock'), and he is resigned to the aggravation he gets. 'The beat constable tries to be friendly with these kids, but there's got to be a bit of the firm hand of the law. Of course, he's restricted. What can he do anyway?'

Break-ins and snatches are a regular feature of life. Curly said: 'I always look when I arrive to see whether I've been broken into. This is the nicking society. Stealing is not looked down upon. You haven't hurt anybody. If something isn't lashed down, tied down with a guard dog standing over it, well, you can nick it. It all helps the family income.' A few weeks earlier he had been robbed during shop hours of £130, and, even though he had a strong suspicion who did it, there was little Birkitt could do once the suspect had denied it. When light-fingered children are around, an Asian-owned shop in the same parade posts four members of the family at strategic points among the sweets and magazines. Curly said: 'The kids are a bloody nuisance because there is no outlet. Mum and dad stay in. The kids want to let off steam; some are even forbidden to go home in the evenings, so they just take it out on the estate.' A few days earlier he had watched boys working out their aggression on the estate's rubbish. 'Any article they got was a challenge; they'd still break it further. There was an old television that wasn't working, so they pulled that out, and smashed it, just banged it in the car park. They obviously got a kick out of it, and they walked away leaving a shower of debris.'

Curly was clear-eyed about the view that many on the estate took of the police. He said: 'They want a policeman when someone nicks their car, but it's fair game when they steal from anybody else. They don't mind as long as it isn't their daughter that gets raped, their flat burgled, as long as the statistics are next door. More people are anti-police than just those breaking the law. They became more anti-Bill when the police got involved in strike breaking.'

'Liz', a divorced mother, is one of Curly's customers. She is tall and elegant, and her flat is an immaculate oasis in the dereliction of much of the rest of St Martin's. She had been brought up in the home counties, sent to boarding school and generally cosseted. Living on the estate as a 'welfare' mother had caused a massive row with her family. She said: 'They live in a very cloistered environment, and seem to think that people like us – me included now – are literally a nuisance to society. They believe that you shouldn't allow your circumstances to make you down and out. But unfortunately, without money you don't go very far. If you say you have thirty pounds a week to live on to bring up two children, to clothe them, to pay the bills, they wouldn't believe you. That's what my father would spend in a night in the pub.' There had recently been a number of local attacks on women, so when Liz went out at night she 'cabbed it' – even half a mile to her best friend. 'I think you're actually safer in Brixton. There's been a lot of break-ins, a lot of undesirables. Gangs of children are utterly unruly. You daren't open your mouth or you'll have no windows. You can't have a doormat because it gets stolen. That's what you're up against.' She was not happy about the way the estate was policed, and was bitter that she had been subpoenaed as a witness after promises that, if she helped the police, she would not get 'involved'. 'I may have seen what went on, but I had no wish to testify against people who lived two blocks down. The police went back on their word.' She knew and liked PC Birkitt, but thought that he lacked backing from the station. 'They don't actually believe that it warrants them being on this estate all the time, but it does. The kids round here could walk rings round the police,' she said.

The saddest remark I heard on St Martin's was made by a mature student who had come as a squatter, and now had a legal tenancy: 'When we first came, we all opened our doors to our neighbours,' he said. 'You quickly learn the codes. People here don't open their doors. If they do, they get burgled.' He was one of a group of professional people assembled by David Gardiner, chairman of SMETRA (St Martin's Estate Tenants and Residents Association), to discuss life on St Martin's, crime and policing. The doors of which he spoke were both literal and metaphorical, friendship was sufficiently likely to be abused that residents learned to distrust their neighbours. In that and many other ways estates like St Martin's are a reverse image of 'normal' communities. Mr Gardiner, a retired marketing executive and an unlikely St Martin's resident, put it graphically: 'As you enter the estate, you pass within a few yards through an invisible barrier to a community where different standards of health, education, policing, and different attitudes of youngsters to older people, pertain. Outside agencies also assume that somehow the estate is separate. Yet what residents dearly want, above everything else, is to be like people on the other side of the invisible wall.'

He described what it is like to return home at night: 'Your first thought is to get to your block safely; when your flat comes into view, you pray that your door will not have been kicked in. I suffer anxiety whenever I return home and turn the corner. I look at the door and thank God that it has not been busted in.' He added: 'We maintain a tolerant dialogue with the people who are oppressing us; there is a curious rapport. The younger kids have street wisdom, humour and tremendous energy. The humour softens the sharp edges of the clash between the groups. A girl said to me recently, "You know, Dave, you're getting awfully crabby. What you need is a wife." The kids want activities, but there is a deep inertia in the system. They spend their time wandering round wondering what the fuck to do, and authority is similarly random.'

Not all Mr Gardiner's group were convinced of the wisdom of opening up the estate to outside scrutiny. One young man said: 'The role of the media is to codify what is morality; the role of the police is not to make people's lives better but to be punitive.' But he added: 'There *are* criminals on this estate; people are afraid to look their neighbours in the eye. Yes, this is a hellhole. Let's do something about it. Kids see the estate as their territory; they will take on anything that comes along. They are hostile to all authority. The police role is to sweep them away,' he said. He himself had done some part-time community work, and a boy had said to him: 'You're a fucking cunt for doing that. You're just another of those people who like telling people what to do.' A teacher said: 'This is a spiritual, not a material, crisis, young people are not lacking clothes, food or even videos.' Charismatic young criminals like 'Norman' fill the gap left by inadequate parenting, he said. 'Because "Norman" is a powerful figure, the level of crime is high. He has cranked his image so hard that he can never back down, but without the lack of parental impact, the poor education, the poor housing and prevalent crime, "Norman" wouldn't exist. He is a weed in a bed of weeds.' This man had been burgled himself, and he did not rate the police contribution to the estate highly: 'They are a little tribe all on their own. It is an inevitable consequence of the way they are treated. They are more and more spurned by more and more people. Everyone has contempt for the police; the very rich treat them like servants, and they are feared by many of the rest of us.' The NACRO report 'Policing Housing Estates' picked up on such disaffection on urban estates, and reported that only 20 per cent of young men in the inner cities felt that their recent contacts with police had been 'very pleasant'. 'The more contact people have, the more critical they are. There is clearly a problem with the way the police relate to the public,' it stated. NACRO would like to see far more than the present 5 per cent of police manpower devoted to home beats. Its report commented:

Beat policing would be more successful if home beat officers were deployed in numbers proportionate to the size, density and difficulty of estates, and if they were committed to this style of policing and prepared to work on an estate for at least two years . . . The deployment of mobile units or squads not local to council estates often causes resentment and hostility. Such deployment should be avoided, unless a situation seriously prejudicial to public order arises which cannot be dealt with by local officers.

Sadly, life on the ground is seldom susceptible to blueprints. I sat in on a community meeting at an estate near St Martin's, at which several community policemen were present. It was both confused and acrimonious, and for most of the evening two or three simultaneous meetings raged. One objective was to start a youth club, but not one resident out of the population of several hundred was prepared to volunteer as a club leader. 'We want,' said one man optimistically, 'someone prepared to throw his weight around and get nasty.' There were good reasons why there were no takers; the women who had run a previous club had been threatened; anyone who tried to discipline the lawless minority would face retaliation. Across the estate several hundred individual fears combined to create this giant collective fear. A widow who had sat quietly through the meeting told me she spent most of her spare cash on locks. Her ground floor flat backed onto a pitch-black area of trees in which anyone could lurk; she had been waiting four and a half years for the council to install some lights. 'I don't get to sleep until two or three in the morning, and I'm lucky to get two hours' sleep. We're very vulnerable to these burglaries.'

What this woman and tens of thousands like her fear is the criminal behaviour of teenage boys. The habitual response by right-wing politicians and commentators is an exhortation to parents and teachers to control children. It is a view shared by many police officers, some of whom will go further and accuse teachers not simply of neglect of their duties, but of political motivation. Jon Bright of NACRO said: 'We know now that exhortation is no solution at all. Kids need boundaries; it's not just a matter for the family. There is nothing out there; very little in terms of the need. Crime prevention is much broader than exhortation. The key is a non-repressive response. It will not, of course, stop all crime, but it may help to get it down on a significant scale.'

Chief Superintendent Street does understand the importance of what is known as 'diversion'. In the summer before I arrived in Streatham, there had been a major disturbance on an estate after the arrest of a suspected robber during a football match. Good police practice is, where possible, to arrest people quietly without confrontation with bystanders; lifting a player during a game broke all the rules, and the police paid the price. Eight players were arrested in the ensuing fracas, and later that night angry residents demonstrated outside the police station. 'Twenty or thirty people jumped up and down; we had a minor siege,' said one policeman. On warm summer evenings the police had already been dealing with regular calls to the estate on which most of the footballers lived, and Streatham's senior management feared that one more spark might ignite a major community incident. Mr Street's response was a 'summer project'. The objectives were to get kids off the streets during the summer holidays; to improve relations between young people and police; and to increase police penetration of the community. If police officers could get to know the troublemakers, they could hope to deal with them without continuously hauling them to the police station – a return, as one officer put it, 'to old style coppering, when a policeman knew every kid on his patch'.

Senior officers also hoped that the experience of relaxing with local youths might help some officers overcome their racial prejudices. One policeman said: 'The thing I learned is that the little black kid is exactly the same as the little white kid. Many people still categorise them as immigrants who don't really belong here. We went through a learning process: kids are all the same, and colour doesn't come into it.' The project attracted over four hundred young people – half black and half white. It opened with a disco, attended by an actor from *EastEnders*, and included a range of sports from athletics to American football; day trips to safari parks, HMS *Belfast* and the seaside; 'specials' like a weekend on a yacht and a day at a flying club; self-improvement classes in subjects including car maintenance, hairdressing and pet care.

Crime figures went down; stress was reduced on the estates; life in an area where few people can afford summer holidays was made more bearable both for the kids and the community. 'There would certainly have been more punch-ups and possibly a major flare-up without it,' said Inspector Don Broadbery, head of community relations. After the project, relations between the police and residents remained good. 'Home beat officers know ten times as many kids now. They can control their behaviour if they know them. "I'll see your dad later" is more effective than dragging them up to the station,' said Mr Broadbery. The project was to be repeated, and several neighbouring divisions decided to copy it.

The cynical might think that the project was old-fashioned window-dressing, similar to the 1930s 'do-good-ery' which brought public school boys and slum dwellers together in summer camps. But from what I heard, and from what I saw of the aftermath, it was a success. Six months later, kids from the estates were still coming to the police station to look at photos, and joshing with the desk sergeant. 'The more political might argue that projects like the Gipsy Hill one are not "real" youth work, because they don't include such things as anti-racist workshops,' said an observer involved in community-based crime prevention. 'Such people never start from the kids' agenda.' In France, after riots in Lyons and Marseilles in the early 1980s, the government itself sponsored projects to get inner city children out of the ghettoes for the summer, which also resulted in a dramatic fall in crime rates.

Harry and Violet Beaton were octogenarian pensioners in one of the St Martin's blocks. Violet was a tiny sparrow, weighing six stone, and together they were almost a parody of indomitable Londoners. 'We never had much money, but we had each other and we always had a good laugh,' they would say. During a five-day period they were robbed and beaten inside their home seven times, and at one point held at gunpoint for six hours by intruders wearing bala-clavas. One morning they were found by the milkman unconscious on the floor. So brutal was their treatment that the story attracted national headlines. The police, frustrated by the lack of co-operation they received while investigating these crimes, branded St Martin's residents 'cowards'. The population responded by accusing the police of allowing the estate to fall under 'gang law'. One policeman was slashed with a knife and another struck with an iron bar while they hunted the criminals.

The horror of that attack galvanised David Gardiner into action. 'Here was a community that couldn't defend its own. We were at a crossroads. Either we got our act together and pulled ourselves up by our boot straps, or we were in terminal decline and nothing would save us from social disintegration,' he said. In a document on squatting, he upbraided both the local authority and the police for failing to protect the community, and he cited occasions when the police had been called by seriously terrified residents and had failed to act:

> Woman pensioner who lives alone hears door of adjacent flat being kicked in late at night. Phones police who arrive in about 15 minutes. Police find two young men on property who say they have just arrived, found door ajar and had decided to squat. Young man asked loudly: 'Who phoned you?' Police decline to say and depart leaving squatters in occupation. Pensioner has since requested a transfer. 'It's too frightening here now.'

To maintain a supply of vacant properties, the squatting organisations needed to terrify genuine tenants into leaving the estate. Tactics included dropping television sets from balconies in the dead of night; allowing baths to overflow into flats below; lighting fires in basements. At one stage their activities became so brazen that men with clipboards assembled their 'clients' outside the local pub, and installed them in vacant flats in broad daylight. Mr Gardiner's exposé led directly to a massive desquat in March 1988, when eighty-six properties were recovered. The operation lasted two weeks, and was notable because the police and Lambeth for once worked in harmony. Lambeth recognised that they were dealing not with squatting by the genuinely homeless but with a massive scam. The organisers were making an estimated £90,000 a year, and the reputation of St Martin's as the place to squat extended as far as New Zealand. The borough was losing an estimated £400,000 a year in rents; its bed and breakfast bill for homeless families soared each month; and both housing staff and tenants became utterly demoralised.

Mr Gardiner lived, when I met him, in what he described as his 'bunker' – a one-bedroomed flat with boarded-up windows and an elaborate chain system for securing his internal doors – and devoted all his time and his considerable marketing abilities to improving conditions on the estate. After the desquat, his next mission was to secure an inner city partnership grant of £250,000 to build a community hall. If not a one-man band, he was certainly the forceful conductor of a tiny number of activists on the estate.

He found the fast turnover of police at all levels discouraging. No sooner had he written a letter describing one Streatham superintendent as 'the new broom', than the man was replaced; PC Birkitt was the third neighbourhood policeman within two years. An unstable community needs stable policing. Mr Gardiner had seen at first hand the calming influence of a neighbourhood beat officer. After a serious confrontation between youths and the police in the summer of 1988, tension on the estate was very high. Police dogs and truncheons had been used to quell the disturbance, and several people, including Norman, had been arrested. Youths began to build barricades and drag trees into the road, and motorists couldn't get home. 'Kids were in a state of semi-hysteria because their heroes had been taken away in a police van; the fact that they had taken on the police represented a new threshold of daring. That was very bad news for the community. The yobs now knew they could stand up to the police as a group,' said Mr Gardiner. By the morning the boys had assembled a cache of missiles – 'half hoping that something would happen' – ready to throw at police vehicles. Outsiders began to arrive, 'chums and friends drawn in by the prospects of a rumble'.

A gang surrounded Mr Gardiner shouting 'cunt' and 'grass' and spitting over his anorak, so that he was forced to go home to wash it. When he returned, PC Birkitt was sitting on a wall talking quietly to the boys. His action, said Mr Gardiner, had a significant impact. Had the lid come off that day, and Molotov cocktails and stones been used against the police, the estate might well have become a future arena for conflict. 'By God, where would we have been then?' asked Mr Gardiner. 'The estate would have become untenable.'

Mr Gardiner does not blame his fellow tenants for keeping their heads down. 'When people hear things at night, doors kicked in, glass smashed, they do not go out because they are afraid they will be set upon. They might call the police, but they would not give their names. The consequence might be a brick through the window or a firebomb. How can people stand up to this force? It is not possible,' said Mr Gardiner.

I met no one on St Martin's who believed that either politicians or senior civil servants had an inkling of what life there was really like. 'They travel up from Edenbridge buried in *The Times*,' said one resident bitterly, adding that his own friends think that he is mad to live on the estate. 'I used to get in a state of stress, but I have reached a plateau of stoicism, and accept it,' he said. This man suggested that the gap in the quality of life inside and outside such estates was now so great as to raise a policing dilemma. 'Do you police within the ghetto, or leave the inhabitants to their own devices containing them with the occasional dust-up?' he asked. 'Do you make a truce? "If you don't leave your area to burgle in respectable areas, we'll leave you alone. If you do, we'll nick you." '

No community could be in greater need of neighbourhood watch than St Martin's, but it is inconceivable that a scheme could be started there. Said one resident: 'Anyone who joined would be branded a police informer. A neighbourhood watch is a nark's charter.' He described his daily return home at a time when he himself was a special target for the youths. 'They sit in front of your door and you have to lean over them to put your key in. It's quite intimidating as they might beat you up if you were to say "piss off". They try to provoke you. If you put a hand on them, they'll kick the guts out of you. Don't think I'm especially isolated. It happens to a lot of people.' He characterised these youths as 'malign' and 'vicious'. 'They know they have the physical strength, and they need money. They want drugs, motor bikes and designer clothes; they're caught up in an acquisitive spiral. All around them they find natural victims, what could be an easier way of making money than preying on them?' Small kids become cadet members of the gangs. It is their job to scout when crimes are planned and to get in through tiny windows. They get a small percentage from the sale of the loot, and are ensnared before they are twelve in the economy of crime. One resident said: 'Ten-year-olds here are not like other ten-year-olds. They're like twenty-year-olds. They're clever. You've got tomorrow's criminals out there on the street.' She mentioned one boy. 'He's not cheeky, he's not funny, he's dangerous. He would not hesitate in hitting you or getting a knife out. He climbs out of the window at one o'clock in the morning. He goes on the buses to the West End. He's a professional pickpocket, and does that for a living – at the age of ten.'

Walking with PC Birkitt, I met this boy and others. The ten-year-old greeted us with: 'Why do you hang around me? I hate fucking coppers.' One passed a screwdriver to another, who threw it in a hedge. Birkitt said: 'I could nick you for that.' 'Go on then, see what happens,' replied the kid. His companion joined in: 'You shut your fucking mouth, arsehole. You fuck off, wanker: you turdish little mother-fucker.' The stream of vile-mouthed abuse torrented forth, some of it directed at me, since I was regularly taken for a CID man (though at least once for a 'dangerous criminal' under arrest). Birkitt said: 'It annoys me that I have to deal with rubbish like that. I could get them for breach of the peace, insulting behaviour or obstruction. But I can't be bothered to deal with offenders like that. It's just not worth it. Arresting them would mean two or three hours' paperwork. They're just more of life's losers who can't keep their traps shut.' But he knew the price he paid for his inaction. 'I'm told that I have to make allowances for that sort of behaviour. Yet I am trying to get respect for the uniform and law and order, and I have to take abuse like that while members of the public are walking past.'

PC Birkitt had surprisingly cordial relations, on the surface at least, with Norman, the chief instigator of disorder on the estate. Norman presented the police with a quandry that was a microcosm of their wider difficulties. If they treated him gently he reacted as if he were 'winning', which boosted the image he projected to the younger kids. On the other hand, tough police action equally enhanced his status. Norman had served one recent prison term. Already a 'legend' before his incarceration, he returned, according to one resident, a 'superman, more cunning, more knowledgeable and physically bigger. He had received his education.' His mini-gang buzzed with excitement in the weeks immediately before his release. There were periods when Norman was arrested almost every other day for offences that ranged from drunkenness to fighting, from thieving to posing as a bogus car repair mechanic in order to steal cars. A wry humour crept into the Streatham collator's entries: 'Young Norman: yes, it's him again. And – would you believe? – bail again. Mind you, the conditions get better.' Over the months these had included various forms of curfew, injunctions to be 'of good behaviour', prohibitions on travelling in the front of a car, on travelling by car at all. One card added: 'Also whilst he was in court he was wearing a white bandage or turban round his head; either he has been injured or he has changed his religion.' But there was not much fun to be derived from Norman's baleful daily influence. 'One or two people,' said one resident, 'behave so badly that it has a massive effect on the quality of life of literally thousands of people.'

Life in a demoralised inner city estate is a continuous struggle between good and evil. The evil influences, represented by people 'like Norman, who are on the estates twenty-four hours a day, are more potent than the sporadic attempts by the authorities to redress the balance. Jon

163

Bright of NACRO explained the notion of an estate 'tipping', that is when the forces of lawlessness are so far in the ascendant that residents with initiative and resource move away and their places are taken by people who represent a hideous concentration of social disadvantage. The estate becomes infamous as 'hard to let'; the professional squatters move in; residents give up – what, after all, is the point of, say, picking up litter, when every square foot is deep in abandoned junk? In this struggle between anarchy and order, the majority are passive onlookers, but the course of their lives will be irredeemably set by the outcome. 'Neighbourhood policing should have its status enhanced; it should be a major step to promotion instead of a relative backwater,' said Bright. In this context the police become an enabling force, creating an umbrella under which the necessary informal community control can begin to blossom. If parents tell a child to behave, they must know that they will be supported if necessary. 'That's different from harassing young people with nothing to do,' said Bright.

Despite the core importance of neighbourhood policing, many officers still regard it as intrinsically 'soft'; several senior detectives spoke disparagingly about it as if it were social work. 'Community policing has little status and sometimes attracts sniping comments in station canteens,' began a feature in *Police Review*. A sustained effort to sell community policing to the troops is needed, and, with a bit of imagination, senior officers ought to be able to come up with attractive and positive aspects of the work to dangle before their men and women. In the words of one inspector, a good PBO is 'an invaluable source of information'. He had in mind one man with whom I spent several afternoons, who had been in the Met for fifteen years and had worked a home beat area for the past three. He was so familiar with some people that he would go straight to their kitchens and put on the kettle. The chairman of his sector working party said: 'When he hasn't been seen for a few days, some elderly people are reluctant to go out.' This PC's technique was to distance himself as far as possible from the arrests

Dog training: preparing the canine response to human yobbery *(Metropolitan Police)*

Women police officers are, in theory, finally equal: (left) two of the tiny minority trained to use firearms − a far cry from the sheltered world of their 1920s predecessors (bottom) *(The Daily Telegraph Colour Library/ Metropolitan Police)*

No substitute has yet been found for mounted police: (left) Saturday routine in the 1980s; (bottom) PC Edward Jeffrey, Streatham's first horseborne officer, patrols the common *(Metropolitan Police/Streatham Society)*

'Riot City', Hounslow: the 'bobby on the beat' is toughened to face urban violence
(Andrew Moore, Reflex Pictures/Metropolitan Police)

Broadwater Farm, Tottenham riots, 7 October 1985: (top) a wary calm the
morning after the night before (bottom) *(Andrew Moore, Reflex Pictures/The
Press Association)*

'When the wheels came off.' Paramilitary response to London riots in 1985: Brixton (top) and Broadwater Farm, Tottenham (bottom) *(Piers Cavendish, Andrew Moore, Reflex Pictures)*

The changing face of Streatham: (top) High Road (with original police station on the left) in late Victorian times; (bottom) St Martin's Estate, 1989 *(Streatham Society)*

A drunk at Euston Station: when everyone else has washed his hands, the police are left to pick up the pieces *(Carlos Guarita, Reflex Pictures)*

that stemmed from his sleuthing. 'I must never be first through the door, or everyone I see on a regular basis will come under suspicion of having supplied me with information,' he said, 'yet most of what I do is gathering information. My brief is to get to know as many people as possible, who's who, who's doing what, what makes the place tick.' He himself does virtually no arresting. He was reluctant to make sensitive visits when I was with him: 'No offence to you. I couldn't make some inquiries with you in tow. Someone might think that you were CID. My contacts have got to live here. A set of four slashed tyres can cost a hundred and thirty pounds.' He suffered, I sensed, from near-permanent frustration because his superiors often failed to follow up his tip-offs. 'It is not enough simply to know that things are going on. Proof is required, which involves surveillance and tailing people. If you go bowling in unprepared, things can go dramatically wrong. Every time an operation is contemplated, it is costed, and, if it's too expensive, it goes by the wayside,' he said.

Each PBO had his style. One, working in an unco-operative community, said that he had to be 'sneaky'. He would ask neighbours seemingly innocent questions, about, for example, a car parked outside the house of a 'disqual' (police shorthand for a disqualified driver). By spending time with people, he picked up information – he had recently been tipped off about a drug dealer – that would never come the way of a street duties policeman simply responding to calls. This officer pursued small crimes like the theft of milk from doorsteps. 'If they get away with it, they'll soon get away with a little bit more.' His main frustration was being diverted to humdrum jobs, like school crossing duties, when he was trying to get to grips with crime.

One of David Gardiner's priorities is to strengthen the link between the St Martin's PBO and the estate by providing a 'drop-in' room in the proposed community hall. A previous attempt to earmark a vacant flat as a police post failed when Lambeth vetoed the idea. But that flat, in any case, would have been useless, since it was at what Mr Gardiner calls the 'epicentre' of St Martin's lawlessness, and anyone going there would have been spotted by the young criminals. A room in a community hall will give residents a chance to talk to the police without drawing attention to themselves.

A call that a burglary was in progress on St Martin's came one afternoon when I was talking to PC Birkitt. With two other PCs, we jumped into a battered police 'GP' (general purpose) car. Although the driver used his headlights and horn to catapult us through the schooltime traffic at a hair-raising pace, when we arrived, the thieves, believed to be two small boys, had fled. The officers broke into a neighbouring squat and called at a flat where young thieves hung out. Nothing was found. The bystanders were not co-operative. One of the relief PCs expressed his anger: 'We get a call and come tearing up here, but no one wants to know. We've got to catch them red-handed. People belly-ache "What are the police doing to catch them?" and then won't lift a finger to help us.' Had PC Birkitt not been on duty when that call came, those initial abortive inquiries would have been the end of the affair, and another burglary would have been 'screened out' as not worth a detective's time. But Birkitt knew and had the trust of some of the reluctant witnesses. None was prepared to make an official statement, but over a period of days he was able to draw out of them descriptions of the suspects, leading him to two boys he had been keeping an eye on. He confronted one, who confessed and then named the other. It was not the Great Train Robbery, but it was one more burglary cleared up; a rarity in these troubled times and a vindication, if one were needed, of 'soft' policing.

7

Voices on the Job

Send for the police, and what do we get? In the first
instance, a blue serge uniform clothing a human being
usually of prescribed stature. The officer will probably,
though not necessarily, be young. In our moment of personal crisis, we will be concerned with only very limited
aspects of this person on our doorstep. Is he courteous?
Does he exude confidence? Does he appear efficient? In
most cases we want a well-programmed machine, not a
fleshed-out human being. The man or woman who stands
before us is interchangeable with any one of the several
dozen who might have answered our call at a different hour
or on a different day. We summoned a uniform, and the
variables of individual disposition, prejudice and faith are
of no concern. Even to supervising police officers, the
troops are often interchangeable. 'I've ordered another box
of policemen, but it will be some time before they get here,'
said a duty sergeant ruefully, when all his men were 'tucked up.'
  But that anonymity does not mean that we are neutral
towards the unknown officer, as we are towards others
who wear uniforms, such as postmen, ticket collectors or
gasmen, civilians like ourselves merely masquerading in
fancy dress while they go about their business. Every policeman is a representative of the force: the sight of him may
move us to feelings of relief, security and trust; or fear,
hatred and contempt. He is the 'law', he is authority. The
good and the bad done by thousands of his colleagues, on
whom he has never set eyes, determine what we feel. Walking beside a PC on his beat, I understood a little of his
special identity. An old woman touched a constable's arm
as if in search of reassurance; foreign students, humping

huge rucksacks and clutching street maps of London, asked the way; aimless youths stared at their feet at his approach. One man wanted to know whether he might park briefly on a yellow line; another abandoned washing his car and went indoors until old Bill had passed. Even when the uniform is stowed in the locker room beneath the police station, our man is still a cop. His neighbours know it; regulars in his pub know it; members of his golf club know it. There are few hiding places from the Constable's Oath.

A detective sergeant said that on holiday he told people that he worked for a 'big legal firm' in order to prevent everyone beside the pool bending his ear with their misadventures with traffic wardens. A detective chief inspector told me that a neighbour built a wall between their gardens when he discovered he was living next to a policeman. A young PC was asked at a party which security firm he worked for; when his host learned he was a policeman, a muttered conversation took place just out of his earshot. He was approached rather tentatively, and asked whether he objected to 'funny cigarettes'. Friends of the same PC, in a pub in his home village, were telling the story of one of their number who, when drunk, had driven his car into the duck pond; suddenly the speaker realised there was a policeman present, and the tale died on his lips. Every policeman has such stories.

An academic with a police think-tank asked rhetorically: 'Who are the police? They are categorised by us, and therefore they stick together. I have met senior officers who say that, after twenty-five years, they have lost much of their personality. It is hard for the rest of us to make friends with people who are able to enforce the law against us; it is difficult to have an easy relationship with such a person. They perforce fall back on each other's company; I suspect it just becomes simpler to play their sport and spend their time together.' There is, he suggested, a very narrow social range between the top and the bottom of the police force. 'Policemen seldom spend money on a shift of life-style. More money means more of the same: more similar holidays, larger TV sets, more expensive cars. An officer may move in his career from the equivalent of a good manual job to senior management, yet his way of life will change very little.' He argued that this demonstrated both that outside influences are 'virtually nil' on many police, and that they are significantly alienated from the rest of society.

Police officers, watching the rest of us from the other side of that gulf, resent what they perceive to be media-inspired antagonism, but my experience has been that most criticism of the police is based on chastening first-hand experiences. While I was writing this chapter I met two 'ordinary' – in that they had no axe to grind – women at supper. A good friend of one had been taken to a police station with her eight-year-old son and kept for several hours because a young officer suspected that the car she was driving had been illegally imported. She was refused permission either to make phone calls or to leave the station temporarily to take her child to neighbours. Her husband, who had the car papers, was abroad. Eventually Customs and Excise were called to impound the car. When her husband returned a few days later, it was soon established that the car was legitimately in the country. Customs officers were beside themselves with anger at the wasted time the whole operation had taken; the woman's previously pro-police presumptions had been torpedoed.

The second woman reported what she thought was a stolen motorbike outside her house. Five policemen arrived at midnight, and peered at it with torches; they radioed for a computer check, and said there was no record of the bike having been stolen. Weeks passed, and the machine, which had been new and shiny, began to rust. The woman raised the matter with a police officer she knew personally. He discovered that the bike's plates had been changed, the chassis number crudely altered, and that the bike had indeed been stolen. A police posse returned (once again at midnight), woke several people up by knocking on doors and with the noise of the loading equipment they brought.

Their local reputation for efficiency and courtesy sank to zero.

Police officers know such stories are frequently true because their own families suffer similar experiences. Several times I was told of policemen's wives who had reported burglaries or been stopped while driving, who had been subjected to arrogance and off hand behaviour which made their husbands cringe. A detective sergeant's estranged wife was burgled. The police asked her, the shaken and upset victim, to go to the police station at eight the following morning. She said it would be difficult as she had children to take to school, but was told it would only take a minute. She arrived to find a 'one at a time' system in operation. When she went to the counter, a PC snapped, 'Wait your turn.' She tried to explain how she had been asked specifically to come at that hour and about the school, and the officer repeated yet more rudely, 'Wait your turn.'

Yet behind their drawbridges, officers discount the public's anecdotal evidence. I was not able to check the police explanations for these particular incompetent and aggravating actions, but I had sat through sufficient sessions of elaborate self-justification to know that the officers concerned would not have been short of explanations. These would, almost certainly, have cast the women in the roles of foolish members of the public. Colleagues, no doubt, would have condemned what happened in each case as 'out of order', but saying 'I am sorry; I was wrong' does not come easily to police lips. The police, like soldiers in war, have a daily intensity of experience that distorts 'normal' life. I felt it the morning of 'Mary's' murder, when my mind wiped out everything and everybody not to do with the murder. Reality was reduced to a stinking corpse and a bunch of detectives on the trail of the killer. Officers see things on a regular basis that the rest of us may encounter no more than once or twice in a lifetime: children crushed to pulp in motor accidents; bodies severed by trains; defenceless pensioners knifed to death in their homes. Daily life, as lived by civilians, is tame. An inspector said: 'We can be flippant about things: unless we were, we couldn't go home at night and sleep. It relieves the tension of unpleasant situations.' Something of the process identified in the United States as the 'Vietnam syndrome' is at work. Police live in a world of danger and sudden action, of high drama and excitement; it is hard to come off such a high. Complaints about waiting a few minutes at a police station or being woken at midnight are insignificant to warriors.

A professional researcher said: 'A policeman says: "I had to deal with a mutilated body this afternoon." "Oh really," answer his companions, and get on with discussing the weather.' The researcher understood how the police felt: he had been to Ghana on VSO, and had looked on those six months as the most important and exciting of his life. 'When I came home, everyone treated it like it had been two weeks in Marbella.' Another police watcher said: 'Police live in watertight compartments, and have great difficulty in communicating what they do even to their own families. They feel that their wives will have no idea and won't want to talk, so they talk about the job incessantly to each other. The barriers between them and their families are higher than normal. How do you communicate what it is like to be banged up for four hours in a van, or how terrified you are? The police are like one giant rugby team.'

That is an apt analogy. The police are rugby mad. A chief superintendent joked that the real mafia in the Met is the rugby fraternity not the notorious Freemasons. Police unity is forged at the beginning of careers. There is no 'officer' cadre, no 'Sandhurst' for police, and all bobbies begin on the beat; twenty-five years later, when one policeman is an assistant chief constable and another, who started with him, still a PC, they often retain a close affinity, surprising the casual onlooker with a familiarity that transcends rank. They have heard the chimes at midnight, and, frequently and crucially, played rugby together.

I became used to being taken to one side, usually by long-service officers – and warned that I would find it difficult to penetrate this closely knit world and might easily misinterpret what I saw and heard. In part, this was a protective ploy. Only the naïve and the wet-behind-the-ears would, I

was told, take the police at face value: I was being asked
to believe that behind the cynical and joky canteen attitudes
– towards blacks or women or 'toe rags' – lurked bloody
good, honest cops, who, if they harboured any of society's
prejudices, as inevitably they must, never allowed themselves to be influenced in the line of duty. In short, however
anti-black in general a policeman might be, he was scrupulously fair when dealing with black people. A senior civilian
working at Scotland Yard said: 'There's a lot of racial
prejudice in the canteen, but policemen don't allow it to
be translated into action on the job. They suppress their
personal views. If they acted out their talk, they'd spend
their whole time smashing blacks on the head.' He added
that the prejudice often stems from personal experience.
Police officers, like everyone else, generalise from what has
happened to them. He had encountered one veteran officer,
whom he described as 'racist, cynical, with an appalling
view of the public'. He said: 'He has no time for anyone
above the rank of sergeant. For fifteen years he was probably a decent cop. But he was stabbed twice, and his arm
was severely broken so he was put on restricted duties.
Each of these violent encounters was with black people, so
he came to think of them as the scum of the earth.' He
knew also of a young police officer who had entered the
force 'well left of centre for a PC', and who had changed
'within a month of going on relief.' He said: 'He had been
abused, spat at, and had already started thinking in terms
of "them" and "us". The only people a young PC comes
into contact with are those likely to be anti-police.'

A very senior officer said: 'Beware of the image police
officers project. They are a race apart; they haven't gone
quite so far as to have a brain transplant, but they are very
different. They have a propensity to wind people up, which
can easily be misunderstood. They delight in a butch,
macho image, and it takes a great deal of care and trust to
understand them. First impressions are so often wrong.'
Later he added: 'Part of their attitude is protective. A PC
came across a horrible rape case, a man with his hands
round the victim's throat. A few days later a sergeant found

the man sobbing uncontrollably in a corner. But, if you'd asked this PC if he had been affected, he would have said: "I'm fine; where's the next job to be done?" A PC is often a poor, little, spotty boy of nineteen with a funny hat on his head, entrusted with awesome responsibility. People the age of his parents, uncles and aunts are relying on him utterly in crises. He cannot be scared or emotional; he has to be strong. Until the outsider is in and has become trusted, it is hard to understand our culture.'

I do not entirely discount what he and others said on this score. It takes time and experience to understand any culture, whether it be Geordie, Afro-Caribbean or the Bill. But it is a convenient smoke screen. Such speakers are often arguing that because not all police officers who make racist jokes are racist, no officer who makes racist jokes is racist. The logic is flawed. People who make racial jokes frequently are racist. Several police officers argued that blacks were thin-skinned; after all, the Welsh get called 'Taffy' and Scots 'Jock' and they grin and bear it. I was reminded of what a black professional footballer had said about racism in the dressing room: 'Sometimes it's hard to draw the line between when people are having a joke and when they're taking the piss. By stopping it straight away, you don't have to draw that line.' Two years before I started on this book, I took a day-trip to Calais. A group of policemen – they actually were members of a Met police rugby team – stood out like sore thumbs, drinking heavily even before dawn. 'These are the only solids we'll be on today,' said one, fishing the lemon out of his gin and tonic. On the way back through customs I overheard them making anti-Semitic remarks. They would have argued, no doubt, that this was their day for letting off steam; the next day, back at the nick, they would once again have been custodians of the law, neutral and unprejudiced in the exercise of their considerable powers. Having spent two or three hours with and observing them, I wouldn't have bet the store on their capacity to divorce their private views from their public functions. Does a man's real personality emerge when he lets his hair down or when he dons his helmet?

Which is the reality, the day-trip hooligan or the impartial figure in blue serge?

The notion that, because a few police are crude, unfeeling and prejudiced, all police suffer from such defects and bias is equally fallacious. Anti-police rhetoric of the 'all pigs are fascists' variety is not only inaccurate and insulting, but also calculated to raise the metaphorical drawbridge outside each police station yet higher. The argument is not whether there should be police forces – even anti-police activists need the police when their children go missing or their homes are burgled – but how the tendencies to abuse, in small as much as large matters, can be curbed. It is harder for a policeman to separate his everyday existence from professional life in the front line than it is for soldiers in shooting wars. Vietnam was 'over there' and one day it ended; it may have taken many soldiers time to unwind, but the vast majority were able to put their experiences behind them. The police never leave their war. One moment the adrenalin is pumping, the next they are required to be utterly calm. A civilian who works with the police said: 'How do you control discipline? An officer may be high after a long car chase. When he finally catches the suspect, he's probably hoping that someone not involved in the chase comes along quickly. You need "Mr Iceman" to pull out of the fridge in the back. "We've stopped the bugger, now you deal with him." ' A chief inspector said: 'We are asking for very rounded people. A flow of adrenalin is followed by a sudden cutting off. You'll rush in and lay about you if you are not careful. What you need to be able to say is "Yes, sir, what's your name and address? Sit over there and we'll sort this out." ' 'Adrenalin' is a constant alibi for police over-reaction.

I wondered whether the officers who told me how hard it would be for me to understand their mores and humour had considered the implications of what they were saying. If I, who was going to have the benefit of several months in their company, would have difficulty, what chance did members of the public who only come across the police once in a blue moon have? Instead of almost glorifying in their close-knit isolation, would they not be better employed reducing the differences between them and the rest of us? It is a paradox that almost in the same breath police claim both to be a tribe apart and to be wilfully misunderstood. Tribes apart normally are misunderstood; hence the need for anthropologists. If they wish to be understood, and I was not sure that deep down all police do, they will have to do more than employ image consultants. The failure is a fundamental one. Many police argue that it is society, not the police, which is out of step, which is surely an impossible creed for an organisation supposed to serve that society.

One senior officer who maintained that Britain has a better police force than it deserves said: 'When I joined in the late fifties many recruits were ill-educated, unsympathetic to the concept of service, rude and uncaring by comparison with the young people of today. Yet today's police, more aware of the world and the issues around them, and able to understand service and accountability, are more widely condemned. It is an injustice. There is a wholly different society, and we, the police, take the brunt of it. People today are much more ready to talk about rights than about duties. A citizen's duty is to obey the law, be decent to fellow citizens, and help the police whose job it is to uphold the law.' Thirty years ago, he said, a tolerant society had a tolerant police force; the two had been evenly matched. Now they were out of balance.

He cherished fond memories of a childhood lived in a harmonious community, a pit village where miners grew prize leeks. Everyone had 'pride'; the village sustained nineteen institutions; Scoutmasters stayed single until their late forties in order to run the village troop; the church organised a literary debating society. 'No one had a penny to scratch their arse on, but our little village was so rich it hurt,' he said. At school, the boys had to put on boxing gloves to test their courage. This man now policed one of London's most troubled inner city areas, with its complex racial and social mix. Harmony and social order, rooted in a common heritage, belonged to another place and another time. His yearnings were human, but nostalgia, it seemed to me, was a liability in the face of the fear, diversity and misunderstanding that washed around his police station like wind-lashed waves worrying an exposed headland.

Our social dispositions remain very largely those of a huge feudal estate, whereon each of us has his place. The police's overt role is to sustain law and order; its unstated, unacknowledged agenda is to defend a dominant social order, which is sporadically threatened by radical change. The scheme of things has evolved since the era in which Sir Robert Peel founded the Met, and the police, with their mandate to protect and conserve, have always lagged half a generation behind. The Queen's picture, adorning many walls in police stations, is a constant reminder of the fountainhead of this desired order. One of the least reverent (and brightest) senior officers I met told me that, when on parade for a state occasion, she once believed that the Queen caught her eye and smiled at her as a royal procession swept up the Mall. This otherwise rather hard-headed officer's face almost shone as she recalled the day, by then fifteen years into the past.

To say that policing is not 'political' in the widest understanding of the word is a canard. The distinction between politics and party politics eludes many canteen sages: the Queen, being 'above' politics, is not political, therefore the social order, which she legitimises, is not 'political'. Although police are, more often than not, conservative both politically and in general outlook, they are seldom keen on party politicians of any stripe. Several officers pointed out gleefully that the same opinion polls that place police near the top of the public esteem usually show their chief critics – politicians and journalists – at the bottom. Tory Home Secretaries get just as rough a ride at Police Federation meetings as Labour ones. Jim Callaghan, the Federation representative in Parliament for many years, who could have played Dixon of Dock Green to perfection, had been popular with the rank and file in a manner that few Conservatives could ever hope to be.

A typical senior officer wanted neither Mr Kinnock nor

Mrs Thatcher telling him what to do. (He had met Mrs Thatcher and found her unbearably patronising.) Politics and politicians, he said, had polarised society, and the police were left in the void. The miners' strike and the printers' dispute at Wapping had brought the police 'into the firing line', and damaged the debatable notion that the police serve the people rather than the state. 'The miners' strike hurt; the police cannot afford to be seen as a tool of government, which was how they were portrayed,' he said. But he had no doubt that the police had a duty to restrain strikers who threatened intimidation and worse. Labour relations, like life, were a balance between rights and duties. 'There is no such thing in law as mass picketing; those big demonstrations are embryo riots rather than pickets. The police must stand between extreme violence and folk going about their normal business,' he said.

Police popularity is also, he argued, related to their pay, which goes 'in peaks and troughs'. Pay used to be roughly on a par with the average skilled wage. When he joined, it had, perhaps, fallen 20 per cent behind, which won the police sympathy. 'At present it is at a high peak, which, together with the perception that we have been used against the unions, makes the police less popular.' He met regularly with representatives of the Police Federation: 'I always remind them that the job does not exist to give them a living – they cannot be allowed to get away with that concept – but to serve London's public. They are now paid on a generous, professional salary scale, and must behave as professionals. However, there is no farm for raising policemen in isolation; they come out of wider society and bring society's attitudes with them, including a materialistic outlook on life.' He added: 'Good police officers are properly paid, but I suspect that an awful lot are overpaid.' He disliked the word 'entitled' which police and others latch on to; the police, he said, were no more 'entitled' than anyone else in public service, like nurses, teachers or doctors. Young PCs are so accustomed to the good times that, if another trough follows the present peak, 'they will be very surprised.'

It is a facet of the war footing the police are on that their daily encounters with people are often difficult and antagonistic to a degree that few others experience. An inspector said: 'Coppers have to create a wall of concrete to protect that little germ of humanity in them that is being jumped on all the time. You cannot perform your job without destroying what you are yourself. People explode before your eyes. It is not aimed at you personally, but if you are over-open you can actually be destroyed.' In its lower reaches the job is very largely a physical activity – walking the beat, nicking villains, driving fast cars. The emphasis is on fitness; the activities advertised on the canteen walls are rugby, soccer, golf, running. The police wish to live near golf courses in Surrey rather than in renovated Victorian terraces in the inner city. A home beat officer, encountering a middle-class house seeker in a decaying area of Lambeth, advised: 'I wouldn't live round here if I were you.' The papers read by the police are almost exclusively tabloid. Many of the brighter officers are, in any case, studying for promotion exams, leaving little time or energy for intellectual refreshment. The ground is fertile for the lowest common denominator to flourish. It makes for a quiet life to succumb to this collective embrace, and to banish disturbing thoughts and private misgivings: the office of constable can be performed almost entirely on reflex actions.

Almost every policeman (I write about policewomen later) I spoke with had joined because he expected an exciting career. For those who were bright and had achieved promotion, the scope of the job had broadened dramatically, setting fresh policing challenges; those who stayed put were in danger of being sucked month by month, year by year into a slough of cynicism and inertia. The unhealthy anti-academic grass roots bias is directly related to one of the police force's central problems: the failure to motivate a PC throughout a thirty-year career.

The Metropolitan Police is like a giant school with too many pupils in the D stream. The bright kids do all right, but they are rapidly removed to the sixth form, from where their impact on the school culture is minimal. Out on the playground it is easy for those left behind to lapse into an uncritical acceptance of some pretty negative attitudes. The majority of PCs will never be promoted, but even those who have no ambition cannot help casting a jaundiced eye on those who are advancing. It is easy, as it is from the back row of the classroom, to invert values. The lads set their own priorities, which have little to do with those being promulgated by the headmaster. Knocking people who dare make an effort, who seek to fulfil their potential, is a British disease which destroys many people's capacity to live fulfilled lives, but it is particularly virulent in hothouse environments such as police stations. An older sergeant, coming upon a younger sergeant studying, said: 'Are you doing a degree or something silly like that?' A civilian attached to the Yard said: 'I often wonder what happens when the bright-eyed young things are got at because they become intensely cynical.' An inspector said: 'Young policemen come here enthusiastic. We disillusion coppers further down. They don't get on the courses they want. I see coppers turning sour. There's no mechanism for turning them back. Some recover, but not many.' A chief inspector said: 'The high ranks have the motivation of career development and prospects to make them do what they are told. We have not yet learned to motivate junior ranks. We like to think that it is a vocational job, and that we are all highly motivated. But a significant number of people regard it as a job, pure and simple, albeit a well-paid one.'

Very few of the police I met had joined out of a commitment to 'justice'. Most had been attracted by their (often inaccurate) perception of the life-style, which was drawn almost entirely from television and film. The few who did talk about 'right and wrong' were keen not to be seen as crusaders. One PC said: 'I don't believe I am holding a flaming sword.' Another, fleeing an insurance office, said: 'I had never done anything wrong myself. I like to think that people can walk these streets we are walking even at one in the morning, so I joined an organisation with that basic aim.' The chief inspector said: 'Most policemen feel

179

passionately about criminals and making arrests. They will quite happily stay late (without overtime if necessary) dealing with prisoners. Our whole being is channelled towards one end, producing people before magistrates. If we lose that *raison d'être*, we may as well pack up and go· home. The vast majority of good policemen, when they have a prisoner or body in their sights, will go on and on. I'm not talking about drunks and vagrants, the rubbish jobs. That's why the Flying Squad and the Robbery Squad are the élites. The officers may be no different from the rest of us, but they are dealing with good quality jobs, dealing with prisoners.' That was a sentiment that ran through the force, like lettering on seaside rock. Even a gentle WPC specialising in domestic violence said: 'As police officers we like to get a result at the end of the day.'

I do not underestimate the problems of trying to change attitudes within a large, bureaucratic organisation, in which the collective influences at the bottom are more powerful than the tone set at the top. I also understand why long-service police are upset that they get less public appreciation than they would like and feel they deserve, for the police *have* changed over the past thirty years, and changed quite dramatically. Some older officers feel the need to pinch themselves when they look back and see how far the force has travelled. An inspector nearing retirement said: 'We are grudgingly, resistingly, being dragged forward.' He paused, and amended 'being dragged' to 'moving'. 'We are a lot more open-minded than thirty years ago, and willing to accept that our point of view is just one of many – all of which may, in part at least, be correct.' He added that the changes had unsettled some older officers. They had joined the job when the police force was still highly autocratic, almost military. 'You were not expected to question decisions; things were very black and white. It is a far more difficult job now for young recruits,' he said. 'When I joined, an individual policeman was a force to be reckoned with. Slowly our authority has been questioned. I don't mind being challenged, because I have to be able to justify what I do, but this came as a shock to some. When I started, you suppressed the opposition: you didn't accept that someone might have a reason to march on an embassy, to shout and to rave. But we came to realise that we were not big enough to police by repression. I'm proud of the way it's done now. We did things in the past which we shouldn't have done, and which, if we are honest, we must admit were dreadful errors.

'We've got to be far more open and talk to people, and they've got to talk to us. It doesn't make policing easier to understand the other person's point of view, but it does make it less likely that violence will ensue. If we hide behind a wall of uniform, we will fail; going out and explaining our policies is the only way forward. People are better educated and want to know "why?" If I'd heard myself speaking like this twenty years ago, I'd have thought "What a load of claptrap!" But life's experiences touch us.' He accepted that 'softly softly' has costs. It irritates people, he said, that there is so much crime at the Notting Hill Carnival. 'We haven't enough people to suppress it; we can't actually prevent anything.' But he added, 'Look at the conditions the Carnival criminals are living in; I'd be rioting if I led such a drab life with no hope.'

Despite having changed his views on the relationship between police and public, the inspector stuck firmly to the old-timers' tenet that formal education was not only unnecessary for the average police officer, but a positive disadvantage. Although five GCE O levels or GCSE equivalent are no longer mandatory for recruits, they remain an ideal. The inspector said: 'I don't think that the possession of five O levels is an indication of a person's common sense. It means that in London people are not policed by their own kind; most people in London do not have five O levels.' The distrust of formal education is endemic. A bright young inspector bridled at the suggestion he might be a graduate. He then laughed, realising that he didn't have to keep up the anti-academic front with an outsider. He wasn't a graduate, but could well have been. It was obviously important to his credibility that he wasn't. The basis of the hostility to learning is that promotion to the ranks of sergeant and inspector is achieved by examination (like mandarins, commented one observer, somewhat snidely). The canteen prejudice is that people who are good at exams are devoid of the common sense required for good coppering.

A detective sergeant suggested that it is as sensible to promote policemen on the basis of exam results as it would be to pick a soccer team according to academic qualifications. Canteen cynicism was, he continued, directly related to 'academic' promotion. ' "Academics" get to inspector as by right, and then they don't get any further. Subordinates can play these inspectors on a string. All policemen are brave because they wouldn't be policemen if they weren't, but what they need is nurturing and teaching. You have got to build morale from the bottom up. The tendency now is for a PC to say: "Oh, it's me grub break, Sarge, I can't do that." ' He suggested that the mandatory two years on the beat should be extended to four, and that NCO ranks that once existed – like station sergeant and first-class CID sergeant – should be restored.

One PC, half-way through his thirty years and a man who might have benefited from a promotion system not based on examinations, carried a series of chips on his shoulder. 'There's a lot of wasted effort in the system. It's all Mickey Mouse leadership,' he said. 'It is hard to know where we are going on this job, or where we'll be in ten years' time. We're bumbling along in our usual way. Robert Mark was the last Commissioner who had a working mind. McNee to his credit didn't try to change much. I'll follow a guy with good firm policies. Newman came in with ideas, and quite frankly we're still struggling with them. He was too intelligent. Day-to-day policing actually comes down to people out there on the streets doing the job. What Commissioners say doesn't count for anything. If PCs don't trust them, they'll go out and do their own thing.'

He said that there was no 'pro-active' policing. No one was asking 'What plan have we got? And what do we do about it?' He complained that PCs coming on parade had a lamentable lack of information. 'Chaps need to know exactly what happened that morning; information that is twenty-four hours old is not worth a light. The computer is largely wasted; it is a management tool. A lot goes in, but not enough comes out. They plot where crime was committed last month and they monitor costs, but they are not really interested in the most important resources – PCs. We are there to prevent crime; if we get a body, we are happy. The organisation, on the other hand, is geared to management.' He complained that traffic rather than crime detection got priority. 'If you park on a yellow line, you'll get done; if you smack someone on the nose, you won't.'

PCs frequently accuse their leaders of failing to articulate the police point of view. A young PC said: 'The public don't realise that we're members of the public as well. They get out of bed the wrong side, and so do we. When we have off days, it hits the headlines; if you only take in what you read in the papers, that's your view of the police . . . always going round making things up and giving people a slap here and there. If you never come into contact with the police, you take everything you read about them as real. The public relations people never get onto the papers and ask "Where did you get your information? How do you justify the article?" '

A lay visitor (to police cells) suggested that, on the contrary, the police are narcissistic in their preoccupation with their own image. He said: 'The police have a much greater desire to be understood than to understand. They welcome lay visitors so that the visitors can see that nothing is wrong and relay it to the community. They have little curiosity in us, and use us to get their perspective to the community rather than to learn the community's perspective of them. Like South Africans and Israelis, they suffer from a siege mentality, continually complaining that they are misunderstood and not appreciated. They are paranoid because all the people they have direct dealing with – lawyers, probation officers, social workers – have a low opinion of them. People who have a high opinion of the police are almost exclusively those who have nothing to do with them.'

A civilian working with the police said that the police tend to believe that their problems are unique. 'Don't you

183

feel that the police are desperately inward-looking? The higher up the ladder, the more officers look inward on the force rather than outward on the community. From early middle management upwards, they are concerned with implementing policies, rather than considering their effect. I say to them, "You see yourselves as a beleaguered minority, but think of other minorities – like British Telecom – who are equally beleaguered when the spotlight is turned on them." The police must expect attention; they are the highest profile institution in the country. I tell them that on balance they get a bloody good press. When things go wrong, they come to me and ask what *I* am going to do about it, why can't I stop these "allegations"? I respond that they are not "allegations". Policemen have gone down for these crimes. How do you counter that? You don't.'

A senior officer explained police sensitivity: 'Before there is any investigation (into alleged wrong-doing), MPs demand, "Sack the lot." Different standards are applied to police than to other people. Venomous and continuous criticism is heaped on our heads. The one or two things that go wrong are taken out of proportion to the thousands that go right.' A policewoman said: 'You see a picture in the paper of a police officer with his arm round someone's neck. You've no idea what happened just before, so you assume the worst of the officer.' A PC said that what really upsets him is the mindless abuse to which the police are endlessly subjected. In the gents in the pub nearest Streatham police station, someone had scraped in the paint: 'Police are pigs. If you like bacon, you like pigs – sliced.'

Most of the attitudes I have reported have been those of male officers. Although a few women aspire to be 'one of the boys', 'canteen culture' is essentially masculine. But the balance between men and women on division is changing month by month. Policewomen have only been entering the force on entirely equal terms since 1985. Before that, despite the Equal Opportunities Act, various games were played – quotas and increased height requirements – to keep the monstrous regiment at bay. They were only allowed to carry firearms in 1985, and issued with truncheons in 1986.

184

Thirty per cent of the Met intake are now women, and they comprise 11 per cent of the force, a figure that is inexorably rising. Already one in four police on the streets are women. These increasing numbers are beginning both to soften the macho image of the force and possibly, some policemen would argue, make police patrols more vulnerable to hooligan assault. Policewomen in the West Midlands have been picked on during disturbances as 'the weak link in the chain'.

In the autumn of 1988, the *Sunday Times* alleged 'Scotland Yard Discriminates Against Women'. The story was more circumspect than the headline, but the gist of it was that policewomen's aspirations were not being met. Women enter the Met in proportion to the number of applications they make, but they are woefully thin on the ground in 'glamour' areas like the CID, Yard specialist squads and firearms training. Two tendencies combine to exclude them from the sharp end of policing: straightforward chauvinism and the old-fashioned notions of chivalry held by many officers. Policemen, in general, believe a woman's place is in the home. I was told at Hendon College that male recruits become upset with instructors who they think drive women too hard. Male sergeants and inspectors tend to assign women to sheltered tasks – in the communications room, in the front office or guarding school crossings. One long-service PC said that it was acceptable for a man to have a facial scar, that was 'macho', but not for a woman; he, therefore, did not want women confronting drunken yobs. The logic of this is that a woman should never leave the police station. If she doesn't leave the station, she does not gain the experience that will qualify her for more demanding and daring work, and the cycle becomes self-fulfilling.

An inspector said that women appear to be more adept at the skills that lead to office-bound jobs – like VDU and message switching operators. 'They seem more willing to take these courses. Chaps don't want to be stuck indoors all the time,' he said. He had started his own career when women officers were almost exclusively concerned with women and children, and the influence of those days was with him still. He admitted he felt protective: 'Women are better off inside, safer,' he said. He felt that women were less assertive, and cited the example of one woman he had come across. She was clearly clever, he said, but she was less effective than most men and lacked self-confidence. 'If you send her for two hours to catch people driving through red lights, she'll come back and say that no one did. Even if you accept that there was a temporary miracle in south London, there were other things she might have done – check tax discs, caution people who drove through orange. I suspect she might not do anything for two hours since she would never want to upset anyone,' he said.

But another woman had won his admiration by averting a potential punch-up by employing her 'feminine' skills. Several officers, including the inspector, had been called to deal with a drunk who was refusing to go in a police van. The inspector began to lose his patience: 'I said: "You'll either go in the van the easy way or the hard way." The WPC, watching this, realised that I was on a short fuse, and said to the drunk: "Listen, pal, they're going to set *me* on you in a moment." The drunk laughed, gave her a quick squeeze and climbed into the van good as gold. Her timing was brilliant, quite perfect. As her inspector, I could not congratulate her enough.'

I was in the area car late one winter night when a WPC was on duty. We had already linked up with her panda car in the search for youths who had robbed two drunks. Ten minutes later, we heard her calling over the personal radio system 'Come quickly, come quickly, for God's sake come.' She was under attack and frightened. We were only a few hundred yards away, but by the time we reached the spot her assailant had vanished, and she was staggering around like a boxer who has just risen from the canvas and not yet collected his wits. She had a cut on the crown of her head that later required several stitches. She had left the panda while her male companion checked a nearby house. A slightly breathless youth approached, and she, suspecting he might be one of the muggers, went to question him. He grabbed her and threw her to the ground, and ran off.

Nothing excites the police as much as an attack on one of their own, and soon the area was crawling with cars and officers. My two male companions were understandably upset. 'Would you let a daughter of yours become a WPC?' asked one.

Another WPC told me that she had been hit only once in five years, and that was during a general fracas involving dozens of police when fists were flying. She said that her feminine approach helped defuse nasty situations. The night I was with her, she was driving a van, and her radio operator was a newly joined male probationer. But at most of the incidents we were called to, members of the public addressed him rather than her. A woman sergeant, writing in a police magazine, complained: 'Since my promotion, having attended numerous incidents with male colleagues of varying rank, I could hardly fail to notice how the male public automatically home in on the male officer, regardless of whether he is obviously immature or turns out to lack knowledge and experience.' Male chauvinism, like racialism, is not restricted to the ranks of the police.

A prejudice common to police and civilian life is that sooner or later women will leave the job to have children, and that, therefore, it is not worth training them for promotion. In fact the discrepancy between time served by women and by men is not great. The average length of service for a woman in the Met is seven years, while for a man it is eleven. But it is tough for a mother to return to a relief, with its demanding shifts. A woman sergeant, who after having a baby was able to get one of the few nine-to-five jobs at her police station, said that she would have quit rather than go back on shift. Her husband is also a police sergeant, and the strain of both of them working has meant that he has not been able to study for further promotion: 'He couldn't consider it while I work. We don't sit down until eight o'clock, and by then he is too tired to study, and anyway we'd have no time together.' A great many policemen and women marry each other, a large number of the romances starting at Hendon. With the proportion of women in the force rising, the number of 'job' weddings

187

is bound to increase. Traditionally, the police have often married nurses, since the two professions are thrown together by their similar shift patterns.

The woman sergeant had gained a place at university, but she had already decided at sixteen that she wanted to join the police and turned the university offer down. She had faced opposition from her father, who thought that she might drift into the police, get married and drift out again with nothing to fall back on. However, she had found that competent women officers survived well. 'I've had hostility, but it has not lasted long. I have known women who have had trouble, but they have not helped themselves by being bad officers. If you are a bad officer and a woman, it is worse than being a bad officer and a man because you are more likely to be picked on. All women get tarred with the same brush. People meet one woman who is lazy, and categorise all women as lazy.' Further promotion, of which she was obviously capable, would be difficult. 'I have a child of two, and I cannot commit any more time to the job than I do now. Mentally I couldn't cope with it. The further up you go, the more criticism you get from PCs and skippers [sergeants], and I don't think I could take that. There is also discipline. If you are not careful, they are doing what they want. Not that I couldn't control people, but if I have words with anyone, I brood over it and take it very personally.'

An ex-WPC, married to a senior officer, still missed the job desperately five years after leaving to have a family. 'They were the best years; we did outrageously silly things that no one would dream of doing now. I would love to go back,' she said wistfully. What she missed was both the stimulation and the status; being 'just a mum' was pallid by comparison. No longer wearing the uniform and not being required to 'take charge', she had felt a loss of self-confidence. After the excitement of the job, she had had to come to terms with the frustrations of being a police wife. When we met, her husband, who had been taking all the overtime opportunities he could, had not had a free week-end for six weeks. She said: 'Often our social life is zilch.

We get invited and just cannot go.' Her husband had recently spent two years in a nine-to-five job on a training unit, which both had regarded as 'bliss'. Her ambition was to return to the force; she and two other ex-WPCs had suggested they should be employed on a job-share basis. 'It is a waste that all our training and experience should be lost,' she said.

With the sharp drop in the numbers of school leavers, all employers have an incentive to hang on to their trained staff, and the Yard is now anxious to find ways of holding women with children. In the winter of 1988/89, the Met's equal opportunities unit was staffed by two men, a fact that naturally delighted the *Sunday Times* in its exposé of sexual discrimination. The unit's boss, Inspector George Waddington, said that the obvious options – job sharing and part-time working – were fraught with difficulties. However, when I met him, the banks had just announced that they were giving their staffs the opportunity to take five-year career breaks with the guarantee of their jobs back, and this was being considered by the Met. Mr Waddington said: 'On division the normal instinct over maternity leave is that the woman has dropped off the edge of the earth, absolute proof that the world is flat. Divisions should be planning, keeping in touch, counselling before the woman leaves, so that her return does not take them utterly by surprise.'

The Met itself had been taken by surprise in 1983, when a woman officer successfully sued the force over discrimination after she had been prevented from working as a radio operator with a traffic division. Her senior officer had argued that the drivers were male and married, and that therefore a single woman might cause a problem. A retired woman superintendent told the *Sunday Times* that harassment in cars was indeed a hazard: 'You'd go out on a job somewhere with a PC. They'd drive you up a dark alley and stop the car. I'd say, "What are you doing here?" and they'd say, "What do you think?" I wouldn't like to count how many faces I've slapped.' While I was writing, the Met, working with the Equal Opportunities Commission

(EOC), had just come to the end of a four-year project to put their house at least formally in order. An inspector writing in *Police Review*, pointed out: 'Equal opportunities can be described as the application of basic justice . . . If the service is seen to be treating its own employees unfairly, what hope can the community at large have of receiving fair treatment from the police?'

Mr Waddington said he was satisfied that Met policies no longer breached equal opportunity legislation: the force was the only one that deployed women throughout the whole range of public order duties. 'We have got to get all twenty-eight thousand officers to abide by force policy. When people say that women can't do the job, the answer is simple. They are doing it now,' he said. All internal advertisements for specialist branches, like Royalty and Diplomatic Protection, stress that the opportunity is open to suitably qualified women officers. Mr Waddington said: 'To decide that women will not be deployed in situations where violence can reasonably be anticipated may be chivalrous, but it is totally against the law.' He added, however, that if there were a major breakdown of order and the Met found that it could not cope because women were not strong enough or were unwilling, the force might have to seek exemptions.

Despite official policy, unofficial quota systems abound. Mr Waddington said: 'A DCI will say: "We don't discriminate; look, we've got three women in the crime squad." If more were good enough, there ought to be more, and if fewer, there should be fewer.' A booklet, produced for the guidance of inspectors and above, also points out that if there is a vacancy in youth and community work (traditionally filled by women), the supervising officer should not automatically reject the idea of a man in the job. A male police sergeant argued that a woman returning from maternity leave should not necessarily be given a vacant nine-to-five job. The implications of equal opportunities are wide-ranging: even the shift system could be challenged if it were shown to discriminate against women. The Met would have to justify it as the only way to police London effectively. As a quid pro quo for EOC support, the Met was preparing a book of best non-discriminatory practice for use by other forces, and equal opportunities law is being accentuated in police promotion exams.

EOC research revealed that most policewomen have the same ambitions as men to be deployed in 'élite' squads. But they are also more committed than men to 'community policing'. Women who had been in the police force before 1974 had joined in the belief that they would serve out their careers dealing principally with women and children. Many felt that both the police and society had lost a great deal when women were removed from their caring role. One recently retired senior woman officer said she considered that women police had been 'disintegrated' rather than 'integrated' as a consequence of equal opportunities legislation.

'People got carried away with the political concept of equality. We were seen as unequal because we were dealing with women and children. To step up, we had to be involved in other things. I never came to terms with that notion. No one stopped to ask what was going to happen to the children: in the fifteen years since, juvenile crime and child abuse have become major concerns. There had been a corps of women who had phenomenal link-ups in the community; their network became a preventative measure. The wisdom was: "Isn't it great shoving all these women off into operational policing?" No one concerned themselves with all those jobs policewomen had been doing. We knew our communities very well; we knew which children were getting into the wrong company,' she said.

She cited one block of flats where youngsters were continuously in trouble. She said: 'You could have built a tramline from there to the police station. We put in a policewoman and she became an "auntie". Officers knew that they could channel the problems of that estate through her. She took an enormous amount of work off the police station, and built up a tremendous relationship with the people. When two neighbours had an argument, instead of giving way to animosity and aggression, they would see "Helen" and she would become an umpire.'

Some women officers had argued that the police should be exempt from equal opportunities law, but, since it was Home Office legislation and the police are the responsibility of the Home Office, that was never going to happen. 'Why on earth were we women police removed from one situation to another? It was a breach of moral contract. It was very very badly handled, and must be one of the darkest corners in the history of the Met,' said the former officer. The presumption behind integration went, as she saw it, to the heart of the 'force' versus 'service' debate. 'Dealing with children was seen to be work for second-class citizens. Yet, as far as I am concerned, if you don't get it right with children, you'll never get it right at all. I couldn't give a toss about burglaries. I was only concerned with burglaries as far as they revealed a social malaise. The wellbeing of children is a greater issue than the loss of property. If what people really want from us is that we arrest as many villains as possible and forget everything else, then we should stop saying that the police are a social care agency. If we are just there to nick people, we should stick to that. We cannot vacillate. The old ethos is coming back. The police are increasingly an enforcement agency; a police force, not a police service.'

When finally she and others like her had to accept 'integration', they were assigned to operational duties. 'I asked no quarter and was given none. I would not back away from anything. I couldn't ask people about things I didn't know, because that would have fuelled their prejudices. I felt that I was under the microscope and knew that I could not afford to make a mistake. I gave my relief a different style of leadership, feminine, but quite strong. Because I was a woman, I had to get right inside them. It was not about me imposing my personality on them. The fundamental error in policing is not to encourage individuality.'

In her first week of operational command, she was called to a jeweller's shop, where thieves had tried to blow a safe with gelignite. The keyholder had not yet arrived, and the only way into the premises was over a ten-foot high wall. Two PCs were standing by, smirking slightly. The inspector ordered them to 'make a back' so that she could climb the wall. 'There was no way I was going to be defeated. I said: "If any of you buggers look up my skirt, there's no time off for a month." That was enough for them; from then on they knew that I would be at the front with them. Coppers have got to be led from the front.'

8

'Fire Up Their Backsides'

> '*When I joined, your word and your uniform were the law. You arrested someone, went to court the next morning, and the case was settled there and then. No one questioned the police.*' An inspector nearing retirement

For the past thirty years the British police have been having to come to terms with a changing social landscape. At one level, this has required *informal* adjustment: life is no longer uncomplicated and hierarchial. The 'bobby' has long since ceased to be a universally benign figure, respected by all save active criminals. But the change has also required the creation of consultative structures to make the police *formally* accountable, and put some bite into the notion that the police are the servants of the community. In the bygone era, when police accountability was sorted out cosily between chief constables and watch committees over a few 'G & Ts', both sides knew where they stood. The police deferred to some people, and a great many others deferred to the police.

Then the police categorised the rest of us according to our class and our criminal disposition. There was a vast gulf between 'good villains', whose crimes required some degree of skill, and 'toe rags', the scum at the bottom of the pile. The categorisations, albeit a little ragged at the edges, remain. There are exceptions, like 'old dears', relics from the good old days stranded on declining estates, but, as a rule of thumb, the worst is often assumed of people in derelict environments. Police, raiding a squat or a 'cardboard city', are prone to abuse their powers in a manner they would not dream of doing when dealing with propertied people. Canteen antagonism to 'rights' is largely rooted in the unpleasant surprises that the police get from time to time when either the toe rags they are dealing with turn out to be better informed and more articulate than they had expected or, more usually, when 'busybodies' or 'dogooders' happen along and assist the underdog. Black people, unless obviously marked out by a furled umbrella, pin-striped suit and Oxford accent, are placed fairly near the bottom of this league of vulnerability.

But life no longer approximates to a Miss Marple story. There is less deference, more turpitude, greater confusion in appearance. Earls' sons sniff coke; JPs and colonels drink and drive; 21-year-old blacks own sports cars; people do know their 'rights'. Unemployment, rotten housing, worse education and racial discrimination make a destabilising brew. The riots of the early 1980s signalled, in the inner city at least, the end of the age of deference. The police were not responsible for the dynamite, but on several occasions, through inept or provocative operations, they provided the detonators. The riots were seen by some who monitor the police closely as a salutary lesson: 'Riots and the prospect of more keep the police on the straight and narrow; they are a constant fire up their backsides,' said one.

Eight years on, the police had developed a two-pronged strategy to cope with the altered social landscape. They had 'tooled up' and were ready to tackle future disorders head-on; and, goaded by the Scarman inquiry into the 1981 riots and compelled by legislation, they had also accepted consultative machinery designed to make them more responsive to public priorities and more sensitive to public concerns. The police, to whom any notion of 'political' control is the ultimate horror, argue that they now have their house in order. 'No one,' a chief superintendent said, showing me a chart with arrows shooting off in all directions, 'is more accountable than the police.' Although these arrangements by no means satisfy London's Labour boroughs, who would like to see the police under direct local control, they are enough to dismay some senior policemen.

A member of a south London police consultative group said: 'Many officers had not been used to public explanation and public anger. Some still find it pretty difficult and irksome.' A member of a police think-tank said: 'The police do not know how to react to people with no tradition of deference to them, and this sets up a potentially hostile interaction.'

The police authority for London is the Home Secretary himself, who is answerable to the people through Parliament. It is this lofty and tenuous relationship between the police and the policed that upsets left-wing boroughs. Their community charge payers sub up half the cost of the capital's force, yet they have no direct handle on police activities or priorities. In their eyes, the new consultative bodies are lap- rather than watch-dogs. Streatham, like Brixton where violence broke out in both 1981 and 1985, is part of the London Borough of Lambeth, and its police have formalised contact with the public at several levels. The most important forum is the borough-wide consultative group, a statutory body with a paid secretariat. A series of divisional consultative teams operate under its umbrella, though in practice these groups are often run with considerable autonomy by local chief superintendents. Streatham organises annual police/public meetings, while at the very local level sector working parties, attended by neighbourhood policemen and active citizens, meet once a month. A panel of lay visitors pays random visits to police station cells across the borough to check on the welfare of detainees.

The machinery, therefore, is extensive, and it is backed by unofficial links, such as dialogue between chief superintendents and MPs, which, I suspect, are the most potent avenues for individual redress. However, the Scarman-inspired process suffers from two debilities: in some left-wing boroughs the local authorities do not participate, and there is a tendency for the police – anxious because other people now exert influence where once they had sole say – to dominate the links. A researcher said: 'The police are instrumental in setting up groups; they have a head start over other contenders for the leadership role. They can marginalise some elements and promote others. The whole philosophy of consultation ought to be to get people to come up with responsibility for their own problems. If the police simply look for the kind of leadership they can work with, the dynamic will fail, and an "Uncle Tom" atmosphere will be created.' This fear contributed to the decision by Lambeth Council, after active involvement in setting up the consultative group, gradually to withdraw. A member of the group said: 'The Labour view was that the police should be "democratically controlled"; some councillors even thought the local force should be under the direction of the council and become local government servants. If the police weren't to be fully accountable in that sense, they argued, then something that fell so far short of that ideal as the consultative group should be avoided, since it was simply a façade, a cosmetic form of accountability.'

In the real world, rather than the brittle, theoretical one in which subjects like consultation and accountability tend to be discussed, links such as those established between PC Birkitt and the housing officials on St Martin's estate are inescapable. A member of the Lambeth Council 'police committee support unit' said, 'The dialogue between the council and the police is like that between Western commerce and the Eastern bloc. There is strong rhetoric on both sides, but behind the scenes there is a lot of toing and froing.' A senior policeman said, with a degree of hyperbole: 'Co-operation can never be upfront, but behind the scenes is incredible'. Senior councillors, he said, would slag the police off, but meet with them every other week to chew the cud. At least one black left-winger, he said, used public hostility to the police as a tactic to reduce tension, believing that strong rhetoric 'lanced the boil'. A Lambeth employee uttered what for him was a dangerous heresy: 'The council and the police actually have a great deal in common: they are both forms of social control. The council is more likely to be in alliance with the police than with the local community.'

Despite this pragmatic co-operation, there remains, on the council side, political antagonism, and, on the police side, deep suspicion of any encroachment upon their cherished 'independence'. The council man said: 'The police might want to be liked, and go out of their way to make friends with the community, but they are not perceived as friends. They come from Scotland or Yorkshire, and have twenty weeks' training: it is unrealistic to expect them to respond sensitively to London's problems. They believe all they have to do is invite people to sit down and discuss a common approach. But the people's historic perceptions are at variance with the police's; there are horrific experiences in the collective memory. It is not as simple as the police make it.' He described how at one meeting, called to discuss the riots that followed the 1985 shooting of Mrs Cherry Groce who was paralysed when accidentally shot by a police inspector, a senior police officer took off his jacket, saying: 'I'm an ordinary person now.' The council man continued: 'The people in the hall laughed. To them all policemen at that moment were one and the same with the person who put the bullet into Cherry Groce. It was a more complex problem than the policeman acknowledged. He thought it was enough to show genuine remorse, but the issue was not just a mistaken shooting – there was a lot more to it than that.'

This council officer argued that police good intentions are frequently at variance with their actions. 'They will go into a school and say: "We're here to help you." A few hours later they are harassing black kids, and people are waiting two hours for a PC to come to their burglary.' He added: 'The police confuse community liaison work with a real understanding of the people and their problems. Trips to Brighton and five-a-side football are not a substitute for recognition of the problem. The police are prone to be either paternalistic or paranoid; their structure leads them to impose rather than consult.' He added, ironically: 'The problem for the council is that the police appear to be offering something worthwhile, and we look negative opposing it.'

The council are not alone in their doubts: I found a number of local people who felt that the consultation machinery was a sham. One said: 'Young blacks have stopped attending. The police speak over their heads: all *they* want is for the group to write to the Home Office to demand more money, and complain that the police are under-resourced. They never consider whether the money might be better spent on something else, say women's refuges.' It was not just young blacks who were missing, but young anybodies. Almost all those at the various meetings I attended were middle-aged or elderly, a solid slice of middle England in tweed jackets, anoraks and dun cardigans.

Edmund Gray, chairman of the Lambeth consultative group, accepted that the group's monthly meetings are not as well attended by young blacks as they had once been, though he suggested that in part this was because community/police tension had declined. The group, he said, is now more normally concerned with burglaries or neighbourhood watch, which tend to be middle-aged rather than young preoccupations. At the meeting I went to, a black man alleged that the police had been stopping expensive cars driven by blacks. A police superintendent rose to make an emphatic denial: the accuser left, looking nonplussed, and another black castigated the group for avoiding the issue and its implications. 'We have no problem when we all agree, over acid house parties, for example, but the awkward questions are ducked,' he said. This exchange illustrated the limits of almost any dialogue between civilians and police when the issues are contentious. One says it is so, and the other says it isn't, and beyond that it is often hard to proceed.

Despite such impasses, Mr Gray argued that it was right and necessary to have 'a forum in which the police are forced to explain themselves. A mechanism by which community views can be put forward pretty forcibly is better than no mechanism at all. It is also a place where people with grievances can let off steam. Psychologically, people find it a help to tell the police how they reacted to operations and to hear whatever explanation the police come up with.' He singled out a previous police commander for praise:

'Very angry people came to meetings and did get explanations and a measure of dialogue with this rather remarkable policeman. He had an impressive ability to respond under pressure to angry people, and a disarming line in explanations and even apologies.' Those are relatively rare gifts. Another member of the consultative group said: 'Senior police officers lapse into thinking that we are there to cushion them against public opprobrium, to reassure the public and give them confidence in the police; they think that consultative groups are a lay arm of the force. We have endlessly to point out to each fresh generation of officers that that is not how we see it.' A Lambeth lay visitor to police cells said: 'We may not realise how *they* can take us to be oppressively inquisitorial; *we*, on the other hand, feel we are just vulnerable members of the public merely tolerated by an all-powerful institution. When we are angry, it is on behalf of the very powerless.' Some police believe that, in allowing inspections of the cells, they have done all that can be expected of them. For lay visitors then to criticise them is taken as gross ingratitude. After a raid on a community of dossers, the visitors claimed to have uncovered some rough and ready police behaviour. The local police chief had been, I was told, 'up in arms' over their findings: he personally had alerted the visitors that the raids were taking place only to find himself facing criticism as a consequence of his efforts to 'consult'.

Police are conditioned to 'take charge'. It is their mission to reduce chaos to order, and this is most easily accomplished by exerting authority. It is, therefore, an unusual senior officer who is at ease with the consultation process. Chief Superintendent Street embraced the philosophy and practice of consultation wholeheartedly. His aim was 'citizen satisfaction', as recommended by Scarman, and he wanted to serve in a police force responsible, as Robert Peel intended, to the law and the people, rather than to the government or an élite, and he believed the way to achieve such a force was to open up to the community. 'I tell them, "We have 300 staff and a budget. What do you want us to do?" This is the way to demonstrate that we are part of the community and not an occupying army,' he said. However, he added that there were certain ground rules that were not negotiable. These included not policing one section of the community more than any other, and concentrating on crimes and not on groups of people who might commit them.

The most important police/public occasion of the year was the divisional public meeting, out of which Mr Street extracted local priorities, and, having married them to the Commissioner's strategy, transformed them into his objectives for the following year. The division's senior management team sat on the stage behind a table draped with the Metropolitan Police flag, and about a hundred members of the public attended. The main presentation was by Superintendent Buchan, who summarised the year's achievements and problems with a skilful blend of information, explanation and apology, which was calculated to draw any stings there might be. In these days of tight budgets, he said, it was difficult to police a high crime area. Officers were young (though mustard keen); arson and murder had drained scarce resources; all categories of crime were up; but the thin blue line would hold. The public, wooed by Mr Buchan's mellow tones and Scottish charm, was generally supportive. People in inner cities live with so many fears that most have a great yearning for the police to succeed. The audience that night were police 'loyalists', who had come bruised and bewildered, desperately tired of the daily struggle against social decay. The police, whatever their imperfections, were their last best hope. Most criticisms were motivated, not by hostility, but by a yearning to improve the service.

At one stage an elderly man did start shouting that his son-in-law was a policeman who had been attacked three times by blacks, and that the answer to crime lay in repatriating 'coloureds'. There were few blacks at the meeting, but one black woman started to walk out in disgust. Mr Street intervened, condemning the man's racism, and, to the approval of the audience, the abusive man rather than the black woman eventually left. One or two potentially awkward issues were neatly dodged – the police had prepared beforehand to cope with embarrassing topics. Mr Street concluded the evening judiciously: 'I do think that we are underresourced. But so then do my fellow chief superintendents. But the Met gets over one billion pounds, and, seen in that light, people are not in favour of us having more. I am not sure that we are using our resources effectively and efficiently. Hence the review.'

One feature of the night was that prostitution, which twelve months previously had been the most contentious issue, was hardly raised. Although 'toms' still walked the middle-class streets near Tooting Bec Common, the police had taken action after what had been a model campaign by local residents to attract resources to their particular problem. The Common has been haunted by prostitutes possibly since Roman times; certainly they were there servicing the needs of a muster camp during the Napoleonic wars, and they returned for similar patriotic duty during the great wars of this century. The demarcation between the Streatham and Tooting divisions runs through the Common, and for many years the prostitutes favoured the Tooting side of the line, so much so that Tooting set up an effective vice squad, which drove the women into Streatham.

One resident, a retired businessman, described what hit them: 'Within the last five years it has become intolerable. The girls go up and down, performing in our front gardens and leaving the evidence behind. You are accosted on your way home, and abused when you go out to protest. I've had to clear human excrement from the garden.' A neighbour said: 'We were physically surrounded, living in a Jekyll and Hyde environment. As the shadows lengthened, so the neighbourhood threw off its guise of being a secure urban area. It tilted, and the pimps, the girls and the punters came out and began to circle. It spoils your joy in living in quite a powerful way; getting up and clearing your front garden of the rubbish, and knowing that you have only got a few hours to be free of it. If you protest, you are told "You fuck off, you cunt." It was appalling, creating a cumulative feeling of stress.'

The residents lobbied the police. 'Police/public relations were falling into an abyss; the police had no idea how disheartening it was,' said a resident who one night called the police to say that he feared that a prostitute was being murdered by a pimp. He was given, he said, the 'bum's rush'. 'The situation was at a very low ebb. I was infuriated by the police reaction. They would retreat behind historical argument: agree it was terrible, but say fatalistically that prostitutes are always with you; claim that in any case they were not a very serious police concern; argue that, if they cleared up our streets, the prostitutes would simply go elsewhere.' A pregnant woman who complained about noise was thrown to the ground and abused (three weeks later she suffered a miscarriage). A man who stood at the end of his drive to deter the women was twice told by prostitutes that they hoped his children would die. One resident said: 'I am not concerned with the morality – they can do what the hell they like as far as I am concerned – but with the public nuisance.'

The residents organised. They carried out traffic censuses, which revealed that the heaviest traffic was between 10.00 p.m. and 1 a.m., when the volume far exceeded the morning and evening rush hours. A lobbying group – Streatham Against Kerb Crawlers (STAKC) – was formed. They went to the police with sound data and local knowledge; they were no longer, in the words of one of the organisers, simply 'bleating and tugging at the police's sleeves'. They stood in the road with clipboards taking car numbers, and within half an hour the volume of traffic had declined by 75 per cent. Public meetings were held; the MP was mobilised; the pressure maintained. One resident said: 'I am a firm believer in citizens taking their share of responsibility. If the police know that the residents are involved, that gives them some motivation and keeps them on their toes. They have got to pay attention to highly skilled professional folk who cannot be ignored.'

Shortly before I arrived in Streatham the pressure paid off, and a five-man 'Tom squad' – a sergeant and four PCs – was set up, which nightly toured the streets, scooping up tarts. The women were booked to appear in court the following day, when they would normally be fined between £30 and £100, and were back in business a few hours later. Yet despite what was essentially a charade, the squad did wonders for local morale. Arrests of prostitutes rose, from 239 in 1987 to 803 in 1988, and complaints fell: the prostitutes were as big a headache as ever, but something was being done. The somewhat cynical police objective – to reduce complaints – had been achieved. The real answer almost certainly lay in a traffic management scheme that would baffle the kerb crawlers, and, as a result of further local pressure, one was being considered. STAKC, however, still believe that more policing can be done. A spokesman said: 'I do not understand why the police don't go after the pimps. They tell us that it is very difficult to prove that they are living on immoral earnings, and that it would tie up several officers for a month to get hard evidence. We rather naïvely thought that was what the police were for.'

As it is, the resources that are devoted to prostitution cause continuous grouse among Streatham officers. An inspector said: 'We respond to letters from MPs, and we listen to the "voice of the community", yet prostitution is not even a crime. Burglaries meanwhile go undetected.' PCs grumbled that they could not get to grips with evils such as rent parties because so many men were assigned to vice patrol.

The job of rounding up the nightly quota of whores was inevitably unpopular. By the time I went out with a squad, the campaign was in its tenth month, and the canteen opinion was that it had achieved all that could be expected of it, and that the manpower should be reassigned. 'If we stayed home tonight, no one would realise,' said a PC resignedly. A colleague briefed me. Between thirty and forty girls (and a couple of transvestites) worked the area: 'It's the bottom end of the market – twenty pounds for a quickie. They are not very attractive; if they went up to town to do the real stuff they wouldn't get a look in.' The ritual was to cruise the four or five side streets looking for a red-handed catch – a prostitute actually getting into a client's car. After a couple of near misses, the squad settled for scooping up four or five girls. The process of arrest is lubricated by a great deal of banter. The women know that if they were to plead not guilty, they would clog up the magistrates' court and decimate divisional manpower. 'If you treat them like slags, they'll hit back. It only works if you keep them sweet,' said a PC.

The prostitutes' language was a stream of tedious obscenity: 'Why the fuck . . . you're always fucking picking on me . . . you're a slag. Sarge . . . you're all cocksuckers . . .' The speaker, nicknamed 'Motor-mouth', was a thin, half-caste nineteen-year-old, who wore a black body sock which she kept hitching up over her breasts. She had scarlet shoes and gloves, and carried a cigarette packet in which she kept her money and a supply of condoms. She turned her attention to me: 'I suppose they've only nicked us to impress this fucking wally', and then taunted a black PC: 'You're good at fucking nicking, but you're not so good at fucking. You're a fucking country boy; you can't fuck like a Londoner.' Occasionally, the bad language gave way to wheedling: 'If you let us go early, you can have a Chinese meal with us. Would you join us, Sarge?' 'No, I'd be living off immoral earnings.'

One by one the women were interviewed, asked the questions they were asked last week, the week before, and would be asked again and again. Motor-mouth, who had just told me that she earned £50,000 a year, was drawing £54 a week in state benefits on behalf of herself and her daughter: all the women were registered unemployed. Another prostitute, short, fair and blobby, was many months pregnant: she speculated whether she could sue the condom manufacturer. 'Who's the father?' asked a PC. 'Your guess is as good as mine, darling.' This woman had once been a shoplifter, but had given it up for prostitution. 'When you're arrested for shoplifting, you go straight to jail: whoring you only have to pay a fine,' she said. Motor-mouth, who had been a 'tom' since she was fourteen, added: 'Going to jail gives you a rest and tightens your fanny.' It also, they said,

205

gave them time to think. 'Life's so chaotic; we're always on the move,' she said.

'Do you use prostitutes?' asked Motor-mouth, and then nodded towards the police filling in forms: 'Many of this lot do.' The sergeant, bent to his paperwork, complained: 'There's as much to write out as if we had arrested a "high class body" [i.e. a professional criminal].' Motor-mouth was quite relaxed by now: 'Actually, I was due for a nicking; I hadn't been nicked in ages.' A PC who had been checking records came back and told Motor-mouth that there was a warrant out for her arrest on a drugs charge. Her jaw froze in mid-sentence, and for the first time in an hour she was briefly silent. The warrant meant that she would be detained in the cells overnight. 'I don't use drugs, I'm a boozer,' she pleaded in vain, her night's work cut short. Outside the police station the released women flagged down taxis, and were plying their trade again within two hours of arrest. Most of them had been swept up forty or fifty times, but the fines were certainly less than income tax would have been on their earnings.

If rank-and-file police resent having their priorities set by pushy civilians, they are equally suspicious of the monitoring machinery set up after the Brixton riots, in particular the lay visitors, who have the right to make random visits to police station cells. A few months before I went to Streatham, visits had been suspended across Lambeth following a row between the visitors and custody staff at Kennington. The police claimed that the visitors had exceeded their brief by giving a prisoner advice relating to his case, an accusation denied by the visitors, some of whom believed that the police were simply looking for a pretext to get rid of them. The police insisted that all future visits be held within the hearing of the custody officer. There was a temporary impasse, with the police asserting privately that the visitors' panel was 'politicised', and some visitors countering that the police had provoked the dispute because they resented young, black visitors. One said: 'We were first-generation black Britons, different in dress, accent, age and manner from our fathers. We were not suitably pliant, and custody officers did not like us in their charge rooms.'

After visits – described by one relaxed inspector as 'pop-in tours of your local nick' – had resumed, a meeting was held at Streatham to explain 'the purpose of lay visits,' as one senior policeman put it, 'to rather suspicious police-men'. He said: 'Policemen are conservative with a small "c"; they are, therefore, shy about innovative ideas, and about being inspected by outside organisations. Lay visitors epitomise the "they don't trust us" phobia to which police are prone.' The meeting, he said, was an appeal to officers to see lay visitors in a positive light, and to understand that they were there to reassure the wider public that all was well, and not to pry into police affairs. Officers were told that, whether they liked it or not, lay visitors were there to stay. This senior officer, at least, was convinced that the visits would benefit the force. He said: 'Lay visitors will discover that we don't beat people up; we do allow phone calls; and that, barring genuine mistakes, everyone gets their rights.'

Lay visitors themselves would not (and could not) go that far. One said: 'It is impossible to give a complete bill of clean health. We do find some malpractice, and we can only sample. We cannot *guarantee* that dreadful things do not go on. However, we are fairly sure that there is no systematic malpractice in the cell wings.' He added: 'There is absolutely no doubt that we have an impact on police behaviour: we meet police officers who admit that things did go on in the old days. We have heard from lawyers and detainees themselves, the old lags who wax almost lyrical about the improvements. We can also measure the physical improvements – blankets, cleanliness and meals – and these have been considerable.' The panel campaigned for paper suits for prisoners whose clothes are removed for forensic examination, and lobbied the Home Secretary for prisoners to be enabled to shave before they go to court. The panel and consultative group are now trying to get showers installed.

The panel by no means claims all the credit for the

improvements in custody procedures. The Police and Criminal Evidence Act (PACE), introduced two years after the lay visitor scheme, prescribes very narrowly how the police must gather evidence and treat suspected people. It requires that a sergeant must be in charge of the custody suite; that prisoners must be afforded such rights as access to solicitors and telephone calls to let people know they are detained; that detailed records must be kept. The Act is treated like the Ten Commandments once were, which is not to say that it is never transgressed, but that it is referred to constantly, providing a step-by-step guide not only to the treatment of prisoners, but also to such matters as searching homes, stopping people on the street and the retention of property. A prisoner is entitled to a copy of the PACE 'Codes of Practice', a substantial digest of the relevant parts of the Act, but I never saw one asked for or issued. Police grumble incessantly about the record-keeping involved – a custody record rapidly becomes a small book – but it was a rod they made for their own backs through abuse of previous safeguards.

Now that the police have PACE, and are learning to live with it, albeit in a slightly ungracious manner, they have a ready answer to allegations of malpractice. Several police officers I was with were asked whether they beat prisoners – the question was usually put by youths whose recently arrested friends had told them lurid tales – and they always cited PACE as their guarantee of good conduct. 'The sarge's job would be on the line.' They usually added that they had seen prisoners get a 'smacking' in a van, but only when the prisoner had started the rumpus. Lay visitors – their mandate is restricted to the welfare of detainees – were concerned that their activities might have 'displaced' police assaults from the cells to the vans (or elsewhere outside police stations), much as police action against crime will often displace it to another neighbourhood. One said that he would like to see detailed research comparing allegations of police malpractice in areas with lay visitor schemes to those without.

Lay visitors in Lambeth serve for three years, and are

selected according to quotas – 50/50 black and white, 50/50 men and women, with a guaranteed age spread, one-third under 30 one-third between 30 and 50, and one-third over 50. Panel members, who work in pairs, send reports both to the divisional chief superintendent and to their colleagues. If a prisoner does make a serious complaint, he is told about the complaints procedure, how to sue for damages, and urged to get a solicitor. If he claims to have been assaulted, he is advised to have the injuries recorded before they heal. I asked one lay visitor how he knew if a prisoner were making a genuine allegation. 'A strong sense of grievance comes across. There are few enough, so when we encounter one we take it seriously,' he replied. Prisoners often want to talk about the right and wrongs of their cases, which causes a problem, since the reasons why someone has been arrested fall outside the lay visitors' remit, but are inevitably uppermost in the detainee's mind. A prisoner will say: 'If you are not concerned, what are you doing here?' Prisoners can be suspicious, believing that anyone who has access to the cells must be hand-in-hand with the police. Despite PACE, each month a few prisoners claim they are denied solicitors. On arrival they should be asked if they want a lawyer; their answer is recorded and the prisoner signs the form. Confused and frightened people, perhaps under arrest for the first time, may not always read carefully what they are signing.

Under PACE, the custody officer is supposed to be independent of the arresting officer, and should refuse to detain a prisoner without sufficient grounds. But the two officers are colleagues, and one lay visitor said that he had never come across a case of a custody officer turning a prisoner away, and that he therefore simply assumed a degree of collusion and co-operation. I did see arresting officers and custody sergeants putting their heads together, both to come up with sufficient reason for their actions, and to ensure that neither was making a bureaucratic mistake. Cell space is limited, and the pressure, certainly with run-of-the-mill cases, is more often to keep people out of custody than to hold them.

In the spring of 1989, the chairman of the Lambeth panel was William Storey, a young black who worked for the research organisation, the Police Foundation. The history of tension between the police and community, he said, meant that local people had to live with the unsettling feeling that riots might erupt again. A community could not develop under that cloud, and better trust between community and the police was a prerequisite for a better quality of life for all. He became a visitor because he was convinced that what happens in police cells is crucial to wider police/community relations, and because he was in no doubt that prisoners had been assaulted in the past. He was happy to recognise the improvements: 'Compared to ten years ago, these things have gone way down. Street allegations have almost disappeared.' A colleague said: 'Perhaps the lay visitor should be saying that, given the conditions in the cells, no man alive could do the job of custody officer. But that isn't the remit.'

I went with Mr Storey not to Gipsy Hill where I would have been known, but to another of the Lambeth police stations. We were courteously received by a youngish sergeant, who was clearly nervous; he had not, he said, come across lay visitors before. We were asked to wait in the charge room while a prisoner, who had been arrested in a provincial town and brought to London, was booked in. In our presence, the prisoner, who wore a torn leather jacket and jeans, was referred to as 'this gentleman'. He had a clutch of possessions in a plastic bag, which were carefully gone through and recorded, and he was asked if he was prepared to talk to us. The sergeant read a rubric (which, obscurely, had been inscribed on the inside cover of a C. S. Forester paperback intended for prisoners' use): 'Lay visitors are ordinary members of the public who make regular, random visits to ensure that any persons detained are being treated properly, and that they are held in reasonable conditions.'

The young man was led to one of the three dingy cells, with high ceilings and yellow brick walls, splattered with graffiti. The heavy wooden doors – on which was inscribed

'SHUT THE WICKET: Remember that the cell wicket must always be kept closed' – had steel linings, and were secured with a lock and large bolt. The prisoner had nothing to say of relevance to us in our capacity as lay visitors, only that his life was in ruins, and he wanted to make a clean breast of what he had done. 'I just hope I don't get a long time,' he said mournfully. In the next cell a young African sat cross-legged on a pile of three blue mattresses: he wore a leather coat and a gold watch, and had a fistful of rings on his left hand. He eyed us suspiciously and, even after several explanations, did not appear to understand why we were there. Observing our notebooks, he muttered something about the press. I was sure that if Mr Storey had not been black and young, this man would not have spoken to us, which confirmed the value of racial and age quotas.

Once he had been reassured, the prisoner startled us by saying that he had been treated 'violently', that he had been given insufficient time to read immigration documents before having to sign them, and that he had had great difficulty in getting access to a solicitor. However, it was clear that poor English lay at the root of his complaints. By 'violence', he meant that the police had failed to answer when he pressed his cell buzzer. He had, it seemed from the confusing entries on his custody record, been misunderstood when he asked for a lawyer. Although he had signed the box indicating that he did not want a solicitor, the arrival of the duty solicitor late the previous night had been noted, and he had had an hour's interview with her at two in the morning. However, by that stage he had already been questioned on his own by detectives for over an hour. With patience, it was possible to piece together both what had happened since his arrest and what he was now saying. His experience provided us with the one substantive case of the night. In his report, Mr Storey outlined the misunderstandings, and suggested that in future more care be taken with prisoners who spoke imperfect English. The only other prisoner was a young lag who knew the ropes.

The sergeant, fussed that we had been so long writing the report, followed us out like a mother hen.

One regular police complaint about the consultative process is that members of the public often fail to see the wood for the trees. A senior officer said: 'Official representatives tend to put the things that concern them first – car parking outside their homes, litter, piles of sand. These minor matters are regarded as deserving of our priority and attention. *We* may be concentrating on five robberies and thirty burglaries, but if *they* haven't been robbed or burgled they may not share our priorities.'

Matching what the public believes ought to be the priorities with professional police judgement and limited resources is probably the crucial skill required by a senior officer. One chief inspector cited a raid on a homosexual sauna house that had tied up forty officers for a complete tour of duty. 'For what? To suppress homosexuality? To quieten the siren voices of local critics? To make Streatham a safer place?' As a result of the raid, four gays had been cautioned for acts of gross indecency; the cases against four others had been thrown out. Eventually, the owner was jailed for six months, which, surprisingly (to me at least), struck the senior police officer as too harsh.

The most harmonious link between public and police is the neighbourhood watch. Local enthusiasm, however, is hard to sustain, and new schemes often become becalmed after a year or so. 'It is easy to pack a hall for the initial meeting,' said one Permanent Beat Officer wearily, 'but often not very much more happens.' I sat in on a meeting on a small council estate attended by two elderly men – one of whom was clearly anxious to get to the pub – two middle-aged men, and a slightly younger husband and wife in whose sitting room the meeting was held and whose son was distraught at not being able to watch television for an hour and a half. Their estate was close to another with an horrific reputation, and their understandable interest was to prevent their neighbourhood going the same way. 'Adults here,' said one man, 'still actually pick up litter.' The scheme was new, and crime had gone down, convincing the members that the orange-and-blue signs attached to lamp-posts and the stickers in their front windows did ward off evil spirits.

This reaction, that crime comes from outside, provokes left-wing scepticism towards neighbourhood watch. A member of the Lambeth police committee support unit said: 'We are not opposed to them, but neighbourhood watch schemes are an inadequate and partial response. They may be of short-term benefit, but are divisive in the long run. They're like circling the wagons; people who don't belong are "outsiders".' He added that watch schemes are only aimed at a narrow band of crime, and make no impact on, for example, child abuse and domestic violence, two of the most prevalent offences within a community. Others do actually oppose neighbourhood watch, arguing that it benefits the affluent and well-organised at the expense of the poor, and encourages the police tendency to view the world in class terms. A pamphlet entitled *Neighbourhood Watch: Policing the People* (Libertarian Research and Education Trust) stated: 'There is reason to believe that crime prevention is but one of the aims of neighbourhood watch within the overall and historical police role of social control.'

Such an ideological approach prevents constructive engagement. A liberal sociologist argued that because of such attitudes, London left-wing local authorities continuously shot themselves in the feet. Outside London, left-wing councils are more pragmatic, he said. He made a distinction between the people who want *better* policing, and their councils who want *accountable* policing. 'Many councils have a tremendous amount of suspicion of anything the police do – even crime prevention. To co-operate with the police is to be an "agent of social control",' he said. 'But people realise that even if the police were "accountable", the service would be exactly the same or even worse than it is now: councils are not known for their efficiency.' Left-wing hostility reinforces the prejudices held by the police, who, in turn, often behave as if apologies simply play into their critics' hands. The sociologist, referring to the 1981 riots, said: 'There should have been an act of police penance. The police always pretended that nothing had happened, and the black community was understandably very, very angry about what went on.'

Bridges between police and public are notoriously fragile. 'They are blown away,' said a chief inspector sadly, 'by one incident, and they hate you with as much vehemence as they hated you before.' He described an effort made by two officers to work with a boys' club. One of the boys was shot with an airgun, and a rumour swept the neighbourhood that the boy – who was black – was dead. The police were accused of not responding to the incident with sufficient vigour and were branded 'racist' as a result. The two officers, who had just begun to have meaningful dialogues with the boys, found themselves back at square one. The chief inspector said: 'It's a very slow, tortuous process. A lot of police see this, and ask "What's the point?" The police are disciplined and an entity; ethnic communities are not, and therefore have to be won over almost literally one by one. Cricket matches once a year are hardly the basis for a trusting relationship.'

A probation officer accused the police of abusing even such links as there are. He claimed that a police officer who had worked hard to be accepted by staff and kids at a children's home later provided information which led to a heavy-handed dawn raid, when doors at the home were kicked in. The local fall-out for the police, he said, was appalling. At root always lurks the tension between community work and arresting people. The same probation officer invited police officers to talk to young offenders. The idea was to show the police as human beings, individuals who deserve respect, and to teach the boys about arresting procedures. The 'clients' got very aggressive, and one police sergeant snapped. 'You stick by your mates, so we stick by ours', he said. The probation officer, who had been trying to confront the boys with the consequences of their offending behaviour, was furious. 'If you're not straight and honest, how the hell do you expect anyone else to be?' he demanded of the sergeant. Later he said: 'The police officers were undermining the moral attitudes we had been trying to inculcate for eight weeks.'

A senior policeman said: 'I know we don't get everything right; we're only human beings. Often there is no "right" answer that pleases everyone. But we cannot have got things wrong to the extent that the GLC and some extreme anti-police groups would suggest. The GLC was a terribly destructive, negative influence.' He leant forward over the coffee table between us. 'In the old days the community basically agreed with the composition of the table, except for a small circle in the middle. Now the circle, comprising areas of disagreement, would touch the four edges of the table, leaving only little segments in the corner which people can agree on.' The police, he suggested, are the only stable element, who hold the ring for the rest of society.

Just as there is often a wide gap between the aspirations of senior police and the foot-dragging of the canteen, so there is a gulf between the ideals of consultation and the reality of street-level contacts between police and public. A researcher said: 'Consultative groups tend inevitably to attract leaders who are more concerned with their own status and careers than with representing people with particular social problems. And good intentions by the police are constantly being blown off course by special squads. A beat PC has just got an estate together, when suddenly the drugs squad arrives, crawls over everyone, smashing down doors, and a lot of good work goes down the drain.' A colleague added: 'The leadership of the consultative process has always been concerned not to upset and alienate the police. Non-answers are accepted, and members of the public stop coming. The police are very comfortable with the process and enjoy it. They arrive, have a drink, give perfunctory answers, have another drink and go home.'

The police, the researchers pointed out, can always dismiss a vociferous argument as unrepresentative of the whole community. 'They say, "We can show that there are other points of view, and therefore we are playing our role in a reasonable way in downgrading that particular consultative noise." It is difficult to deal with this. If you don't get your act together and don't make a noise, you are never heard; if you do, and the police don't like what they hear, then you are not "representative".' A civilian at Scotland Yard, however, who watches police/public relations closely, said he felt the police were too prone to listen to the most vocal people. 'They rush into policies because loud voices *are* allowed to penetrate,' he said. In order to challenge police priorities effectively, civilians need more information than they are likely to have. A researcher said: 'We owe the police collaboration because we and they have common aims, but on what basis do we owe deference to a body that gets millions of pounds to catch people who break the law, and who make such a poor stab at it? If you raise the fact that their performance is abysmal in terms of crime figures, they turn to the fact that they do not have enough men. "Of course, with limited resources I cannot do the things the public wants." They are educating us in a partial view of the problem.'

From the police perspective, consultation confers legitimacy. The researcher continued: 'It is usually introduced after a crisis to get the police back on the streets and to restore confidence. If there is public trust in the lay visitors' scheme and the consultative group, it becomes possible for two policemen to walk down the road without getting spat at. The police might be able to do something about illegal parking without attracting a hostile crowd. Hard-nosed police will say: "We have got to have consultation, but it is quite separate from the job we have to do." CID and special squads are ninety per cent impervious to consultation.' A colleague, who had been listening, said that he had seen CID officers change stride at the sight of a lay visitor in the charge room.

These researchers' joint view of the consultation process was essentially jaundiced. They argued that the police do not recognise that what is demanded of them will in the end benefit them. One said: 'The power of consultation to influence what is happening is very limited; the power through head office is very strong. Consultation in the end is toothless; the police are not required to listen.'

216

A huge chasm loomed between this and the police perception. A very senior officer told me: 'I don't want to be a member of an unfettered police force; that is a very dangerous concept. And I don't want a tame consultative group, but one that addresses the real issues that concern people. The whole process is about influencing people. It is quite legitimate for the local community to sit down with the police and ask, "What is to be your style of policing and your priorities (because we should like to influence them)? Have you got the right numbers of officers in the right places? Is there a right amount of activity in the right areas?" It is desirable that this should be done in the public arena. We should encourage that sort of dialogue. If we jointly identify, jointly analyse and jointly apply solutions, we should get it right. Consultation ought to be in a much more creative mode; not just responsive to last year when things went wrong.'

9

'Mrs Thatcher's Bootboys?'

Flying into Heathrow Airport one winter's evening, the captain of a Nigerian Airways flight was appalled to see just below his port wing what appeared to be a crashed plane, surrounded by flickering flames. Convinced that there had been a disaster, he radioed a 'plane down' alert. It was a wholly understandable false alarm. The pilot had, indeed, seen a plane and flames, but the plane was an ancient, engineless Trident, set on permanent concrete mounts, and the flames came from a rain of petrol bombs as Metropolitan Police officers staged a simulated riot. The captain was flying over 'Riot City', nine acres on the edge of Hounslow Heath, equipped not only with the plane, but with a network of streets complete with 'shops', a 'bookie's' and 'restaurants', a London Underground train, and vast hangars, inside which police officers practise with plastic bullet guns – weapons yet to be used on the streets of Britain – and occasionally with CS gas.

The existence of Riot City is hardly a state secret; six thousand Metropolitan Police officers train there regularly, and it is, as the Nigerian pilot proved, visible from almost any flight landing at Heathrow from the east, but it is not widely advertised either. The site, the only purpose-built police riot training centre in Europe, is tucked behind a private housing estate. There are no signs directing the visitor, nor any clues at the gatehouse as to what goes on behind a perimeter fence of the sort that surrounds low-security jails. Were it not for a board advertising the current state of alert, the complex might be taken for one of the many warehousing depots that dot the flat and featureless hinterland of Heathrow.

218

The relative anonymity is part of the necessary security for a sensitive police installation (anti-bomb and mortar patrols guard the perimeter), but there is also a compelling public relations reason why what goes on in Riot City is not a high-profile police activity. For the Hounslow site is, in police terms, the equivalent of the strategic hideaways in which the US Air Force continuously prepare for a war they desperately and sincerely hope will never be fought. Dressed in visored helmets and flame-resistant overalls, and armed with body-length transparent shields, several hundred police officers each week face bricks and petrol bombs in preparation for urban violence on a scale not yet experienced in Britain.

Watching one cold January night from a rooftop at the junction of 'High Street' and 'Victoria Street', as fleet-footed instructors acting the part of rioters bombarded greenhorn cops with petrol bombs and wooden bricks (real bricks had once been used but were withdrawn because too many police were being injured), the scene below was realistic enough to prompt sharp memories of Belfast and Brixton, St Paul's, Bristol, and Toxteth, Liverpool. The acrid smell of burning petrol, the savage shouts, the clatter of missiles, the dark figures behind their Roman shields, now cowering, now charging, may have been no more than sophisticated and violent play-acting, but to a spectator they were a reminder that there is at the heart of British society a fissure that, given provocation, ill luck or a long, hot summer, could again shatter the surface serenity. There are even circumstances – a world recession, a plunge in Britain's economic fortunes, escalating unemployment – in which that fissure could split asunder to become a permanent gulf between those who are comfortably off – who are increasingly retreating behind electronic gates or leaving the cities for the suburbs – and those who have almost none of the late twentieth-century goodies. Perceptive officers, who know that the force has not yet overcome the 'political' image created by the miners' strike and by Wapping, view the prospects of policing fresh social tensions with alarm. One senior officer had, when I met him, recently been involved in policing demonstrations by nurses; the police had tried to be low profile, he said, and to project a soft image. But demonstrators had chanted 'Mrs Thatcher's bootboys' at them. 'That hit deep within me,' he said sadly.

The police may debate the competing merits of 'force' versus 'service', and the outcome of that debate may have a significant impact on whether fresh urban riots do occur – but once all the wheels have come off, and shops are being looted, cars burned, streets barricaded, the police have only one role. They become a civilian army charged with re-establishing the *status quo*, and they will employ what force they consider necessary, including certainly the use of plastic bullets and CS gas, to hold the streets. If they were to fail, the government would turn to the military, indicating that, so great had become the loss of social cohesion, British citizens were beyond the control of civil power. The Metropolitan Police may be playing war games at Riot City, but potentially the training has a deadly application.

The training at Hounslow represents the ultimate police response to the breakdown of law and order, but the police are also prepared for less dire, more mundane eventualities. When I arrived at Streatham, a bright young sergeant, shortly to leave on promotion to inspector, was completing a year-long update of the division's contingency plans. Each duty inspector has a copy, and the master plan – two inches thick in a blue folder – is kept in the front office. A conspiracy theorist would find it a disappointing document, dealing, as it does, in an unemotional way with the practicalities of both public disorder and potential disasters like train smashes. (Streatham is criss-crossed with commuter lines, and the Clapham rail crash of December 1988 happened in the next police division.) The plans contain few subjective judgements. One entry did read: 'A large number of Brixton council house tenants have recently been relocated on this estate [not St Martin's], and may well present a problem in the future.' There was a specific section on St Martin's itself, underlining its rundown condition, the influence of some local criminals and the estate's proximity to Brixton. It was 'imperative', said the manual, for St Martin's to receive 'high-tension policing during any disorder in the Brixton division.'

The plans were, said the sergeant, 'a fool's guide to the galaxy'. They lead the duty inspector step by step through any foreseeable sequence of events until the disaster or disorder is either in hand or becomes too big for local control. Some divisions have particular public order responsibilities – obvious ones being airports or major football grounds – and draw help on a regular basis from the rest of the Met on a system of mutual 'aid'. Each week lists are posted announcing 'the following have been selected . . .' for duty at a soccer match or demonstration, as if the officers themselves were playing or demonstrating. It is popular work, as it breaks the routine, pays overtime, and normally involves little danger since a very high proportion of such events take place without significant trouble.

Public disorder has high priority in inner London. The Streatham sergeant said: 'More than our fair share of aggravation is centred around London. We are probably, therefore, more efficient than country constabularies who don't deal with it with the same frequency.' Certainly, senior officers are constantly vigilant for tension indicators that might signal a 'Broadwater Farm' about to explode on their patch. I talked at some length to a senior officer who had been involved in the Met's post mortem into Broadwater Farm, a double disaster for the police in that they failed both to anticipate it and to control it – blunders that cost PC Keith Blakelock his life.

This officer said that if the situation in Broadwater Farm had existed in isolation, there would have been very little excuse for what happened, but at that period twenty-four separate locations within the Met had been reporting rising tension. He said: 'If you work in a high tension area, you get used to it. You cannot be constantly raising the alarm or you become like Matilda shouting "fire". On some London estates home beat officers are subjected to such abuse that they come to regard the abnormal as normal. If anything like that were to happen in Bromley or Epsom, the local police would flood the centre with tension indicator reports.' There is also powerful psychology at work: the junior officer who shouts for help looks as if he cannot cope. I had seen how reluctant PC Chris Birkitt had been to accept reinforcement on the St Martin's estate (although in his heart he wanted it), because it would have signalled, to both his superiors and the local population, that the estate yobs had him on the run. The senior officer said: 'At every level we're expected to come up with solutions, not problems. Those above you want to have alternatives to choose from; simply to go to a superior officer with a problem is frowned upon. To raise a panic shows a lack of bottle; in a macho service it looks as if you cannot cope. So you have to be careful how you couch your reports. Each level has its checks, so, as Broadwater Farm was beginning to bubble, very little was getting to the centre.' Yet the evidence of impending disaster at Broadwater Farm was plain enough: local officers had discovered dustbins packed with empty bottles, clearly destined to be made into Molotov cocktails.

The Streatham contingency plans dealt with both local response and the assistance they could call upon. 'If it does get out of hand, we press the button and it goes to the big boys at the Yard,' said the sergeant. In force-wide operations, both the levels of command and the severity of incidents are categorised by colour. The strategic commander is designated 'Gold', the operational tacticians, of whom there may be two or three, 'Silver', and the significant ground commanders 'Bronze'. The colour coding of incidents ranges from green for normal through amber, blue, red and finally black which denotes a major disorder. The response, through a series of so-called 'waves', can be stepped up from providing units of the Territorial Support Group (each unit comprises one inspector, four sergeants and forty PCs) to 'draining every single police station of every single officer'. As an example of how the system works, the sergeant said that if St Martin's goes 'a bit funny', the response might be 'blue', denoting that the incident was beyond divisional control, and outside officers would be drafted to patrol the estate.

The plans give guidance on such matters as at what stage it is prudent to withdraw from an incident; when the police station should be protected; how to deal with dead bodies; which way to direct traffic if the High Road were to be blocked by, say, a chemical spillage. The necessary equipment for handling these eventualities, right down to the books for entering such details of disaster as the property found on corpses, is stored in the police station basement. The advice for handling the public is essentially non-confrontational. 'Tactic One' is to 'be helpful and co-operative, treat the public as a customer'. Although officers are entitled to be 'firm and restrictive', and finally may use 'lawful force', they are instructed to return to Tactic One as soon as possible. Initial failure to gain control leads, senior officers are advised, to escalating, manpower-intensive problems. When 'high tension' policing *is* necessary, its objective is both to 'deter and discourage would-be criminals' and to offer the 'essential level of support for the community to enable them to continue their lawful business'.

During an emergency, the police are divided into two categories. 'Defenders', local officers who know the area, are tasked to protect previously identified vulnerable premises, such as Territorial Army drill halls, banks, off-licences, chemists, political party offices; 'enforcers', drawn from the TSG, operate under the guidance of local officers. The divisional detective chief inspector takes charge of intelligence (the contingency plans place great stress on 'rumour control'). Each sector of the division is profiled, and potential trigger points identified. Influential civilians, known as 'community intervenors', should be co-opted for their knowledge and calming influence, and neighbourhood watch co-ordinators used to reassure local residents. There are 'rendezvous' points, so that outside reinforcements do not blunder straight into the action – 'They could start World War Three without us even realising there were units on our ground,' said a Streatham officer. At the back of the blue binder are listed the home addresses of all the officers in the division, together with their ages, dates of entry to the force, and their local police stations.

An inspector, who had been a police constable in Brixton during the 1981 riots, said: 'We were not organised as we should have been. We were told "You, you and you, get into that van." We found we were on a shield detail with no training; we didn't even know how to hold the shields.' We were only wearing ordinary helmets.' He rejected the contention that equipping the police in paramilitary style simply raises the stakes and makes violence more likely. He said he would like the Met in future to go 'the whole hog' with baton rounds (plastic bullets) and CS gas. He held a book a foot or two from my face to show how close rioters get to the front line of police. 'They would not approach that close if there was a guy kneeling there about to fire a baton round; they wouldn't come within six feet of the shields,' he said. 'The police should react more nearly to the level of violence used against them. We cannot justify the number of injuries that we suffer. Casualties are too high; we're not cannon fodder and we should be afforded more protection than we get.'

During the Wapping printers' dispute, each night started, said the inspector, with ordinary PCs – 'guys out of the canteen' – having things thrown at them. It was not until officers had been hurt that units in riot gear were deployed. He said: 'Take your lager louts on a Saturday night. It is a one-way street of violence with police ending up in hospital with broken noses. No one is saying, "Hey, this can't go on." Police are pushed and shoved; blows are exchanged. Police go down in a hail of this, that and the other. I'm damn sure that if there were a line of twelve yapping Alsatians across the road, the protesters wouldn't come anywhere near those police officers. That's the degree of protection we ought to be afforded. Look worldwide: in Germany you don't see them pressing up against police like that any more, and their police never seem to sustain the injuries we sustain.'

About sixty Streatham officers were shield-trained, which

224

committed them to a two-day session at Hounslow every six months. TSG officers, the front-line troops for riot control, spend twelve days a year at Riot City. According to one instructor, they are not popular with the staff, often acting like overgrown schoolboys: the week before my visit, they had deliberately set off the alarms. The TSG have a reputation for arrogance, and some divisional officers fear that its units are capable of similar excesses to those that had discredited its predecessor, the Special Patrol Group. These doubters regret that the TSG concentrates so much on public order. Any 'élite' corps, trained to a pitch for confrontations that seldom happen, can over-react. The TSG is not the CRS (the French riot police), and there are safeguards to prevent its units becoming a police force within a police force – service in the group is restricted to four years, and the length of time two officers may remain partners is limited – but one former SPG officer acknowledged that the TSG is a more macho outfit than the SPG had been.

At the time of my visit to Riot City, the facility was commanded by a self-confident, ambitious Ulsterman, Chief Superintendent George Crawford, a former first-class rugby referee who achieved fame in 1985 by leaving the field during a match as a protest against violent play. He had been a ground commander in Brixton in 1981, and for several years had taken charge of the shield-equipped units at the Notting Hill Carnival. The Hounslow complex cost £10 million to develop, and has an annual budget of £2 million. It is, said Mr Crawford, a 'Rolls-Royce' site; even the CRS only have ex-army camps in which to train. Like the rest of his staff – five senior officers, three sergeants and forty PCs – he wore a blue pullover, blue overall trousers, and soft-soled boots, which gave him and them the air of commandos rather than of policemen. Riot City is, he acknowledged, a macho location, where it would be easy to become infected with the notion that the world is a hostile place. 'You can actually be fighting the war every day,' he said. 'Police officers' attitudes change out there. They are placed in an arena where in the main they have got to be seen as bigger and stronger, and to have more bottle than the next man.' He was concerned that officers did not confuse the training for the real thing. 'Anyone who has actually been in the middle of a serious riot and says he enjoys it is a fool. Simple as that. It is the most frightening and dangerous thing you'll ever do, and quite truthfully your life is on the line. The one thing that is difficult to put across here is that this is play-acting.'

Mr Crawford admired the senior officers who volunteer for shield training when they could be sitting quietly behind their desks. Shoulder to shoulder with their men, their reputations can be 'killed stone dead' by one bad decision, he said. 'They have got to be capable of dirtying their hands, getting in amongst the men, and stopping any behaviour that's less than satisfactory. That is their job. Total control and domination of the officers they are working with.' An inspector told me that, when violence breaks out at a demonstration, a busload of coppers are hard to handle. 'Their instinct is to pile out and get stuck in. It is difficult when you see your colleagues being assaulted, not to react with excessive force,' he said.

Riot City is dominated by a control tower. One million pounds' worth of video equipment scans the mocked-up streets, and a sound system allows the riot 'controller' to intimidate the trainee officers with sounds such as the shattering of plate glass. It was nearly dark when I began my tour, and newly arrived officers jogged gingerly in the gloom, limbering up for the 'riot' ahead. Mr Crawford first showed me the 'violent man' complex, in which instructors wielding iron bars defy trainees to disarm and arrest them. 'It actually happens every day somewhere in London,' said Mr Crawford. In real situations his own instructors – most of whom are superfit; several are international weight-lifters – act as 'SWAT' (Special Weapons and Tactics) squads, sometimes alone, sometimes in conjunction with Scotland Yard's firearms branch. (An officer of the rank of commander can authorise the use of lethal firearms, while only the Commissioner or his deputy can sanction non-lethal plastic bullets and CS gas, a distinction that underlines the relative political sensibilities of the two ultimate police responses.) A much publicised raid on a Yardie stronghold had first been simulated at Riot City. 'It's all about professionalism, having the expertise and doing the job well,' said Mr Crawford. In one hangar stood a gleaming row of armour-plated Landrovers, which each weighed three and a half tons and cost £50,000. They can be driven at ninety miles an hour, which they were when SWAT teams rushed to Hungerford after Michael Ryan went on the rampage. But at four miles to the gallon, they are not the ideal vehicle for pottering around in. They provide police critics with a handy metaphor for modern policing: they bristle with armour, are excellent at fast response, but inappropriate for the day-to-day business of old-style patrolling. (The police had argued that they should be painted dirty grey as in Northern Ireland, but it had been considered politically advisable to make them a highly visible white.)

Mr Crawford showed me TV pictures of riots that took place before the police were properly organised. Police believe the character of street violence changed at the Notting Hill Carnival of 1976, when officers scrambled to seize dustbin lids to ward off missiles. Shields were used for the first time in 1977 at Lewisham, when a National Front demonstration was attacked by anti-fascists. But officers were still not trained, and Mr Crawford's TV pictures showed disorganised police scurrying this way and that like rabbits caught in a bright light. In 1981 at Brixton, police still wore regulation helmets, which are as useful against flying bricks as a silk parasol against a downpour. Thereafter came what the police would describe as necessary 'professionalism', and what their critics see as a paramilitary tendency out of keeping with the desired aim of policing society by consent.

The Hounslow site was bought from the Ministry of Defence in 1981, and in September that year the Association of Chief Police Officers (ACPO) met to consider the altered urban and political landscape; two years later a working party, which took advice from the Royal Hong Kong Police, produced a 'Public Order Manual of Tactical

Options and Related Matters'. The manual was 'restricted' to the 270 officers of ACPO rank. (ACPO represents the leadership of the forty-three forces in England and Wales and the Royal Ulster Constabulary and enjoys a special relationship with the Home Office.) The switch of emphasis and its implications for resources, recommended by a small group of unelected people meeting in private, flew in the face of Lord Scarman's report on the 1981 disorders, which had advised that changes in policing should be made with the co-operation of, among others, Parliament and local communities. The new practices were condemned by TV journalist Gerry Northam in his 1988 book *Shooting in the Dark*. He wrote: 'The stage had been set for the most significant shift in police strategy Britain had known for a century and a half, but nothing was made public. The preparations were carried out in total secrecy.' The police, with their proclivity to screen out what they don't wish to hear, had leapt on Scarman's recommendation that they should be better equipped and trained, and had ignored his caveat about accountability. To the police, equipment and training are operational matters, and, therefore, of no concern either to police authorities or to the wider public represented through consultative groups. The film of bewildered young cops staggering around London's streets made it clear that professionalism had been, as Scarman said, necessary; but, by acting in secret, the police had fuelled the suspicion (and hatred) that contributes to making street confrontations so antagonistic. When the police fight demonstrators or urban rioters, there is paranoia on both sides of the front line.

A number of senior police from the Middle and Far East had visited Hounslow, and had, I was told, expressed amazement at the kid glove tactics that the British police employed. 'We'd have shot everyone – none of this nonsense – blasted them to bits,' said one visiting officer. British police love stories like that: it is a way of saying to their liberal critics that, by comparison with what happens elsewhere, the British police are civic minded and reasonable, and that it follows, therefore, that complaints about their transgressions are trivial and carping. In fact, favourable comparisons with brutal, inefficient forces elsewhere merely confer a seal of approval that reads 'these goods are not as shoddy as some others available elsewhere.'

The Riot Act was removed from the statute book in 1967, and riot police work on the principle of 'no more force than is necessary'. But rank and file officers tend to regard major street violence much in the way that a regiment regards past battles. Officers talk about a 'return match' with the Broadwater Farm rioters; in the collective mind, despite the life prison sentences handed out to those convicted of PC Blakelock's murder, there remains a substantial score to settle. The next London riot will require strong police leadership. One intelligent and fast-rising police officer, talking about preparations for disorder, said that if people were killed, the police would have to be ready to defend temporary mortuaries against rioters seeking to recover the bodies of their 'brethren'. He carefully avoided the word 'coloured', but the implication of his remark was unmistakable.

By the time Mr Crawford and I had finished our film show at Riot City, the shield-training outside was in full swing. In a riot, the front ranks of the police are the foot soldiers, deployed in units of five linked like the first two rows of a rugby scrum behind three long shields. From behind them operate the snatch squads, mobile officers with short, round shields, the medics, the photographers, and 'evidence gatherers' who are wired for sound. In the confusion of a riot it is far easier to seize people than to build a case against them that will stand up to cross-examination many months later in court. The police also use video cameras to identify offenders: their cameramen mingle with the hordes of others – professional and amateur – who now tape demonstrations.

Some of the trainees, including senior officers, rehearsed street manoeuvres under the direction of constable instructors; others, using their shields as umbrellas, stormed buildings beneath a hail of bricks thrown from upper windows (police fighting their way into houses, often to dislodge squatters, have had objects as heavy as refrigerators dropped on them); still others practised holding their ground and their nerve while instructors hurled petrol bombs at them. (The Hounslow training centre buys three thousand empty milk bottles a month.)

After an early supper, all the officers underwent baton-gun training. The technique was for the shield serials who had been bearing the brunt of a confrontation to fall back, their places to be taken by fresh cadres trained to open their ranks to allow the baton gunners clear lines of fire. Within the limited space of the hangar, the exercise was slow-moving and unrealistic. Rioters could certainly have charged the front line long before the baton gunners had taken up their positions. The present gun – the L67 baton discharger – was developed in 1942, and is little more than a pistol with a stock welded on one end and a 38 mm barrel on the other. It is far from accurate, and the police fear mistakes and legal action if it is ever fired in anger. The consequences of a poor weapon or its inefficient deployment have been highlighted by experiences in Northern Ireland, where sixteen people have died after being hit by plastic bullets. The search is now on for something accurate and non-lethal to take its place. Home Office scientists, under pressure from ACPO, have been testing a number of non-deadly 'stopping' weapons, including a British-made gun, the Arwen Ace, already used by many American police forces.

The final exercise of the night was a pitched battle between the trainees and the instructors, who, dressed in running shoes and tracksuits, clearly revelled in their fleet-footed opportunity to run rings round the nervous and unpractised divisional cohorts. The trainees' brief was that a petrol bomb factory was hidden somewhere in Riot City; they had to sweep the area to locate it. (The heat of the petrol bombs warmed the cold January night three storeys above the fray.) The 'rioters' led them a merry dance, and won hands down. There was, I suspect, great relief beneath the helmets when a whistle blast announced the end of hostilities. The following day the trainees, who included a few women, were to test themselves in the 'violent man' complex, and practise search techniques in specially adapted houses and vehicles.

A few weeks after visiting Riot City, I went with a serial of Streatham officers (one inspector, two sergeants and twenty PCs) to a mass demonstration of students protesting against government proposals to replace student grants with loans. The march through central London was expected to be peaceful, but a similar protest three months previously had degenerated into violence when mounted police guarding Westminster Bridge clashed with students trying to reach Parliament to lobby MPs. The police claimed that the trouble was provoked by a small group of determined lefties who had taken charge of the head of the march and led it from the agreed route. The confrontation was the most violent on London's streets since Wapping, and the day ended with seventy arrests and a large number of injuries. Many of those caught up in the violence were unworldly middle-class kids and, whatever the origins of the skirmish, the police image took a battering. A sixth form student at my son's college had the lead letter in the *Independent* a few days later. She first described what she saw: 'Panic broke out. People were screaming and desperately pushing away from the centre of the road. I could see mounted police charging straight through the middle of the crowd. I saw a boy fall to the ground and smash his head as he was trying to run. My friend was hit in the face by a policeman, and others were pulled off buildings where they had climbed to escape the charging horses.' She then reported what these scenes had done to her attitude towards the police: 'I have always defended the police in arguments with friends. I believed that they were our protectors and our safety. This has completely changed my whole outlook, not only on the police but on our society today. Mrs Thatcher travels around the world extolling the virtues of our free and democratic society, and yet the Government resorts to unnecessary and wanton brutality to quell the voices it does not want to hear.'

The demonstration I attended was staged on a Saturday

when Parliament was not sitting, so it was hoped there would be no set-piece confrontations with the police. Student leaders and senior police had been meeting for weeks to agree the route; the National Union of Students were to provide two hundred and fifty stewards; key buildings like the South African Embassy and 10 Downing Street were to be heavily guarded.

The Streatham detachment met in the canteen shortly after 8 a.m. They were led by an inspector, John Walsh, who the previous day had attended a Scotland Yard briefing on the demonstration. He reminded his serial, which included one woman sergeant and three WPCs, about the previous violence. The ground rules this day were to let the fifteen thousand demonstrators 'within reason do what they want while marching along, and hope that it will be a peaceful day . . . the stewards want a peaceful march as well, but you will have some militants there who will see it as a means of making a political point, however valid that might be'. There would be police horses, which, although they were not to be deployed unless there was trouble, might provoke students with memories of the battle of Westminster Bridge. Shield serials were to be kept out of sight, unless needed. The police commander for the day, designated 'Gold', was Deputy Assistant Commissioner Bob Innes, coincidentally the DAC for Four Area and therefore for the Streatham division. The officers were told to bring their truncheons, just in case, and finally advised to bring a good book, as they would be several hours in the coach.

Our first stop was a huge feeding station at Buckingham Gate, close to Scotland Yard. The streets nearby were packed with police buses, and we queued in the drizzle. It was still over three hours till the demonstration, but students in black leather jackets clutching loud-hailers and banners were already meandering towards the Embankment assembly point. Breakfast was excellent: it is force policy to keep the troops happy with decent 'grub'.

The three PCs nearest me at breakfast were graduates, two of whom had been on demonstrations during their student days. Their policy, they said, was to chat with the

232

protesters; usually it worked, but one recalled a demonstrator who simply replied 'class war' to every remark addressed to him. Later in the bus, as we watched rather unkempt and scruffy young people gathering for the march, the collective mood was less mature. 'What wouldn't I give for a flame-thrower,' said one PC, and got an appreciative guffaw for his sentiments.

We did, as Mr Walsh had forecast, wait several hours in the bus. The boredom and frustration caused by being cooped up for hours before the action started appeared to me to undo any good that a decent breakfast might have achieved. (The early arrival also adds substantially to the hefty overtime bill for such days.) Mr Innes said later: 'There's an old policing principle about dealing with public order that we should "take the ground". If you leave it too late, the police coaches start colliding with transport for the demonstrators. If they get on the ground before we do, there's a right hotch-potch, and the day starts with conflict. Whereas if our policeman are on the ground early, the day takes the shape we want.' The prompt arrival is part of the new 'professionalism'. Older officers remembered disasters early in their careers; one had been on a bus that had been thronged by already gathered demonstrators, and another, travelling on public transport, had emerged with his serial from an Underground station to find himself at the heart of a mini-riot.

A senior officer said that police had to show more discipline during a protest march than usual, both because inept reactions could provoke trouble, and because they were being watched by many thousand people and by the media. He said that 'discretion', by which he meant not arresting people, was vital, unless the demonstration threatened to get out of hand. Acts of minor lawlessness that might normally lead to arrest should be overlooked. Officers had to play the numbers game. One counter-demonstrator, provocatively heckling a march, might be safely arrested; five hundred marching in opposition would have to be carefully policed. For a supervising officer, the key was not to transmit worry, 'even if everything is about to go pear-shaped'.

Mr Walsh kept his serial as informed as he could. The more the officers knew of the full picture, he said, the easier they would be to control if trouble were to break out. The serial's assignment was to police the head of the march, a high visibility role that would require exemplary behaviour. 'I want you ten yards apart. I don't want you creeping up behind one another and having a chat. Press and media are going to be there because there was trouble last time, so we don't want to direct any attention towards ourselves in a bad light,' he said.

The march, led by the women's section of the National Union of Students, was uneventful until a small group staged a sit-down on Lambeth Bridge. The target of their anger appeared to be the NUS leadership as much as the police, for what the more militant demonstrators took to be pusillanimous tactics. While the vast majority of marchers disappeared towards their planned rally in Kennington Park and radio messages flew the few hundred yards between New Scotland Yard and police on the spot, heavy rain, sufficient to dampen the strongest ardour, soaked seated protesters. The soggy and raggedy rearguard stumbled to their feet, and set off in pursuit of their compromised comrades. The Streatham serial, after failing to find its bus for a while, returned to base eight hours after setting off. The following day the Yard would mobilise again; fifteen thousand 'Not in My Back Yard' citizens of Kent were to march through central London to protest against the route of the Channel Tunnel rail link.

If there is one aspect of police work as politically sensitive as the control of public disorder, it is the use of firearms. And if there is one other Metropolitan Police installation as guarded and out of public view as Riot City, it is the weapons training centre at Lippitts Hill in the middle of Epping Forest. Three horrendous shooting errors in the mid-eighties – the gunning down of film director Steven Waldorf, who had been mistaken for a wanted criminal, the paralysing of Mrs Cherry Groce by an armed police inspector hunting her son and the accidental killing of John Shorthouse, the son of a man wanted for a serious crime –

had indicated that the police were either trigger happy or inept. Such highly publicised mistakes, together with the ambushing and shooting of armed criminals in operations that appeared more in character with the SAS than with the tradition of unarmed bobbies, revealed that the police were 'tooled up'. Officers openly carrying weapons, including sub-machine guns, stalked the concourses at Heathrow; diplomatic and royalty protection officers bore arms as a matter of routine; officers in fast response cars stocked with small arsenals patrolled the motorways. These changes appeared to signal that, just as the country had woken one day to find it employed police forces equipped and trained for paramilitary operations, so armed police had surreptitiously stolen into cop shops all round the country and walked off with dear old Dixon's size-ten boots.

As a matter of historical record, British 'bobbies' have been armed in the past. In the 1870s and 1880s, the era of armed burglars like Charles Peace when guns could be bought and sold without licence, constables were issued with revolvers to go on suburban patrol. Immediately after the First World War the Metropolitan Police was armed to counter an IRA offensive. The Met today possesses 1,600 weapons as against 2,000 in the 1920s, when, one senior police officer estimated, there were nearly 2,000 armed police on duty every night. There were armed motor patrols – their recent reintroduction created a minor furore – and an armed guard on every gundealer in the capital. The police were once again heavily armed during the Second World War, but by the mid–1960s they had few weapons and, as the proportion of ex-servicemen in the force declined, a diminishing reservoir of skill.

The present arrangements – a corps of full-time arms experts responsible for both training and major operations, backed by 'authorised firearms officers' (AFOs) on division – have evolved since the murder of three plain-clothes, unarmed officers in a 'Q' car near Wormwood Scrubs Prison in August 1966. It was not the shooting itself which led to reform – unarmed police, like unarmed anybody else, will always be vulnerable – but the chaotic state of preparation and training that the hunt for the principal gunman revealed. Harry Roberts, who is still serving a life sentence, had trained as a British serviceman in Malaya. Shortly after the murders, he equipped himself with a sleeping bag, rucksack and tinned food, and lay low in Epping Forest. Five hundred police were assembled to hunt for Roberts, and six revolvers were to be issued. But, when it came to handing them out, it emerged that there were only two authorised shots amongst the five hundred. In his book, *London's Armed Police*, Chief Inspector Michael Waldren described how two of the remaining weapons were issued to men who had served in the army, and the last two to officers willing to 'have a go'. As a result of this near fiasco, the Metropolitan firearms branch was established. Known for most of its existence as D11, it is now designated PT17, and has its headquarters at Old Street police station in east London and its principal training facility at Lippitts Hill. The science of policing is constructed brick by brick in reaction to events, and each major armed incident since the hunt for Harry Roberts – such as the Knightsbridge Spaghetti House siege in 1975 – has refined operational practice.

Mr Waldren was the Met's chief firearms instructor at the time I was writing this book. It was he who was called to inquests and trials to explain police practice on the increasingly frequent occasions when police shot a criminal dead. He articulated well the unique responsibility of an armed police officer: 'What causes such great feeling about the carrying of weapons? Why is there such a big gap between this and what a police officer normally does?' he asked rhetorically, and answered his own questions. 'The difference is that in normal police operations there is no intention that someone should die. Using a gun is a big leap. We have no death penalty. The highest judge in the land cannot condemn someone to death, but in effect that is what a police officer might be doing when he squeezes the trigger. In certain circumstances, he is justified, and that conveys an enormous amount of power. That feels wrong, and therefore we say as a society: "Hey, mister, if we are going to give you such authority, you better be able to justify it, and prove you got it right." '

PT17 is tiny, only seventy-seven officers. The most experienced, known as 'Level One', comprise the Met firearms instructors, from whom one team – an inspector, two sergeants and six PCs – are set aside on twenty-four-hour standby for a week at a time to respond to major incidents. Level One officers also advise and sometimes accompany officers from specialist squads on robbery operations. (The fatal shooting of six armed robbers in four incidents between 1987 and 1989 were all carried out by Level One officers.) They have access to a wide range of weapons, including pump-action shotguns, sub-machine-guns, Browning pistols and a variety of high-powered rifles. Level Two marksmen – eighteen officers divided into three teams – serve for two years before either being further trained for Level One or returning to division. They are armed only with standard revolvers, and their intended role is restricted to checking buildings, searching and containing. If the incident escalates, for example into a hunt for a dangerous person, if hostages are taken or automatic weapons suspected, a Level One team takes over. On division there are between two and a half and three thousand AFOs, whose role is restricted to initial response and containment. Cherry Groce was shot by a divisional officer, and the emphasis since that incident, which sparked riots in Brixton in September 1985, has been to deploy fulltime, professional marksmen.

One December day long before dawn, I joined a Level Two team at Gipsy Hill police station for an operation that would, before the shooting of Mrs Groce, have been handled by the division. PT17 officers were already donning body armour and buckling the shoulder and belt holsters that carry the standard police weapon, a Model 10 Smith & Wesson .38 Special. A few days earlier a WPC had been called by a man who complained that a neighbour had been taking pot shots at his dogs with an air rifle and with a gun that fired the red paint pellets used in war games. The policewoman visited the 'gunman' and discovered that his bedsit was an arsenal of what looked to her untrained eye like real weapons, including a powerful rifle, ammunition and combat equipment. He was naïve – 'You won't tell anyone, will you?' – and had been solicitous towards her, saying that he would go to her defence in the street, if need be, with his bayonet. But his room at the top of the house, could, she felt, be turned into a redoubt. She visited his local pub, and chatted to people who knew him, determining that he was certainly a screwball and might conceivably be dangerous. He had claimed to casual acquaintances that he routinely carried weapons, and, since the Michael Ryan massacre, no chances have been taken with the 'Rambo' types – those, in the words of one PT17 officer, who 'boast of going out into the wilds and strangling rabbits with their bare hands'.

Under the command of a Streatham inspector, the PT17 team together with divisional officers split into three vehicles, and parked at strategic points near the 'gunman's' front door. It was a street of reasonably substantial, Edwardian semi-detached houses, some of which were divided into bedsits and some of which had been reconverted into family homes by the professional classes. There were five of us – three PT17 officers, large men made extra bulky by the flak jackets they wore beneath their combat uniforms, the WPC and myself – in a rather battered general purpose Vauxhall Cavalier saloon, which attracted surprisingly little attention from the gradually accelerating stream of early morning workers. As often happened, the communications played up. One of the PT17 men's covert radio appeared to be dead. 'Communications are the worst thing in this job; we can send people to the moon, but we can't speak to each other next door. We have been on a lot of jobs recently that have failed at the last instant because of communications,' he grumbled. 'Sometimes I think we'd get better results with tin cans joined together with pieces of string.' He suggested that the Met put relay stations on tall buildings across London, so that officers everywhere had access to a strong signal.

The targeted man had a previous minor conviction, so

we had with us a copy of his criminal record, which showed a wild-eyed man with long, lank hair. Our wait lasted two hours; from time to time the PT17 sergeant left the car and slipped into the garden behind the suspect's house to see whether there was a light in his room. Night shaded into day, and we felt over-exposed. The cars moved to another street while the sergeant observed the suspect's front door from the comfort of a nearby house. 'The bastard's going to be fed cups of tea; the advantages of rank!' half-grumbled one of the PCs.

But there could scarcely have been time to get the kettle on before a shout came over the radio 'Left, left', meaning that the suspect had set out and turned left from his front gate, and was therefore heading straight towards us. Two armed officers leapt from the car, pulled on cotton caps emblazoned with the word 'POLICE', and seized the suspect at the corner of the street. There were no dramatics; he was not flung to the ground, and the police did not draw their weapons. The suspect was searched and a cosh found up his sleeve – 'That's ten for starters,' said a PC. He was handcuffed and taken back to his bedsit, which was – just as the WPC had described – either a fantasist's den or the hideaway of a very dangerous man.

He was bitterly upset at being arrested. 'I'm not a criminal, I'm not a violent person. I'm not a terrorist; I wouldn't have asked the young lady in if I thought it was wrong. I'm not going to run away,' he said when his arms were pinioned behind him. When he talked, he compensated for his handcuffed state by emphasising points with his knees. The WPC gave him a cigarette, removing it from his lips each time the ash threatened to fall. One wall of his shabby room was a shrine to violence, stacked with combat equipment: a camouflage jacket, webbing belt, bandoliers of ammunition, torches, gas masks, binoculars, smoke grenades, a variety of coshes, handcuffs, a cigarette lighter fashioned like a hand grenade. The initials 'SAS' had been indelibly written on ammunition pouches, and there was an SAS cap badge on a khaki beret. Scattered around the room were helmets, boots, belts and knives. There was a crossbow on which the letters 'PLO' were engraved and four or five full-sized guns, including two .22 air rifles and a replica AK–47, for which he said he had paid £184 two days previously (there is no law against the sale or possession of replica weapons). The police went methodically through the equipment, while the handcuffed man sustained a running commentary: 'That one does no more harm than a water-pistol . . . you can't take my stuff away . . . I do it for a hobby; it's like playing golf . . . It's all paid for and everything.' On the wall opposite the shrine, above a rack of 'combat' videos like *Rambo, First Blood* and *Young Warriors*, were pictures of the man playing war games in some clearly foreign location and also in his back garden. Beneath one, of himself and a friend clutching rifles on a mountainside, he had written his name with the rather pathetic additions 'VC, SAS (Capt.)'.

The suspect said defiantly: 'To be honest, I do the "business", probably better than your people. I've done the training in Israel, Cyprus and Lebanon. Over here, though, it's civilised, and I just keep my gear.' The inspector, having decided that the man, despite his big talk and his agitated state, fell basically into the harmless (rather than Michael Ryan) category, treated him gently: 'It's all got to be done properly for everyone's peace of mind. It's better to be overcautious and to get it right. You'd expect us to be professional.' While this conversation went on, other police lifted carpets, levered themselves through a trapdoor into the roof, took the bed apart. Satisfied that what they saw was all there was, the police gathered together those items, including the crossbow and some ammunition, that were possibly dangerous, and we and the suspect returned to the police station.

It had been, as one of the PT17 men said, 'a very low-key, straightforward job', and, as such, far more typical of armed police operations than the shoot-outs that make headline news. An inspector said that in the first half of 1988, PT17 officers only removed their guns from their holsters on 50 per cent of operations. However, he added: 'We are deploying more trained, armed officers against criminals, and criminals are prepared to use their weapons, not simply firing a shot through a bank ceiling. The level of violence now used by criminals is much greater than it was, therefore officers must be prepared to fire to ensure their own safety.' He listed four circumstances in which shots were likely to be fired: when the criminal was known to be 'especially dangerous', perhaps having declared that he would never surrender to police; when criminals take drugs to give themselves courage; when criminals had previously fired guns; and when the weapons carried were, like pump-action shotguns, particularly awesome.

'The price we pay for countering these threats is that we are seen to be much more overtly armed. But still the first person likely to respond to an armed incident is an unarmed police officer, and criminals are prepared to use guns against him,' he said. (A few days earlier a PC panda driver had been shot dead in Coventry.) Despite this, trained police officers are not in favour of arming all police. The inspector said: 'Arming all would be useless. The man with the gun has got to want to use it and be capable of using it.' His argument was that few would wish to have the responsibility. 'Once you have pulled the trigger, if there is any suggestion of wrongdoing, you are before the courts. There is no hiding; you risk your career and even gaol. If you *arrest* the wrong person, there are no terrible consequences; if you *shoot* the wrong person, there are.' All the PT17 officers I met made the same point: a decision they have to take in less than a second may later be judged according to different criteria in the unhurried, calm environment of a court. A senior PT17 officer said: 'It is very difficult to convince yourself that the jury decision is based on the same information that the officer had when he made his decision to shoot. The jury has all the surrounding circumstances. With the benefit of hindsight, maybe the officer would not have pulled the trigger.'

I was to be exposed later on a range at Lippitts Hill to just how difficult it is to decide when to shoot, but I did feel that officers' protests about the jeopardy they face would have been more convincing if courts did occasionally

241

find individuals culpable. Anyone entrusted, in Mr Waldren's graphic analysis, with something of the powers of a hanging judge must understand the implications.

I was told that no reliable psychological tests exist to determine someone's suitability to handle firearms. 'It would be nice if there were a test or yardstick we could apply, but the present tests are not worth the paper they are written on,' said the inspector. Training officers rely on their perceptions on the range, and they reject officers who are either over-eager or too withdrawn. The inspector continued: 'You have got to make a value judgement. Being with someone tells you an awful lot about him. A supervisor gets the feeling "there is no way that person should carry a gun".' He agreed there was 'glamour' attached to being armed – like driving fast cars or being in the CID – but said that, for that reason, no policeman is allowed to carry weapons until he is at least twenty-five and has had five years' service. 'That way the gung ho is knocked out of him. Until then, he hasn't really worked out what being a police officer is all about, never mind being an armed one. We want enthusiasm, but we want it controlled,' said the inspector. When a police officer does shoot someone, his authority to carry a gun is automatically suspended until his reaction to the shooting has been assessed and the incident investigated.

The recent deaths of criminals at police hands raise the natural question as to why police do not shoot to wound or disarm. The inspector said: 'It is a misconception that police officers are marksmen who can shoot in the leg or shoot a gun out of a man's hand. It is not possible at the level of training and skill that we can afford. After fifteen years, it wouldn't be feasible for me.' Mr Waldren said: 'Everyone has a mental picture of the circumstances in which they would use a firearm to defend themselves. But you ask any of the guys who've actually fired a shot, and it's not the way they imagined it.' Critics, he said, cannot think themselves into the situations that face armed officers. 'Lots of experts will write things about how I should have taken a rolling dive, and come up and kneed the gunman.

Who are these people who have written all this nonsense? They have never done it in their lives. Either they are leaping on the bandwagon, trying to make names for themselves in the security field, or they are politicians trying to get their names in the paper. It all adds to the pressures on the poor chap who's fired the shot.'

Mr Waldren no more wanted an all-armed force than did his inspector, denying that it would do anything to prevent massacres like Hungerford. (Such bouts of uncontrolled slaughter are, of course, far more common in the United States, where every police officer carries a gun.) 'Every step you take along the way of giving police a particular firearm or a particular set of body armour has to be carefully considered, because you can never go back. All we may have done is give the police officer some protection, but that may change the public perception of what is going on,' he said.

'There was an awful lot of fuss recently about how we acquired machine-guns. We'd had them since 1975. The only difference was that they hadn't been seen like they are at Heathrow. As long as people are not aware of what we've got and what we're doing, most aren't bothered. Most of us, myself included, get indoctrinated by what we see on TV. When the good guy gets shot, he's shot in the shoulder; if you shoot at a car, it will explode; it is possible to wing people, to shoot them in the leg; when you shout at a man "give up", and he's a baddie, but not too bad a baddie, he'll give up. All these are total myths.' He told the story of a recent ambush at a post office. PT17 officers surrounded a robbery gang as they tried to escape, and one of the criminals went for a gun. 'By all the rules that bloke should have been shot. I would have shot him, but they didn't. They leapt on him instead. The gun was a toy. Now what kind of idiot, when he is surrounded by police with real guns, would go for a toy. He's got to be nuts. No one on TV would do that; he'd throw his hands up and shout "It's a toy, it's a toy." Life isn't like that, but that is what the public expect. So when they read that someone's been shot in an armed robbery, they believe there has been an escalation in police methods. What you read in the paper will bear no resemblance to what actually happened. You end up with innuendos and semi-criticisms that are based on a story that didn't happen. Minds are made up on faulty information: it is very frustrating.'

Lippitts Hill, the Met firearms training centre, is based on a former Second World War anti-aircraft encampment and PoW camp. Inside the gate there is a large concrete statue of a seated man created by a German prisoner; and pictures of PoW soccer teams and of an ornate Italian chapel fashioned out of a Nissen hut hang on the canteen walls. Elderly Germans occasionally arrive at the gates asking to be shown round: they must feel a strong sense of familiarity, since Lippitts Hill, with its creosoted huts, clearly remains much as it must have been in their day. The camp was bought by the Met in 1960, and first used as an adventure training site for police cadets. It still serves other purposes as well as weapons training: it is the Met heliport; police horses retire to its meadows; and a high mast beams 999 calls throughout north London. The complex includes one fifty-metre and three twenty-five-metre ranges; an indoor shooting gallery in which still and moving pictures are projected onto a bullet-proof screen, where I was to discover that deciding when to fire a gun is a hair-raising business; a house and series of rooms, where trainees learn to search, negotiate and – when necessary – take by storm; and, of course, an armoury. The courses range from the basic ten-day technique and tactics given to divisional AFOs, to six-week instructors' courses. The day I was there, diplomatic and royalty protection officers were being trained in body-guard techniques.

My guide was Inspector Alex Moir, a Scot from near Aberdeen, who had managed to combine a childhood ambition to be a policeman with a love of shooting: 'To be able to hit something from a thousand yards is always an achievement; to hit it in the middle is even better.' He had given up chances of promotion to stay with firearms. Mr Moir explained the narrow distinction between 'shoot to kill' – which, if deliberate and unnecessary, would be a criminal offence, whoever pulled the trigger – and 'shoot

244

to stop' – which, when dealing with someone who might shoot back, is essential. 'The gun may be the only thing left to stop someone killing you. You are doing to him what he would otherwise do to you. For the greatest chance of hitting him, we must aim at the largest bit, not the bits that move, because they could have moved in the time it takes to squeeze the trigger. There is no way you can guarantee that you will kill someone with a bullet – there are people walking round with all sorts of bullet holes in them. Equally there is no way you can shoot not to kill,' he said. 'Yes, you must try to avoid the use of deadly force, but the bottom line is to stop a man if his actions threaten another life.'

My visit to Lippitts Hill took place before the April 1989 shooting of two armed robbers after a bungled post office robbery in north-west London. However, following the deaths at police hands of four men in the previous two years, there was already considerable concern (among civil libertarians, if not the wider public) about the police tactic of allowing a crime to reach the point at which the use of firearms became likely. Critics pointed to the danger to which members of the public are exposed, and argued that the laws of conspiracy exist to enable the police to pre-empt serious crimes. The penalties for conspiracy are at least as severe as those for the commission of major crimes. They rejected the police argument that juries wilfully acquitted guilty professional criminals, asserting that the fault lay with the police for presenting cases inadequately.

Mr Moir, who shared the hostile police attitude towards conspiracy charges, outlined the options available when police get information that an armed robbery is about to take place. They can attempt to scoop up all the people known to be plotting the raid, and prosecute them for conspiracy, with what he would see to be the difficulties of making the case stick. They can allow the robbery to go ahead, and seek to arrest the criminals later. 'Unfortunately during the robbery two people die, and the next day's headlines are that the police knew about the robbery and did nothing about it,' he said. 'The third option is to arrive

armed, with superiority of weapons and numbers in order
to try to avoid shooting, when the criminals are there in
their stolen vehicles, stocking masks on and guns in their
hands. You arrest them just before they carry out the robbery, which is the only time that you can prove that they
were in actual fact going to commit it. It's a finely tuned
decision. They have a choice. Most immediately drop their
guns, but some don't. You then have three-eighths of a
second and later ten weeks in court to decide whether you
were right or wrong. You must go for the body, because
you need forty per cent luck to shoot something out of
someone's hand. Yes, you could shoot him in the leg, which
would bring him down, but what happens if he fires as he
is going down?'

The main reason why more criminals are shot now than
were a few years ago, most police would argue, is that more
criminals carry weapons. In the early seventies, said Mr
Moir, an armed team were committed perhaps once every
six months; now they deploy a team two or three times a
day. In 1987 there were roughly five robberies a day involving firearms in London. Priorities had to be decided, said
Mr Moir. 'Are we looking for the most dangerous man in
London? Or is it something we can put off until tomorrow?'
He said that on the day that Steven Waldorf was mistakenly
shot, Scotland Yard received a telephone call from a perplexed reporter on the *Chicago Tribune*. That week seven
innocent people had been shot by the Chicago police, he
said, and there had not been a whisper to compare with
the British ballyhoo over one shooting. Although that argument has a comforting air about it, it proves no more than
that the police are vastly quicker on the draw elsewhere.

Mr Moir said: 'Firearms are just another tool in the
policeman's tool box to be used at the right place and time.'
Had the Metropolitan Police got it right? 'Probably the
number of times we issue guns is about right,' he replied,
'but no two calls are alike. Sometimes we find we need
more men and weapons; sometimes we go with too many.
It all goes back to the accuracy of the original information.'
I asked whether the police, by increasing the number of

weapons at their disposal, had made it more likely that criminals would go to crimes prepared to use deadly force. 'We could say that we will no longer be allowed to carry guns. Then we could not make mistakes. You could write a thesis on that one,' he replied, laughing at the notion. 'We could go to the next armed robbery with nothing – a loud hailer perhaps – and see how we got on.' Then he asked seriously: 'What causes villains to shoot with no police present and no resistance?' (While I was writing this chapter, two security men in the Midlands were shot and seriously injured by a gang who fled empty-handed.)

My tour of Lippitts Hill started in the armoury, a well-guarded, single-storey building. Mr Moir showed me the full range of guns, from the Mark 10 Smith & Wesson and Browning pistols through to Remington 870 12-bore pump-action shotguns, Heckler and Koch MP5 sub-machine-guns, and a variety of rifles, including Enfield 7.62mm sniper rifles, with which a good marksman can hit a man-sized target at up to six hundred yards. The collection included sawn-off shotguns, regularly used by criminals, and Mr Moir showed how these can be carried without being obvious beneath a coat – often hung by a piece of string. Why, I asked, did robbers favour the shotgun over handguns? Mr Moir simply pointed first a revolver and then a shotgun at me, and asked which was likely to influence me to open the till fastest.

We visited the house where police practise ending sieges and capturing armed criminals. (With a bit of plaster and a lick of paint, the house would have been fit for habitation.) One door is steel-plated so officers can practise smashing locks with sledge-hammers. 'It is,' said Mr Moir, 'extremely difficult to swing a sledge-hammer in a confined space.' But, he added, trying to kick in a plywood door can prove more hazardous. 'Your foot goes through, and won't come back again. You have a foot inside and a police officer outside.'

He took me to the short indoor range where officers are taught how to decide when to pull the trigger. Training is standard for all officers, so that, if something does go wrong, investigators know exactly how the officer concerned has been taught to respond to any given situation. Here, on his own territory, Inspector Moir soon demonstrated just how difficult it is to make a judgement when facing an armed man. He projected a number of still pictures onto the bullet-proof screen: they included a man lying asleep in bed with a revolver by his ear; a man grasping a shotgun which pointed at the ceiling; a man with an axe apparently about to cleave a PC armed only with a truncheon; an armed man wearing a stocking mask and holding a gun, who is bending over a prostrate body; and a man apparently slumped over a bar facing a barman with his hands up. Each picture presented a less than clear-cut situation in which the risk of shooting unnecessarily was finely balanced against the dangers of holding fire. My initial instinct was not to fire if possible, which is how, I was told, the large majority of officers approach these situations. When Mr Moir pointed out which of my hesitations had probably cost lives, I became, not gung ho, but certainly more prepared to shoot.

Next he showed moving pictures – a man who had seized his wife and a hostage from a battered wives' shelter leaping pell-mell from his car brandishing a revolver. I hesitated again, and the hostage was shot. The next video showed a gang running from the scene of a robbery towards a getaway car: that time the situation was (happily) too confused to shoot, but I was asked to describe the fleeing men and could not begin to, given the speed of the action. Mr Moir said: 'The aim is to change general thinking. We are turning a man from an unarmed to an armed PC.' It is a momentous step, and as I ineptly tried to decide when to pull the trigger I thought of Mr Waldren's image of the hanging judge.

I don't doubt the competence or integrity of the PT17 officers. But that much power must be kept in check by close supervision. Some barristers believe that the police could bring successful conspiracy charges if they were to prepare their cases more professionally. A determination by a judge and jury is obviously a better way to resolve criminal responsibility and just punishment than shoot-outs on the streets. For the moment the public may be prepared to accept that, since armed criminals understand the risk they are running, they have only themselves to blame for the fatal consequences. The police know there is nothing more fickle than the public mood in these matters. A run of 'success' can induce over-confidence. The British like their police to be unarmed. It would only take one error or one stray bullet for PT17 themselves to be back in the firing line, and with them the wider force.

10

Some Modest Reforms

The day I sat down to write this concluding chapter, the Metropolitan Police suffered an horrific own goal. The months I had been at work exactly coincided with the period the Met had devoted to responding to the £150,000 report into the force image that had been commissioned by Sir Peter Imbert. This had found that London's police operated in 'an atmosphere of shabby confusion'; that police officers felt both isolated and bewildered; that the public was often ill-served; and that a minority of officers were rude and insensitive. Imbert's response had been to launch yet another initiative to improve both image and performance. This was to be known with woolly imprecision as the 'Plus Programme', which sounded more like a worthy late night Channel Four offering than a clarion call to an embattled police force. Unluckily for Sir Peter and the Met's public relations staff, on the day of their press conference a High Court jury awarded £30,000 damages to a man whose confession to an armed robbery they decided had been fabricated by Flying Squad officers. Since the law moves with the alacrity of a hobbled goat, the wrong the jury redressed was by then seven years old. But the impact of the verdict swamped Sir Peter's PR exercise. *The Independent*, for example, reported the damages award across four columns on the front page, adding at the foot of the story the ironic cross-reference: 'Met's new image, page 6'.

The issuing of an instruction to police officers – that, for example, there shall be no more racial prejudice – is often mistaken for the desired deed itself. The tendency stems from a naïve belief that the best of intentions promulgated at the top are, by some process almost of osmosis, automati-

250

cally translated into good practice at the bottom. To errant members of the rank and file, force policy is rather like religion on Sundays for backsliding Christians: the distinction between right and wrong is fully understood, but not always adhered to in the rough and tumble of daily life. Sir Peter reinforced his 'Plus Programme' by issuing a booklet entitled 'Making It Happen' to the troops. The previous similar publication, issued by Imbert's predecessor, Sir Kenneth Newman, had been widely used, one retired chief superintendent told me, to prop up wobbly canteen tables.

The police shelter behind the reassuring notion that such abuse of their powers as there is can be laid at the door of a convenient bunch of scapegoats known popularly as 'rotten apples'. It is true obviously that criminal malpractice – at least of the order that winds up before High Court juries – is restricted to a relatively small number of evil policemen. But the question whether there is something endemic in police culture that nurtures the rotten apples is seldom addressed – at least by the police themselves. It is easy to blame wrongdoing entirely on the individuals who are caught and disgraced. In the community at large no man, as John Donne taught us, is an island; in a tightly knit, highly structured organisation like a police force, that famous aphorism is yet more true. The police are a tribe – many officers I spoke with were happy to accept that shorthand definition – and members of a tribe not only share characteristics, they take their tone from the tribal leaders. The attitudes and faults detected by Wolff Olins create an environment in which abuse ranging from the most trivial incivility to the public through to major criminality is an ever-present threat: moral turpitude is indivisible.

Two days after the (for the police) unhappy coincidence of the evidence-fixing case and the Met's fresh image campaign, two distinguished Parliamentarians, Lord Bonham-Carter and Frank Field MP, wrote to *The Independent* pointing out that not only was the fabrication of evidence against an accused person not unique, but that the response by the leadership of the Metropolitan Police was, on such occasions, woefully inadequate. It had proved impossible either to prosecute or to discipline the officers involved: a Scotland Yard spokesman made one of those promises of action which newspapers print in the interests of 'balance', but which are not worth the few lines they occupy at the foot of the story. 'We will study the case and if any further evidence against the officers comes to light then we will refer it to the Director of Public Prosecutions.' This after seven years, two previous 'inquiries' and a court case. As a popular newspaper might say: 'Pull the other one, Sir Peter.' In the case of a notorious attack on youths in Holloway, north London, by officers in a transit van, the men concerned were not even identified for many months. A very senior policeman told me they never would have been, had not the press kept up a sustained and vociferous campaign.

Lord Bonham-Carter and Mr Field had been pursuing yet another case, in which a jury believed a defendant who claimed that police officers had planted drugs on him. This man was also paid damages. They wrote: 'No disciplinary action has been taken against any of the officers involved in the case despite the fact that they had planted drugs on him and lied under oath.' In passing, they had some fun with the platitudes with which Sir Peter Imbert launched his campaign – 'compassionate, courteous and patient, acting without fear or favour or prejudice to the rights of others'. But their serious thesis was that, if it is as difficult as the hand-wringing leadership of the Met would have us believe to rid the force of corrupt police officers, it ought not to be. 'A first step would be to alter the standard of proof required in police discipline cases to that required in the armed forces so that those who transparently prejudice the rights of others are punished,' they wrote. The Met tendency to put image before substance leads the force unerringly towards the sort of ambush it suffered with its 'Plus Programme' campaign. Just imagine how different the press response would have been if Imbert had announced that he was immediately suspending the officers who, in the judge's words, had 'cooked up' the wretched suspect's confession. Instead of worthy, instantly forgettable headlines tucked on inside pages – 'Imbert outlines "compassionate" role for Met' (*Independent*) – Sir Peter would have commanded the front pages – 'Commissioner acts to clean up Yard'. Tolerance of officers who abuse their authority in such a terrifying manner – the wrongfully accused man was held in custody for seventy-six days, and, partly as a consequence of his ordeal, his marriage broke up – should simply not be possible in a disciplined service, dedicated at great public expense to the maintenance of 'law and order'. Imbert should put as much energy into acquiring new powers to rid himself of cheating coppers as he did into lobbying for the right to silence to be abolished. That he doesn't, sends a message to the canteen far more powerful than all the ten-point creeds and booklets destined to prop tables.

Individual officers are against sin within their own ranks, but they are seldom against the individual sinners. I had several conversations with officers who followed unequivocal statements that corrupt police should be booted out with impassioned defences of the particular officers who had actually been caught. Who is to blame them when general condemnation at the top is seldom matched by specific action? Many officers argued that it is pointless using civilians to investigate police malpractice, since even policemen often find it impossible to penetrate a force or group of officers who have closed their ranks against outside inquiry. At the moment that is clearly so, and the rules need to be changed so that the heat is on not only officers under suspicion, but also those inclined to protect them. It should be a severe disciplinary offence for a police officer not to co-operate wholeheartedly with complaints investigations.

A force that tolerates a climate in which rotten apples mature on the bough also runs the danger of allowing the diktat of its officers to become synonymous with the law. This tendency is to be observed on public order occasions, when police officers will impose arbitrary and authoritarian decisions on citizens going about their lawful business. During the visit to London of Soviet leader Mikhail Gorbachev in March 1989, all manner of people were inhibited from parading their views – including the Women's Committee for Soviet Jewry and a group demonstrating against the conviction of the 'Guildford Four' bombers. On television I actually saw a cadre of KGB men in black leather overcoats asking London bobbies to move demonstrators further away from Number 10 Downing Street, a request that the men in blue almost fell over themselves to enforce. By whose consent were those citizens of Britain being policed? Bernard Levin, the *Times* columnist, who witnessed some of these events, commented that all people entrusted with power – particularly power tricked out in a quasi-military uniform – sooner or later want more. If not given it, they will take it, he wrote. To which I would add the qualification – unless they are capably restrained.

Of course, the best senior police officers deplore the seeming ease with which their corrupt or overweening colleagues skip out of retribution's way. They have at least as much reason as the rest of us to wish devoutly that police malpractice should be punished fast and effectively. It is the force to which they belong that loses credibility; it is their colleagues who will not be believed under oath in court; it is their men on the beat who will suffer the disrespect that gathers about an institution that cannot put its house in order. I first covered police affairs twenty years ago. Then officers said frequently that, while there had been abuses in the past, the force had finally established a tight grip on wrongdoers. A police generation later I was told the same, and, if I still have breath to inquire in twenty years' time, no doubt I will be told it again. Sir Robert Mark came and went; the 'firm within a firm', the inner core of corrupt detectives, were said to have gone with him. Still juries sustain allegations of framing and fabrication.

The tragedy of Imbert's seldom-ceasing verbiage is that it not only does nothing to allay the gathering perception that all is not well, but it also sustains the belief among his officers that they live within a protective cocoon, safe from the consequences of public dissatisfaction. If confidence is to be restored, something clearly has to be done about the national complaints procedure. At present, the prospect of a complaint is about as threatening to most officers as a shower of rain to a duck. The bald figures are that of the 5,548 cases referred to the Police Complaints Authority (PCA) in 1988 (these would have been the 'serious' complaints out of the tens of thousands that are made annually against officers), only 50 resulted in criminal charges, 111 in disciplinary charges and 655 in admonishment or advice. There was no action taken in respect of 86 per cent of the complaints.

There are, without doubt, a large number of malicious complaints, often made in an abortive effort to pre-empt charges, which inevitably submerge those in which the complainant has a genuine sense of grievance. Often the complaint itself has roots in poor relations between the aggrieved person and the police, which makes it hard to disentangle truth from emotion. One night a group of Streatham officers discovered a man with a torch and a tool kit working on the lock to a block of flats. Naturally suspicious, they investigated. At some stage, believing either that the man was not co-operating fully or that he was about 'to do a runner', they apparently asserted their authority. The man was black, and an employee of Lambeth Council's emergency repair team. According to the officers, had he made that immediately clear, none of the subsequent 'misunderstanding' would have occurred. I was not there, and cannot, therefore, enter into the right and wrongs of a grievance that seemed set to meander through the labyrinthine complaints procedures for many months. But in such cases there are often several mutually antagonistic assumptions at work. The complaint itself is a symptom of the bad blood between two hostile parties. The issue is further confused because in the macho world of policing, a complaint can easily be seen as evidence of good coppering. A former Brixton detective said that they could tell when they were beginning to be effective because the complaints poured in. Since this is clearly true, it makes it very easy for the complained-against officer to confuse the 'tactical' complaint against him, which is a sort of battle honour, with the genuine, which ought to be a matter of shame.

Although the PCA is headed and run by civilians, the investigations into complaints are carried out by other police officers, leaving many complainants feeling hard done by. Police argue strenuously that civilian investigators would simply break their lances against the 'wall of silence' that the police throw up on these occasions. Yet it is scandalous that it is harder to bring police officers to book for wrongdoing than it is the members of almost any other profession. The present flawed system often leaves the police at least as unhappy as the complainant. Complaints can take well over a year to resolve; one PC who had served as a probationary detective claimed that he had never been confirmed in the rank because there were always outstanding complaints against him (made, according to him, because of his legitimate zeal). Officers say also that ill-founded complaints are often 'conciliated' so that, although they have done no wrong, what amounts to an admonishment goes on their records. A sergeant who failed to give a prisoner a meal was 'advised' as to his future conduct, although he had presumed, since the hour was late and the prisoner had not asked for food, that the man had already eaten.

Police men and women need the knowledge that they will be hit swiftly and hard if they depart from the straight and narrow (so does anyone else entrusted with power), but, more crucially, they need the faith of the people they police that the force has got its house in order. If the police get this wrong, nothing else matters a great deal: the efficiency of detectives, the skill of firearms officers, shield-training, driving expertise are as of nought. No doubt General Pinochet's police had their skills, certainly the KGB, whose representatives saw fit to tell Met officers what to do in Downing Street, do; but that is not what they are known for across the world. Everything else pales into insignificance beside the probity of the police. Any police officer who thinks I am creating a mountain out of a molehill should consider the clearly identified recent deterioration in police/public relations: 'POLICE: PUBLIC ALARM GROWS' roared a *Daily Express* front page splash headline in March 1989. The nature of our society, less tolerant and less pleasant today than it was a quarter of a century ago, is at stake.

One reaction to this crisis, and the one adopted by several left-wing councils, amounts to little more than a blanket condemnation of everyone who wears a blue uniform as a 'pig' or 'fascist hyena'. Extreme caricatures may relieve feelings, but, far from improving the quality of policing, they exacerbate an already perilous situation. It may be that, if we were fashioning a police force from scratch, we would not start from here. But here we are, with a force whose roots go deep into our culture and history, and the challenge now is to ensure that it is the best possible force, representing the needs of society rather than either merely its own interests (which is an ever-present danger) or a powerful sectional cause. If there were to be an economic catastrophe in the near future, which is by no means a wild surmise, the fault line in British society between the comfortable and the underclass might become a chasm. The police, with their recently acquired riot control training and equipment, could be required to 'put down' what might amount to insurrection in the inner cities. Policing, despite the conventional protestations by police officers that they stand outside politics, is a highly 'political' issue.

The government has got to put the public interest before the police interest, and this means discounting the habitual police sensitivity to criticism. The police must moan more than any comparable group of people. Officers will scour a report – like the four-volume Policy Studies Institute investigation into the Met – solely in search of adverse comment. Emerging triumphant, like miners returning from their workings clutching a nugget of gold, they will feed the criticisms to colleagues who have never set eyes on that or any other inquiry into the police. The report is then branded 'anti-police', and officers feel thoroughly justified in casting aside any constructive suggestions it might make as the work of prejudiced critics. As I have been writing, I have sensed a notional canteen scrutineer peering over my shoulder and ready to pounce triumphantly wherever I have reported something that his colleagues might find uncomfortable. The process often goes one stage further. A senior member of the Police Federation said: 'A large number of people are untouched by policing; they therefore take their tune from articulate, vocal critics who have access to the media. Such critics sow seeds in other people's minds.' The logic of this argument is that all criticism of the force has its roots in the malice of those motivated against the police – usually conceived as an 'industry' or tightly knit group of politically hostile activists. Such people exist, but their voice is feeble when set against the pro-police efforts of the media. Consider the impact of a television programme like *Crimewatch UK*, on which never a word of criticism about the police is voiced.

Because of the recent increase in public unhappiness, demands have been growing for a Royal Commission. I would like to suggest a few modest reforms, that for implementation do not require all the huffing and puffing and expense of such an inquiry. When Sir Joseph Simpson became Metropolitan Police Commissioner in the 1960s, the fact that he was the first head of Britain's largest force to have risen from the rank of PC was hailed as a great breakthrough. I believe it is time once again to appoint a commissioner who has *not* worked his way through the ranks. Tribal loyalty bred within a tight-knit institution is all-pervasive; after twenty-five or thirty years' submersion within it, no man conformist enough to reach the very top is going to find it easy to shake free of his tribal identity. However consciously such a man tries to be dispassionate, there must remain calls deep within him, similar to the calls of patriotism that sometimes blind us to our country's faults, that make it extremely difficult to act with detachment.

The job must not go to a time-server drawn from the lists of the 'great and the good', who himself would be in danger of being institutionalised as soon as he had got his feet under the desk. I suggest that the next commissioner should be appointed with the expectation that he remains in the job for a minimum of ten years: recent commissioners have come and gone in about five, which effectively means that, however energetic they have been, they have been unable to do more than grab hold of some small part of the massive animal. For one man (or woman) to make a genuine impact, even in ten years, the Met must be reduced in size. The number of officers and civilians together is now 44,000 people, and is growing all the time, as is a budget of over one billion pounds. From the divisional perspective there is often despair at the thought of the pyramid stretching into the bureaucratic stratosphere. A detective chief inspector, asked at a meeting whether he had yet a reply to a memo he had sent to the Yard, replied, only half facetiously: 'No; I only sent it four months ago.'

A chief superintendent said: 'The division is the basic element. Yard bureaucrats couldn't run a pillow fight in a dorm. What is the point of having a consultation system, finding out what local people want, and then having priorities dictated by the Yard?' Those in charge of the Met's considerable purse, he said, pay little attention to what communities need, but dole out the money – 'more of the same, more of the same' – in the traditional ways. His division had recently been criticised for having cautioned fewer offenders than the Met average. The inspectors, said the chief superintendent, had simply take the crude percentage of cautions out of the total number of arrests without verifying which were suitable for a caution. 'People are making assumptions about you and your competence on the basis of this sort of information. You can live with that. But they are also allocating resources on those flawed assumptions,' he said.

Another senior officer said that the intended devolution of power to the front-line forces – a central facet of the most recent Met reorganisation – had simply not happened: 'The idea was that divisions should have authority and accountability; in reality they have no control over resource whatsoever. There is an unhealthy competition for power, and a struggle to push chief superintendents down in their place. To make the existing system work, you have to trust the chief supers. At present they have all the responsibility and none of the power.' Senior officers get almost no financial training. A civilian employee said: 'We're not talking about peanuts. It can be laughable to listen to financial discussions – they're childlike.' Nor do they have adequate office support. When Mr Street explains his function to members of the public, he compares his role to that of 'chairman of the company', yet he has no secretary, and, if he is out of his office, his phone can ring and ring.

A senior provincial officer suggested that the Met should be split into four quarters – north, south, east and west. But to divide London that way would create a bureaucratic and jurisdictional nightmare. It would be far better to shave off the suburban areas – those parts of 'Greater London' that lie beyond the embrace of the London postal districts – and to return them to the home counties forces. It is a nonsense that the 'London' police boundary should run through farms and woods deep within counties like Surrey and Hertfordshire. With the Met at its present size, the most energetic commissioner – even if his tenure were increased to ten years – would inevitably leave office with his work half done. A senior member of the Police Federation pointed out that when Sir Kenneth Newman retired as Commissioner in 1987, he departed burdened with honours and with plaudits ringing in his ears. Yet a few months later, his successor had commissioned the Wolff Olins inquiry into the regrettable state of Met morale and public relations. 'The new leadership accepts that this critical report is an accurate portrait of the force,' he said.

A 'civilian' commissioner (technically all commissioners are, for some arcane reason, civilians) would need support from others not dripping in tribal woad. I believe that the police ought to have an 'officer' class. This idea always raises a howl of protest from the anti-'academics', who believe that graduates and others who find it easy to pass promotion exams are rapidly elevated to positions beyond their competence. A civilian working with the Met said that some officers were indeed over-promoted, but that the problem was not that these people were too clever, but that they were not clever enough. One of Britain's brightest young policemen was Malcolm Sparrow, at thirty-one a chief inspector with the Kent force, who had a first-class degree from Cambridge, a Master's degree from Harvard and a PhD. If he had stayed in the police, there was every chance that he would have become a chief constable, perhaps even commissioner at the Met, but he quit, and chose instead an academic life in the United States. He told *The Times*: 'The last ten years have been very worthwhile, but the prospects for the next ten years would have been largely administrative and involve wading through bureaucratic treacle. I am not convinced this would be the best use of my talent, nor do I think that it is the best preparation for being a chief constable.' He argued the case for appointing top people who have not had to make the laborious climb up the promotion ladder. 'If I arrived [at the top] by that route I'd be a little bit cynical, my brain by no means as creative and energetic as I'd like it to be.' Under the present system, having resigned, he is lost to the British police for good. 'It would take a brave chief constable to make an exception, because of the resentment from senior officers who consider that the only way for promotion is through the ranks,' he said.

The canteen attitude towards such a man would, without doubt, be 'good riddance'. A detective sergeant articulated the prejudice against learning: 'You haven't got to have a poxy GCSE in geography or home economics to be a policeman; you only need to be able to add up and to write down. What damn good is a university graduate who has been reading architecture at Cambridge, who has come in as a graduate entry? That guy's going to be a senior manager one day. I know inspectors who would never make coppers as long as they walk, and sergeants who couldn't organise a barbecue in a churchyard. These are the people you are putting the young recruits under.' Because of their deficiencies, he said, these graduates often have to be 'carried' by their subordinates, who keep them out of trouble. (He was, ironically, determined that his own daughter should go to university.)

This 'them and us' prejudice against well-educated colleagues is underpinned by the hourly wage system, which not only means that some PCs spend a great deal of their time watching the clock and worrying about overtime, but that they also grudgingly measure out the service they offer against the ringing of a cash till. Some police officers become 'overtime barons', salving their consciences for the small amount of time they spend at home by buying their wives the latest household machines. A senior officer said: 'That is no substitute for the presence of a husband/father in the home.' Police divorce rates are well above the already high national average. My next reform, therefore, would be to incorporate all overtime into the basic wage, and tell police officers to plunge into their jobs as do other people on decent salaries. There would be a massive share-out available – £60,000,000 is paid annually in overtime in London alone – boosting police salaries well into the comfort zone. The Federation fear of mass exploitation would soon evaporate when their supervising officers discovered the realities of man management that did not rely entirely on goading their troops with overtime. Discontented police report sick a great deal more than contented ones, which would provide one simple way of judging which senior officers were handling their men well.

A form of merit payment ought to be introduced. Sir Peter Imbert has hinted at it, provoking inevitable howls from the Federation. But rewards based on effort and ability, as opposed to payment according to seniority in a given rank, follow naturally from the introduction of a salary system. 'Uniform carriers', so long as they do the bare minimum to steer clear of disciplinary attention, are guaranteed regular increments. Such a reward structure is not a great incentive for enthusiasm, and can even reduce the ambition for promotion. A senior PC calculated that he would be no better off as a sergeant, and was not, therefore, going through the sweat of sitting the promotion exam. He would, I suspect, have made a good sergeant.

If the incentives for individual performances have to be made more efficient and meaningful, so an improved way of measuring force performance must be devised. Crime and clear-up rates are both unfair and almost meaningless as yardsticks for how well the police are doing. Whether, for example, theft is reported is almost entirely dependent on whether the loser will be seeking an insurance pay-out. I came across quite serious crimes that were not reported – like the break-in at 'Curly's' shop on the St Martin's estate – while I myself reported the theft of a bicycle the day I started writing this chapter. One obvious first step would be to measure and publish response times, much in the way British Rail report the percentage of trains that are on time. Mr 'Vance' had to wait an hour for a PC to stroll round to his 999 call; in San Diego, California, the target response for such a call is seven minutes.

Whatever the outcome of the internal debate between police 'force' and police 'service', policing will always be a public 'service' in the widest sense. A service industry has customers, and customers must have criteria with which to judge the quality of what they are getting beyond the merely anecdotal. Policing is far wider ranging and more demanding than running an airline or a hotel, but it would benefit from absorbing the positive attitudes of industries that are dependent on customer goodwill. A smiling, pleasant face is not the be-all and end-all, but it does no harm. Imbert has talked about making the reception areas of police stations less forbidding by introducing something of the atmosphere of the public areas of banks and building societies. At present it is often a nightmare getting into a police station: once, when I had an appointment to see a deputy assistant commissioner, I had to go to a public phone in the street to let his office know I had arrived. There is no reason why simple forms – those required when reporting minor accidents or producing drivers' documents, for example – should not be filled in by members of the public. Anything that relieves the bottlenecks at police station counters will dramatically improve police/community relations, and increase the likelihood of members of the public coming forward with gobbets of information.

The aim of all reform should be both to reinvigorate

the police and to draw them closer to the community. Redesigning the shift system would certainly help lower the barriers between police and public. If only those police who were needed to provide emergency response were on duty through the night, the majority of cops could work hours more like those kept by the rest of us, which would help their social integration. Mr Street's proposals to give the majority of divisional officers geographic responsibility are a sensible way of returning policing to the community. I believe that recruiting ought to be carried out on a local basis, with a guarantee – to those who want it – that their service will be local. (In London, recruiting by borough might conceivably attract more applicants from ethnic minorities.) Training should be integrated with further education in the community; the twenty weeks that recruits spend at Hendon – during which they virtually never get out except at weekends – inevitably start the process of isolating young officers from the rest of society.

A retired chief superintendent said: 'If you don't get close to your community, the gap between public and police widens and widens, and extremist groups can capitalise. The short-term concern may be burglary, but long-term it is the community. The aim on division must be to get the police to be part of the people and the people part of the police.' But this officer was very despondent, and had retired prematurely because he felt that every time he got the burden almost to the top of the hill, it rolled back down again. 'I wouldn't be one of the nodding heads, and I paid very substantially for having vision. A police force is always capitalising on what happened yesterday, so vision is a handicap. I have seen the light die in lots of people'e eyes in that force. I was not allowed power because I was vociferous; and, because I would not toe the party line, I was "neutralised".' He continued: 'There is not much chance for the Metropolitan Police unless there is a Royal Commission. I think the police are heading for a great crisis. The sensitive officers – those who believe they are there to serve the public and not just to catch criminals – are getting demoralised and depressed. The core of the Met – which is about care and compassion – is slowly being torn out. They'll be left with officers concerned solely with enforcement. They'll be the people they recruit, and so it will go on and on and on.'

He was also concerned that little is done for the true welfare of police officers. He said: 'Welfare is not just money, eyes and teeth – but minds. A boy who witnessed the Harrods bombing, who had been an excellent officer, simply fell apart. No one suggested anything constructive, or even put two and two together. Policemen are walking around full of anger and pain. Policing is an ideal vehicle for such people, because they can always find a situation to give vent to that anger. The trauma may go back a long way, but the police will pick up the tab; the working environment is akin to a pressure cooker in which the steam cannot get out. An officer told me recently: "Sometimes I come on duty hoping that someone is going to upset me." If you internalise your anger, you'll hit back. Highly professional officers let it all bounce off and fall to the floor.' The present structure of the force and relationships within it, he argued, militate against individuality. He said: 'I tell chief superintendents: "You have got to exert yourselves as individuals and not merely as senior officers." They find themselves running towards the finishing line, and someone is always moving the tape. No one ever pats them on the head; they work in a vacuum. The paradox is that no one ever told them what their job was anyway. They are aspiring to some "x" factor that is not laid down anywhere.' He added that after a career in the police, even intelligent senior officers often find it hard to operate in an unstructured situation.

If successful officers who have had stimulating careers have difficulty in retaining their individuality, it is inevitably even harder for their juniors to survive for thirty years without becoming submerged by the system. The retired officer said: 'The biggest influence is the mafiosi in the canteen. Night duty and the isolated environment will bring it out. Their defence against the bosses is mockery. What they see at ground floor level is a lot of words flowing from on high that don't do a lot for them. In the three years that I was a divisional chief superintendent, nothing passed through this chain of command to make the lot of the policeman on the street easier. Most police officers are totally confused about police objectives. Can you be surprised that they have their own culture?' The public, he argued, is so bombarded with crime figures that they lose the capacity to grasp essentials. 'The truth is that twenty-eight thousand police officers cannot police several hundred square miles and eight million people,' he said; it was up to individuals to take care of their own property, leaving the police free to concentrate on keeping people safe. He asked rhetorically: 'What is the investigation of theft for? All that time and petrol?' And answered: 'To provide the Home Office with statistics, so that everyone can say "Isn't it terrible?" And for the benefit of insurance companies so that they can validate claims. The police need a new and open mind at the top. You cannot expect change to happen like that' – and he clicked his fingers – 'you have got to recruit and train people to different criteria to meet that change. If you are going to have a divisional chief superintendent as "chairman" of the company, you have got to train him and give him the resources.'

Most officers join for the money and the prospects of an exciting life, but there comes a point several years into a career when the money is taken for granted and the excitement begins to pall. What then? It is clearly hard to motivate a PC through the declining years of his thirty-year stretch. A member of an independent think-tank said that in his experience the most contented (and, therefore, the best adjusted) officers were those committed to a speciality, like driving, dog handling or river police, with which they were comfortable. He said: 'They are relaxed socially and suffer none of the cultural drawbacks of ordinary policing. They are professionally competent; don't drink excessively; have stable families.' The two or three days I spent with officers from the PT17 firearms branch confirmed that: they seemed free of the restless, rather querulous spirit that afflicts some long-term rank and file officers.

Endless obeisance is paid to the theory of enhancing the importance and responsibility of the PC, just as it is to promoting the autonomy of the division. At Streatham an attempt was certainly made to involve police constables, but, in practice, they were often omitted. One PC, who had ambitions to join Special Branch, was recommended by his inspector to work with the crime squad. But, with no explanation, another PC was selected, which bewildered and disappointed the original applicant and aggravated his inspector. Police orders require that some jobs, such as the investigation of a fatal accident or a search, be carried out by officers of certain rank, which can restrict PCs from performing tasks at which they might be very competent. Older PCs are often to be found mooching in out-of-the-way jobs, or hopping from one task to another, like migrating birds constantly unhappy about their landfall.

Policing by consent embodies the notion that we are policed by our peers. Police officers base their distrust of 'academic' colleagues on the grounds that the academics are not representative of the community they police. Yet they seldom pursue the logic of that argument to complain about the lack of black faces in their ranks, which, in areas like inner London, is such a bar to good community relations. I suggest that there ought to be positive discrimination along the lines adopted twenty years ago in the United States, even though it would be at odds with the unforced snail's pace social evolution to which the British are accustomed. Applicants of suitable character and aptitude should be given a crash course to bring them up to the starting line. The majority of London police officers come from far-flung parts of the British Isles and Ireland (whose citizens are, rather mysteriously, eligible for recruitment), and many have seldom seen a black face let alone got to know a black person. They will live, almost certainly, in such Caucasian suburbs as Epsom and Orpington. Sheila Ward, a former chief superintendent at Streatham, said that, in the absence of sufficient blacks themselves in the ranks, the main way to combat racism was to recruit officers who were familiar with minorities. She always advised young people

anxious to join the police to spend time in organisations
that included blacks where they can discover for themselves
that blacks 'are just as capable of decent human emotions
as they are'. A chief superintendent said: 'Officers who have
not worked in "ethnic" areas are uncomfortable when they
have to. At the Notting Hill Carnival they can be disorien-
tated by the ninety per cent black faces; they think that
every single one of them is going to mug them and ravish
their wives. They can actually be thrown by the colour of
skin, and a war situation develops. You can tell the guys
who work in black areas, because they are in amongst the
carnival goers, having a chat, having a glass of beer.'

Most of my modest reform proposals require a consistency of purpose which it is hard to achieve in a force that
plays musical chairs at a frantic pace. Senior officers such
as divisional chief superintendents and detective chief
inspectors should be assigned, as are officers in the armed
services, for minimum periods of three years. Each time I
was away from Streatham for more than a week, I returned
to find new faces round the table. This was destabilising
even to me as a casual visitor, so I could understand how
severely it demoralised the PCs. The 'guv'nors' became
an impersonal cast of interchangeable characters, which
encouraged the natural canteen cynicism. Initiatives were
often shrugged off on the assumption that the driving force
behind them would not be around long enough to see them
through. In offices, nothing seemed permanent: one man
had stacked his trophies (the police love to give one another
wooden wall plaques) on top of his filing cabinet, a statement that there was no point in screwing them to the wall
since he was unlikely to occupy the room for long. A
member of the Lambeth consultative group complained
that it was hardly worth obtaining a pledge from senior
officers in the borough, since the next moment they had
gone and been replaced by someone who denied all knowledge of the commitment.

Mr Street asked me after I had been in Streatham a few
months whether I thought the division was undermanned,
and several of his colleagues regularly stressed what they

claimed were staff shortages. I suspected that they hoped that what I wrote might, in a small way, be ammunition in their ceaseless guerrilla campaign for more officers. Certainly there were days when the men and women on duty were perilously thin on the ground, but a visitor to a police station is also struck by the slack in the system. The demand for a police service is open-ended. There is now one police officer for every 400 Britons; forty years ago it was one for every 700. What is the right ratio? One for every 200, for every 20? I would like to see Mr Street and other divisional chief superintendents implement his reforms of the relief system, and to see how much more work officers could fit into their days once they had freed themselves from their obsession with overtime payments. Then it *might* be possible to judge the real shortfall, if any, in manpower. The Met tendency is to throw men at some problems, and pay cursory attention to others. Conscientious individual officers become bewildered. In their own minds they work their socks off, yet the job never gets done, and both their masters and the rest of us take their efforts for granted. A very senior detective said: 'Most police officers do think they are doing something very important. I have never seen anyone writing about how passionately the police feel about what they do, in the way the doctors and nurses are written up. We attempt to be custodians of the law, yet we are bombarded with comment that we are inefficient and unsympathetic. Is it any surprise that we suffer from a siege mentality? It seems at times that every fucker is against us. A writer may offer a door through which the true message gets out.'

'What is truth?' said jesting Pilate; and would not stay for an answer. I did stay, but after six months spent largely watching police at work, the answer remains elusive. 'Are you pro- or anti-police?' The question lay in ambush for me as I did my rounds. Twenty years ago I reported a demonstration in central London which had, for most of the afternoon, been pleasant, but which had turned ugly towards evening. When I returned to the office, there were two pictures on the night news desk: one of a policeman holding a bunch of daffodils and the other of an officer, with truncheon drawn, belabouring a demonstrator. 'Well,' demanded the rather gruff night editor, 'which was it? a picnic or a riot?' 'A bit of each,' I replied, which was not the answer he wanted, but he ran the two pictures side by side across the top of the front page. A man with two young adult daughters said they had both recently been stopped by the police. One had been Breathalysed (she passed), and the police officers could not have been more courteous or correct in their behaviour. The other was standing on a street corner with her boyfriend early one Sunday morning when police officers drew up and started questioning the young man about why he was wearing a studded leather belt. They were rude, aggressive, and behaved as if they were tempting him to react. As a result of these two experiences, the man's daughters now have diametrically opposed prejudices about the police: it was almost, he said, as if they had encountered different species.

Jekyll and Hyde is such an overworked concept that one hesitates to employ it. But there is a dark side to the collective police personality. It is to do with power, with isolation, with human frailty – intangibles over which the best police chief has little influence. But it is also to do with organisation, control, example. In the New York Police Department an 'Internal Affairs Department' patrols the streets checking on officers; 'field' officers act as moles, looking for signs of racism or brutality; a sergeant has to attend the scene of every potential arrest to ensure that it is justified. These safeguards may have been introduced as a result of abuses – police 'reform' is almost always reactive – but policing is too important to be left to trust and luck.

Yes, most police are decent people; yes, they approach their job with the best of intentions; yes, policing is a lot more brutal and unsatisfactory elsewhere in the world; yes, we now have some structures in place for dialogue between them and us. And yet we have a self-confessed crisis. By all means put pot plants and comfortable chairs in the front offices of police stations; end the 'Sellotape culture' by issuing as many pinboards as are necessary; give the police woolly pullies; issue every man with ten principles to stuff in his helmet when he goes out on the beat. But also put the fear of God into him that if he transgresses he will be booted out; if he is idle he will be retired; if he is arrogant he will be disciplined; if he is discourteous, he will be on the carpet. The time for hand-wringing is long past.

11
Guildford and After

The day this book was published in hardback, the 'Guild-ford Four' were cleared of IRA bombing murders for which they had served fifteen years in prison. Public concern about the police exploded; it was as if someone had turned the gas up full beneath an already simmering pan. Whatever one's view of the customary virtue of the police, there could be no excuse for or escape from the fact that a handful of Surrey officers had mercilessly concocted evidence against four young Irish drifters for horrendous crimes. The Lord Chief Justice of England, Lord Lane – a man implacably opposed to the kind of media-sustained campaign that had been waged on behalf of the abused quartet – said the police who secured the convictions through 'confessions' must have 'lied'. He could not, alas, find the words to apologise to the victims of this monumental miscarriage of justice.

The dismal police perversions were spelled out at the Old Bailey – the Four were sitting in the dock they had occupied when they were imprisoned for life – by Mr Roy Amlot, QC, for the Director of Public Prosecutions. The story he had to tell was of fabrication of evidence and perjury by at least five policemen. They had 'seriously misled' the original court, and thereby 'contaminated the case for the prosecution'. The only saving grace from the police point of view was that the frame-up was discovered by other police – from the Avon and Somerset force – who had been asked to investigate facts presented by Cardinal Basil Hume on behalf of the campaign to free the Four. It was remarkable that the Surrey officers had allowed the notes which gave the game away to moulder all those years in the files. Had they taken the pragmatic course adopted by some other police under investigation for wrong-doing, and shredded their handiwork, the Four would almost certainly still be in prison.

At the original trial, Sir Michael Havers QC (as he then was), leading for the prosecution, said: 'Accusations of the most appalling kind have been made against the police during this trial. If true, there has been a really gigantic conspiracy between the two police forces – the Surrey police and the bomb squad – through officers of all ranks. If the allegations are true, there has been a most appalling perversion of justice.' We cannot, of course, retrospectively hear his tone of voice, but the jury was clearly being invited to dismiss as utterly fantastical the notion that police could plumb such depths. Similar words loaded with incredulity were spoken by the judge at the trial of the 'Birmingham Six', another group of convicted Irish pub bombers who still languish in prison although their case is alleged to bear the hallmarks of that of the Guildford Four.

The legal establishment is chronically conservative, and can be terrifyingly out of touch. It, too, was implicated in the long incarceration of the Four, whose appeals had foundered both on the narrowness of the rules and the clear scepticism of the judges. But in the months since I finished the first edition of *The Force*, faith in the probity of the police has been buffeted as if by gales in a hurricane zone. Today it would be a brave or imprudent prosecutor who suggested to a jury that allegations of police wrong-doing – on whatever scale – were simply the last, desperate throw of cornered criminals.

A few weeks before the Guildford Four case, Geoffrey Dear, the then chief constable of the West Midlands (England's second largest force) removed his entire serious crime squad of fifty-three officers from operational duty after widespread allegations that they had been fabricating evidence. Some cases had been thrown out by juries, and several prison sentences had been set aside on appeal. The widest ranging inquiry yet into police malpractice under the supervision of the Police Complaints Authority (PCA) was undertaken by the West Yorkshire force; men in prison were interviewed, and one hundred allegations made.

Hard on the heels of these damning accusations came the acquittal of Kevin Taylor, a vibrant Manchester business-man who had been a friend of John Stalker, the former deputy chief constable of Greater Manchester. The associ-ation between the two was used to discredit Mr Stalker while he was investigating the alleged shoot-to-kill policy of certain detectives in the Royal Ulster Constabulary. Although Mr Taylor had no convictions, he was said to have mixed with criminals, some of whom went by the sobriquet of 'the Quality Street Gang'. Mr Stalker not only attended Mr Taylor's parties, but had holidayed with him in Florida. It was a patently tenuous link between a senior policeman and the underworld. Mr Stalker was quickly reinstated, although he did not return to the Ulster inquiry, and shortly afterwards left the police to become a writer and broadcaster.

Mr Taylor could not put his life together so easily. A laborious case was made against him alleging that he had defrauded a bank, although the bank had no complaint and had actually made a handsome profit out of his business activities. Both Mr Stalker and Mr Taylor were convinced that the police had prosecuted Mr Taylor in order further to discredit Mr Stalker. The Taylor trial lasted sixteen weeks before the judge, disturbed by police irregularities in obtaining evidence, threw out the case. Four years pre-viously, in order to gain access to Mr Taylor's bank accounts, detectives had, apparently, falsely claimed to a judge that they were looking into drug-money laundering. The files relating to the evidence used in that application had since gone 'missing'. In the meantime, Mr Taylor had been ruined: his business had collapsed, he had had to sell his home, his health had deteriorated, and – when I lunched with him during the trial – he was living on state benefit.

The public uproar over this further twist to the Stalker affair was immense. Once again there appeared to have been an abuse of police power, and Mr Stalker further alleged that he had documentary evidence implicating

senior civil servants (at the very least) in his removal from
the Ulster inquiry. There were calls for a judicial inquiry,
but these were brushed aside by the Home Secretary, David
Waddington. Newspapers had a field day. *The Independent*
intoned: 'The condition of the police in Britain can best be
described as one of institutional rot. Too often insensitive
in their dealing with the public, sometimes aggressive in
their stance towards ethnic minorities, trade unions, the
media and anyone else who dares to criticise them, a significant minority of police officers convey the impression
that they see themselves as a thin blue line defending, not
the public against crime, but a besieged citadel, manned
by themselves, against the public.' The Manchester police
authority, accustomed now to local earthquakes, was
requested by the DPP to hold an inquiry into the Taylor
affair. It seemed likely that an outside force would be
invited to carry out yet another probe into police malfeas-
ance. *Quis custodiet ipsos custodes?* (Who guards the guards
themselves?)

By early 1990, the investigation of complaints was beginning to absorb an unconscionable amount of scarce
resources. The *Sunday Times* calculated (before the Taylor
fiasco) that the annual cost ran at over £50 million, enough
to pay for an extra 2,000 officers. The Metropolitan Police
employ 273 full-time officers on complaints and corruption
inquiries, and the Royal Ulster Constabulary 142. Twenty-
one out of forty-three forces in England and Wales were
then occupied with inquiries into other forces, and all forty-
three, of course, constantly conduct their own internal
investigations into less serious complaints. As Mr Stalker
said succinctly: 'An experienced senior detective is more
likely to be investigating police misbehaviour hundreds of
miles away than catching criminals on his own patch.'

Yet the PCA has depressingly little to show for this
gigantic effort and investment. Public faith in its efficacy,
already fragile, was severely battered by the dismissal of
the more serious charges against officers alleged to have
used violence against print union pickets outside Rupert
Murdoch's Wapping newspaper plant. The Appeal Court

ruled that there had been procedural irregularities in the early stages of the investigation. As I write, the probability is that the less serious charges will also be dropped, and that if any disciplinary proceedings are brought against the accused officers they will also founder. In simple terms, not one of 440 allegations has resulted in successful action against an officer.

Apart from the procedural laxity, suspected officers had once again proved the validity of hanging together lest they should hang separately. According to some who followed the case closely, the senior investigating officer from the Northamptonshire force was treated like a country bumpkin. *The Independent* commented: 'The tough east London officers, mainly from a division known as the territorial support group, greeted him with even more hostility than is normal for an investigating officer.' The dismissal of the allegations without them being tested in court was, added the paper, possibly a 'lethal' blow to public confidence in the complaints procedure.

There was further controversy when someone leaked the main points from the Northamptonshire report to the BBC. This was said to have found that there had been 'undisciplined and uncontrolled actions often involving the indiscriminate use of truncheons'; that some officers lacked 'both adequate supervision and self-control'; and that 'no person could be considered to be in effective command and control'. A representative of the Metropolitan Police Federation spoke on behalf of the capital's officers: 'Northamptonshire police should stay in their green fields and leave things like Wapping to the forces that can cope with them.'

The failure of the Wapping investigation reinforced the public perception that police investigating police (albeit under the supervision of the PCA) is at best unsatisfactory and at worst futile. Even making a complaint is bruising and requires unusual persistence. A man who complained of police rudeness and inefficiency when he tried to report an assault on himself found that his letters to the relevant duty inspector were ignored. Action was only taken after he had written to the commissioner, and the two officers were eventually found guilty. The complainant was articulate and middle class; he knew police procedures well, and had written a detailed memo about what happened immediately after the event. Such experiences, spread anecdotally, do not encourage others to bother unless the presumed offence is dire.

The saddest story about the complaints procedure concerned a Kent PC, Ron Walker, who discovered that his detective colleagues were merrily clearing up crimes by leaning on convicted criminals to own up to offences committed by others. On the basis of you scratch my back with a few phoney 'TICs' – 'taken into account'; crimes that a convicted criminal admits to though he is never tried for – I'll scratch yours with a good word to the judge or whatever, Kent shot up the efficiency ladder. Why the bosses never became suspicious about their detectives' apparently outstanding clear-up rate was never explained, but the process continued at a gallop until Mr Walker gathered the courage to name names in a 27-page report. It proved to be an act of professional suicide. First (despite guarantees that what he was doing would be utterly confidential), word of his action was instantly spread among his colleagues, forcing him to remain at home on full pay for the duration of the inquiry; secondly, the initial team of investigators from the Met allowed six months to pass before they began looking for incriminating documents. These had been shredded. The Walkers lived in a police house, and – true to the tradition of police solidarity – they were ostracised by their neighbours. 'Those friends we had disappeared from sight, just like that. It's the police force. That's what happens when you break ranks,' Mr Walker said. He retained his sanity, he said, by playing with his cats. Eventually, a second inquiry made some progress, but the derisible upshot was the dismissal of one officer, limp-wristed fines for five more and relatively minor disciplinary action against thirty-three others, all of whom remained in their jobs.

Mr Walker was too frightened of the probable reactions of his colleagues to return to work and – having been threatened at one stage with disciplinary action himself – quit the force without compensation. He said: 'I find the whole thing simply unbelievable and astounding. No one will ever come forward in future to complain about police malpractice if this is the way they are going to be treated. Although I have been vindicated, I would not advise anyone else to do what I did.'

While Mr Walker suffered his long purgatory, there were complainants who got both satisfaction and substantial redress for wrongs done them by the police. The route they took was not through the PCA but through the courts, where juries began to award substantial damages to those who had been framed or beaten up (or often both). Mr Rupert Taylor, a black lay preacher from Notting Hill, was awarded £100,000 for being wrongfully arrested, strip-searched and having – to the satisfaction of the jury – cannabis planted on him. (Costs were estimated at a further £100,000). On the day after Mr Kevin Taylor's acquittal in Manchester, Mr Milton Morris, a black window cleaner, was awarded £25,000 for malicious prosecution. He alleged that the Metropolitan Police had planted fibres from his clothing on a mask and overalls abandoned after a bungled armed robbery. Mr Morris had spent nine months in custody.

Bitter criticism after the Wapping débâcle and dissatisfaction over what happened to PC Walker stung the PCA chairman, Judge Francis Petre, into action. There was press talk of a public relations campaign to persuade people of the PCA's effectiveness. Judge Petre gave interviews, his photograph revealing a benign, jowly man in late middle age, clasping a pipe and wearing the customary striped shirt and spotted tie of his class and calling. His words were soothing. Speaking of the hostility of the Police Federation to the PCA, he said: 'Areas of some tension are inevitable, and we seek to treat them with respect and courtesy while maintaining our integrity.' He gave his interviews in the presence of a press officer from the Central Office of Information. Yet the judge and his colleagues are not civil servants, and stress their independence. Curious. The chairman was, apparently, unperturbed by criticisms: 'I think the present system, whatever the public perception, is as good as you will find anywhere in the world. I've not come across a better one.' That may not be saying a great deal.

Shortly before the first publication of this book, I had my own brief experience of the complaints procedure. The publisher had – as a courtesy – sent proofs to a number of policemen and officials who had been involved with the project. There was a short silence, and then the phone erupted. The calls chiefly came from friends at Streatham, warning me both that there was some grave unhappiness with what I had written – one officer was described as 'chewing the lampshade' – and that I would be hearing from the Yard's complaints investigation branch in respect of an 'allegation' made in the book. The two were coupled so closely that I assumed (quite possibly wrongly) that the displeasure was the direct reason why an incident in the book had been referred to the complaints department.

The anger, I am glad to say, (which may have been exaggerated by my informants) evaporated like dew beneath a warm sun. Hostile reaction was understandable. If someone had come into my professional life with complete freedom to write what he wanted, I, too, would surely have been wounded by some observations. In such circumstances the eye is drawn unerringly to the criticisms, and it may take a period of reflection before they can be seen in context. A few days after the outbursts, police officers whose first reaction had been hostile had undergone a sea change; they talked positively about the contribution they hoped the book could make to police *perestroika*. I was delighted. I had always feared the publication might shatter friendships I had made while researching the book. In the event, everyone (I think) at Streatham proved big enough to accept the criticisms – however much they hurt personally – as a necessary and legitimate part of a book that sought to be more than Yard-approved window-dressing. The warts are the essence of its credibility.

The complaint, on the other hand, could not go away. Once formally made, it set in motion the slow workings of a pedantic machine. (A senior officer told me that it took six months to discipline a basically good cop who had trouble getting to work on time. By the time the case was ready, there was a file several inches deep. The man, who had reformed in the meantime, was fined two days' pay.)

The complaint was made by senior officers against the PC who is reported anonymously in Chapter Three as having slipped something into the pocket of a drug suspect. The officer involved was, apparently, returning the 'something' to a young man who had thrown it to the floor; the young man naturally protested. At that moment a senior officer entered the room, and commented light-heartedly 'I see, we have the first allegation of planting'. At the time I had been reasonably sure that the officer was doing no more than he said (though I was perturbed by his over-aggressive attitude to his prisoner), and I was able later to check with another PC, whom I knew, that – in his opinion at least – this was the case. The suspect later agreed to be cautioned for 'possession', which is a legal admission of 'guilt', so, despite his protests, he presumably accepted the accusation made by the arresting cop. He had also complained at the police station, but – being a mere suspect – had not been sufficiently believed for his allegation to be taken seriously.

Some senior officers, I gathered, felt that I had failed to live up to the standards that I had been seeking to impose on them. I had asked for corrupt and inefficient cops to be driven ruthlessly from the force, and yet here I had been, with a possibly bent cop under my nose, and had done nothing about it. My answer was that I was not there to report every police peccadillo to the authorities, and that, had I become an on-the-spot nark, my Streatham sojourn would have ended in tears. PC Ron Walker's ostracism would have had nothing on mine. The suspect had, in any case, complained; to me what was interesting was that his protest had been so readily dismissed according to the 'he would, wouldn't he' formula. Most substantive complaints are, presumably, from suspects; dismissing them so lightly is a powerful way of keeping the numbers down, a genuine 'Catch 22' for aggrieved prisoners.

My justification for not being more co-operative was based on two principles – the (hotly contested) duty of journalists to protect confidentiality, and the unfairness that a man's career might be blighted not so much for what he had done (many officers assured me that such minor misdemeanours are legion) as for doing it in front of an outsider. He presumably took me for part of the operation, a drugs analyst or a licensing officer perhaps. I had, when asking for access to write the book, given a blanket undertaking that I would not identify anyone without his explicit approval; some undertaking that would have been had I tamely identified the erring PC.

I was asked to go for an interview at the Metropolitan Police Complaints Investigation Branch at Tintagel House overlooking the Thames on the Albert Embankment (from where a special squad under Detective Chief Superintendent 'Nipper' Read broke the Krays' gangland empire nearly a quarter of a century ago). I was courteously questioned by two senior officers. They had taken the trouble of preparing some of what they wanted me to say (uncontroversial stuff about who I was and the book), and wrote down my answers to other questions in the form of a statement. I was not prepared to change my mind about helping them identify and convict the erring officer. If I had, I would not have been of much use; I could not even have described the officer concerned. I did agree to be a witness in the event of a disciplinary hearing, though I pointed out I would and could go no further than I had. Six months have passed without word from my inquisitors; I expect, none the less, that I shall hear more.

Between the two editions of this book there have been both reforms and talk of reform that meet some of the points I made in my recommendations. Sir Peter Imbert, the Metropolitan Police Commissioner, floated the idea that the burden of proof in discipline cases not involving criminal accusations should be reduced from 'beyond reasonable doubt' to 'the balance of probabilities'. Sir Cecil Clothier, Judge Petre's predecessor as PCA chairman, advocated that collective action by officers to frustrate an investigation into police malpractice should be a disciplinary offence. The height requirements for Met police of both sexes was abolished – largely in the hope that more Asians would be attracted to the force.

I returned to Streatham a few months after the division had occupied its refurbished police station. Graffiti had already been etched into the cell walls, and cops were chaffing that the revamped custody suite was cramped and badly laid out. Officers complained also that there was only one interview room equipped for tape-recording, and that this was inadequately sound-proofed. There was, however, a high tech control room under the permanent supervision of a sergeant, and Chief Superintendent Street was about to implement his reforms of the relief system. Half Streatham's PCs were to be assigned to neighbourhoods, returning the bobby to the beat and matching the hours they would be on duty to the demands of the job and the needs of the community.

Streatham had had a good year statistically in 1989, with arrests up by nearly 30 per cent and many crimes – including burglary – down. Mr Street saw the improvement as a vindication of community policing; higher arrest figures suggested greater local trust in the police. He was devoting more police attention to quality-of-life crimes, such as criminal damage; he sensed that, in part as a consequence, Streatham's citizens had more pride in the community and more self-confidence, qualities inextricable from the maintenance of law and order.

There had, inevitably, been both concern in the community and grumbles in the canteen about Mr Street's intended reforms; at first at least, he was going to have to press-gang officers into the sector teams. The teams will have responsibility for the full gamut of police work; they will not be there simply to look reassuring on the streets and to drink cups of tea with chosen cronies. The beat officers are to be the front-line troops who will, for example, get the resources for campaigns against burglary; they will be expected to carry out arrests on their territory. 'We are police officers, paid to do the unpopular tasks as much as the popular ones. The PCs will not be on these teams for a holiday. I will be watching them closely and expecting results,' said Mr Street.

He had embraced Sir Peter Imbert's 'Plus Programme', welcoming it as an effective tool with which to shape attitudes. There were regular meetings to discuss how the Imbert philosophy could be injected into the everyday life of the division; the local press and the community were both involved. Mr Street had even taken a leaf out the San Diego police manual, and was planning a slogan for his division: 'Serving the Local Community'. A suggestion book had been pinned to a wall near the canteen, and thus far – and somewhat to Mr Street's surprise – the entries had been constructive rather than mickey-taking; Mr Street made himself available early each morning to any officer who wanted to see him. It appeared from my relatively brief return visit that Mr Street (and his colleagues) had taken a decisive grip on the division. A few days later Peter Imbert paid Streatham an unannounced call, and found the divisional 'Plus' team in session; the discovery clearly bucked him.

I had what amounted to a summons to see Imbert. I had heard that he was upset that I had made my proposed 'modest reforms' – which included a few sharp digs at him – without seeing him. My reason for by-passing him was that I intended this book to be a portrait of what police actually do, not an apologia for their shortcomings. I did not, therefore, interview either academics or senior officers, active or retired. The analogy in my mind was that of the theatre critic or sports reporter, who wants to judge a cast or a team from the performances he sees on the stage or the field of play rather than from long interviews with the director or manager.

Imbert saw me in his extensive, panelled eighth-floor office at New Scotland Yard. He wore a well-cut, grey pin-striped suit, and was courteous and complimentary about this book, which he had gone through carefully, marking passages in pencil. That week he had, he said, recommended it to a meeting of his senior officers. But he clearly felt that I had sold his Plus campaign short, and he returned several times to phrases – such as 'Imbert's sel-dom-ceasing verbiage' – that had wounded him. He is stak-ing his claim to be a reforming commissioner on an assault on the canteen culture and its malign public consequences. He would like Plus to take root tomorrow, he said, but realistically it needed a two-year lead time. The strategy to sell Plus to his 28,000 officers is to be based on a pincer movement, first convincing senior officers of its necessity and merit, and then concentrating on the rank-and-file so that the everyday working life of London cops becomes suffused with the programme's high-minded principles. The battle between the notions of 'service' and 'force' was over, said Imbert, declaring 'service' the undisputed cham-pion philosophy for the Metropolitan Police. He added that on occasion – such as the arrest of reluctant criminals – force was an integral part of the service.

'If officers are not prepared to accept the values of Plus and live by them, then indeed there is no role in the organis-ation for them,' Imbert said. I repeated a story I had just heard of a man visiting a hospital who had been told by a policeman to 'fuck off' when he had tried to peer inside one of the army ambulances then in use during the ambu-lance crews' industrial action. Imbert, who was disturbed by the anecdote, said: 'We must capture and harness the canteen culture so that it turns on its head. If telling some-one to "eff off" is thought to be macho, it must be turned round to be totally unacceptable to everyone in the organis-ation.'

He came back to this anecdote several times, on one occasion commenting that the officer concerned might have had just those heroic qualities needed to deal with an armed robber, and on another that he might have been com-passionate at moments of human crisis. Despite Imbert's obvious sincerity about trying to rid the force of offensive attitudes, these qualifications disturbed me. The police have a mountain to climb; every shattering headline proclaiming another Guildford or West Midlands sets back a quietly incremental reform like Plus by several months. If public trust in the police is to be restored, the force can no more afford PCs telling citizens to 'fuck off' than it can afford further scandals. In almost every other service industry, abusive language of that sort would result in instant dismissal, whatever the compensating merits of the sinner. Imbert is, of course, aware of the challenge he faces. Even so, I left after a wide-ranging, two-and-a-half hour conversation sadly unconvinced that Plus would prove a match for the enormity of Imbert's task – the fundamental recasting of a tribal way of life. Naturally, I hope I am proved wrong.

A year has passed since 'Mary' the murder victim, was buried. On another wet, windy day I visited her grave. There was no headstone, though someone had left an 'M' fashioned from pink plastic roses, and there were other artificial flowers. The wet clay had sunk beneath the level of the surrounding turf, and the depression had filled with damp oak leaves. A solitary crow on a bare, black tree cawed harshly. 'Ali' has not been found – dead or alive.

Paul Foot
Who Framed Colin Wallace? £4.99

'The finest and most alarming example of professional investigative journalism I had ever read.'
Robert Kee, THE SPECTATOR

This book was rushed out 48 hours before the new British Official Secrets Act. In it Paul Foot has meticulously researched and written a shocking exposé that the Government would like to ban.

'An exciting, brilliant and profoundly disturbing book. Everyone concerned for the character and quality of our democracy should read it.'
Robert Kee, THE SPECTATOR

'Strengthens the case for a judicial inquiry into MI5's activities in Northern Ireland in the 1970s.'
THE DAILY TELEGRAPH

'His story is worth reading for its insights into the murkier side of life in Britain.'
THE GUARDIAN

'No fair-minded person can read this book and doubt Wallace's story. . . . The story is too big, too powerful, too troubling.'
R W Johnson, LONDON REVIEW OF BOOKS

'If what Wallace describes in this carefully researched book is true it makes fiction look tame. It also leaves some very difficult questions at the door of the British government.'
IRISH PRESS

John Costello
Mask of Treachery £6.99

'In 1979 I cornered and flushed out the then Sir Anthony Blunt, a smooth, tough and seasoned spy if ever there was one. Now, MASK OF TREACHERY causes my heart to miss a beat or two. . . .'
ANDREW BOYLE in THE DAILY TELEGRAPH

'New and explosive material about the activities of Anthony Blunt. Costello shows how the old spy became a homosexual mole for Stalin inside Buckingham Palace, when he carried out a secret mission in the American occupation zone of Germany on behalf of King George VI. Blunt recovered royal family papers and among the documents was hard evidence about the dangerous political flirtation between the Duke of Windsor and Hitler. As a reward Blunt became Keeper of the King's Pictures and allegedly used his position to provide Stalin with information from the pinnacle of the British establishment.

This fascinating book asserts that Blunt's knowledge provided him with a gold-plated insurance policy. For years his threat to reveal the royal secret saved him from exposure.'
THE DAILY MAIL

'Costello's assertions about Blunt and Britain's band of upper-class traitors . . . raise questions about the incompetence, self-protectionism and curious sexual habits that were rife among the British ruling elite.'
INTERNATIONAL HERALD TRIBUNE

Researched from British Intelligence files available in America but classified in Britain. *Mask of Treachery* could not have been written under the Government's new Official Secrets Act.

Hugo Young
One of Us £7.99

With new material for the paperback edition

The definitive biography of the leader who has intrigued the world
more than any of her predecessors since Churchill by one of Britain's
most distinguished and respected political journalists.

'A magnificently authoritative work, a textbook to its epoch and a
Baedeker Guide to one woman and the political landscape she has
dominated for ten years.'
THE SPECTATOR

'This book has persuaded me that biography of the living can be a
serious historical exercise, avoiding by an equal margin the pitfalls of
breathless urgency and of crude partisanship.'
ROY JENKINS, THE OBSERVER

Edwina Currie
Life Lines £4.99

'One of the secrets of political success is the resilience normally only seen in cartoons. Drop them, eat them, electrocute them, trample on them, kick them over cliffs and they – the cartoon characters and the politicians – are indestructible. I found it impossible to dislike Edwina Currie. She is professional, chatty, confidential, disarming, genuinely caring, and indefatigable.'
LESLEY GARNER, THE DAILY TELEGRAPH

'On the occasion I sat next to Mrs Currie at dinner I must say I warmed to her. The party lost some of its entertainment value when its agricultural lobby decided that she was, after all, not quite fit for human consumption. Now she has written a book which, coming as it does in the twilight of the Thatcher years, might serve as a valuable postscript to that period.'
JOHN MORTIMER, THE SUNDAY TIMES

'Who will not remember the political storm, the writs, the fury of the farming industry, the gloating jibes from her own party as well as the Opposition? What she went through – even if much of it was self-inflicted – was enough to traumatise even the strongest.'
ANNE de COURCY, EVENING STANDARD

'Underneath that bright'n'breezy exterior is an essentially well meaning politician . . . as an attitude shifter and leader in public opinion, none can deny the part that Edwina Currie has played in building a more health conscious Britain.'
DERBY EVENING TELEGRAPH

'No beating about the bush with Edwina . . . in telling her version of events we are left in no doubt that she is still smarting.'
VAL HENNESSEY, DAILY MAIL

All Pan books are available at your local bookshop or newsagent, or can be ordered direct from the publisher. Indicate the number of copies required and fill in the form below.

Send to: **CS Department, Pan Books Ltd., P.O. Box 40, Basingstoke, Hants.   RG21 2YT.**

or phone: 0256 469551 (Ansaphone), quoting title, author and Credit Card number.

Please enclose a remittance* to the value of the cover price plus: 60p for the first book plus 30p per copy for each additional book ordered to a maximum charge of £2.40 to cover postage and packing.

*Payment may be made in sterling by UK personal cheque, postal order, sterling draft or international money order, made payable to Pan Books Ltd.

Alternatively by Barclaycard/Access:

Card No. ☐☐☐☐☐☐☐☐☐☐☐☐☐☐☐☐☐☐☐

Signature:

Applicable only in the UK and Republic of Ireland.

While every effort is made to keep prices low, it is sometimes necessary to increase prices at short notice. Pan Books reserve the right to show on covers and charge new retail prices which may differ from those advertised in the text or elsewhere.

NAME AND ADDRESS IN BLOCK LETTERS PLEASE:

....

Name ————————————————————————

Address ————————————————————————

————————————————————————————

————————————————————————————

————————————————————————————

3/87